T0224359

Raspberry Pi OS System Administration with systemd

The first in a new series exploring the basics of Raspberry Pi Operating System (OS) administration, this volume is a compendium of easy-to-use and essential system administration for the novice user of the Raspberry Pi OS.

The overriding idea behind the system administration of a modern, 21st-century Linux system such as the Raspberry Pi OS is the use of systemd to ensure that the Linux kernel works efficiently and effectively to provide the three foundation stones of computer operation and management: computer system concurrency, virtualization, and secure persistence. Exercises are included throughout to reinforce the readers' learning goals with solutions and example code provided on the accompanying GitHub site.

This book is aimed at students and practitioners looking to maximize their use of the Raspberry Pi OS. With plenty of practical examples, projects, and exercises, this volume can also be adopted in a more formal learning environment to supplement and extend the basic knowledge of a Linux operating system.

Robert M. Koretsky is a retired lecturer in Mechanical Engineering at the University of Portland School of Engineering. He previously worked as an automotive engineering designer at the Freightliner Corp. in Portland, Oregon. He's married and has two kids and two grandkids.

Raspberry Pi OS System Administration with systemd
A Practical Approach
Series Editor: Robert M. Koretsky

Raspberry Pi OS System Administration with systemd: A Practical Approach
Robert M. Koretsky

Raspberry Pi OS System Administration with systemd

A Practical Approach

Robert M. Koretsky

CRC Press
Taylor & Francis Group
CHAPMAN & HALL

First edition published 2024
by CRC Press
2385 Executive Center Drive, Suite 320, Boca Raton, FL 33431

and by CRC Press
4 Park Square, Milton Park, Abingdon, Oxon, OX14 4RN

CRC Press is an imprint of Taylor & Francis Group, LLC

ISBN: 978-1-032-59635-8 (hbk)
ISBN: 978-1-032-59634-1 (pbk)
ISBN: 978-1-003-45553-0 (ebk)

DOI: 10.1201/b23405

Typeset in Palatino
by Newgen Publishing UK

To my family.

Bob Koretsky

Contents

Series Preface

This series of books covers the basics of Raspberry Pi Operating System administration, and is geared toward a novice user. Each book is a complete, self-contained introduction to important system administration tasks, and to other useful programs. The foundation of all of them is the systemd super-kernel. They guide the user along a path that gives the "Why" and "How to" of those important system administration topics, and they also present the following essential application facilities in three volumes as follows:

Volume 1: Raspberry Pi OS System Administration with systemd

Volume 2: Raspberry Pi OS System A not administration with systemd and Python

Volume 3: Raspberry Pi OS Text Editing, git, Virtualization with LXC/LXD

They can be used separately, or together, to fit the learning objectives/pace, and interests of the individual, independent learner, or can be adopted in a more formal learning environment, to supplement and extend the basic knowledge of a Linux operating system in a classroom environment that uses the Raspberry Pi OS.

In addition, each book has In-Chapter Exercises throughout, and a Question, Problems, and Projects addendum to help reinforce the learning goals of the individual student or reader.

An online Github site, with further materials and updates, program source code, solutions to In-Chapter Exercises , plus other supplements, is provided for each volume. It can be found at:

www.github.com/bobk48/RaspberryPiOS

The fundamental prerequisites of each volume are (1) knowledge of how to type a syntactically-correct Linux command on the command line, (2) having access to a dedicated Raspberry Pi computer with the latest Raspberry Pi Operating System already installed and running on it, (3) being a privileged user on the system that is able to execute the **sudo** command to assume superuser status, and (4) having a basic knowledge of how to edit and save text files in the **nano** text editor.

All instructions in these volumes were tested on either a Raspberry Pi 4B, or a Raspberry Pi 400, both with 4GB of memory, and the latest version of the Raspberry Pi OS at the time.

Volume 1 Preface

Background

This book is a compendium of easy-to-use and essential Raspberry Pi OS system administration tasks for the beginner. The Raspberry Pi OS is derived from the Debian branch of Linux, and as of this writing, Debian Bullseye was the most current version of that operating system. To present the system administration topics and commands here, I have selected some very basic stuff, and a few more advanced concepts, topics, commands, and details that might not appear in a more complete system administration book.

The overriding idea behind system administration of a modern, 21st-century Linux system such as the Raspberry Pi OS, is the use of systemd to ensure that the Linux kernel works efficiently and effectively to provide these three foundation stones of computer operation and management: computer system concurrency, virtualization, and secure persistence.

And this control of the kernel by a "super-kernel," which is what systemd essentially is, must also promote the highest level of system performance and speed, given the use cases the computer might be put to, and the perceived needs of the target user base that the computer serves. Unless a novice user, or even a more seasoned system professional, has not only a basic, but also a more complete knowledge of how systemd controls and oversees every process operation of a modern Linux system, they will never be able to master administrating and implementing the kind of functionality that their use case(s) might ultimately require. Particularly for the user base on the system, and the demands that user base makes.

Everything illustrated in Chapters 0, 1, and 2, in the specific form (and the syntax of commands) found there, is explicitly applicable to all Debian-family distributions, including the Raspberry Pi OS, and also to all other versions of Debian, including Ubuntu, and Linux Mint, RedHat-family CentOS, and Slackware distros, such as SuSE. The major areas of development of Linux over the last several years has been the expansion of the role that systemd plays in every aspect of Linux operating system use.

Certainly, out of the multitude of possible topics we could have presented, the ones you find detailed here have basically been selected in somewhat of a subjective way. That selective way was mainly guided by these concerns:

a. The secure maintenance, in terms of concurrency, virtualization, and persistence, of a single Linux computer system that an ordinary novice user can install on her own personal computer.

b. How important the topics are in a perceived ranking of essential Linux system administration tasks.

c. How systemd plays into the maintenance regimen chosen by that ordinary novice user.

d. The overall pedagogic integration of the selected topics presented on system administration with each other.

e. How well these topics serve to prepare a student for entry into any chosen Information Technology or Computer Science profession, or how someone already in those professions can use this book to better their practice of that profession. In other words, for educational and continuing education audiences.

f. To some degree, making it possible to extrapolate these topics (for audiences in e.) from a single computer system environment to a broader and larger-scaled computing environment, such as is found on small-to-medium sized servers, or to cloud-based, virtual computing.

How to Read and Use This Book

Note

The premise and prerequisite of this book is that you know what the correct form, or structure, of a single Linux command is, and how to type one in on the console or terminal command line!

Just to review, the general syntax or structure of a single Linux command (often referred to as a *simple command*) as it is typed on the command line, is as follows:

$ **command [[-]option(s)] [option argument(s)] [command argument(s)]**

where:

$ is the command line or shell prompt from the Raspberry Pi OS;
anything enclosed in **[]** is not always needed;
command is the name of the valid Linux command for that shell in lowercase letters;
[-option(s)] is one or more modifiers that change the behavior of **command**;
[option argument(s)] is one or more modifiers that change the behavior of
  [-option(s)]; and
[command argument(s)] is one or more objects that are affected by **command**.

Note the following six essentials:

1. A space separates command, options, option arguments, and command arguments, but no space is necessary between multiple option(s) or multiple option arguments.
2. The order of multiple options or option arguments is irrelevant.
3. A space character is optional between the option and the option argument.
4. Always press the <Enter> key to submit the command for interpretation and execution.
5. Options may be preceded by a single hyphen - or two hyphens, --, depending on the form of the option. The short form of the option is preceded by a single hyphen, and the long form of the option is preceded by two hyphens. No space character should be placed between hyphen(s) and option(s).
6. A small percentage of commands (like **whoami**) take <u>no</u> options, option arguments, or command arguments.

Everything on the command line is case-sensitive!

Also, it is possible, and *very* common, to type *multiple* Linux commands (sometimes called *compound* commands, to differentiate them from simple commands) on the same command line, before pressing the **<Enter>** key. The components of a multiple Linux command are separated with input and output redirection characters, to channel the output of one into the input of another.

As stated in the Series Preface, the fundamental prerequisites of this volume are (1) knowledge of how to type a syntactically-correct Linux command on the command line (as detailed above), (2) having access to a dedicated Raspberry Pi computer with the latest Raspberry Pi Operating System already installed and running on it, (3) being a privileged user on the system that is able to execute the **sudo** command to assume superuser status, and (4) having a basic knowledge of how to edit and save text files in the **nano** text editor.

An online Github site, with further materials and updates, program code, solutions to both In-Chapter and End-of-Chapter Problems, Questions, and Projects, and other supplements, is provided for this book. It can be found at www.github.com/bobk48/RaspberryPiOS

All command line instructions in this volume were tested on either a Raspberry Pi 4B, or a Raspberry Pi 400, both with 4GB of memory, and the latest version of the Raspberry Pi OS at the time.

Routes through the Book

Browse the Table of Contents.

Select a topic that interests you.

Do the Examples or all the command line materials presented for that topic.

Maybe pick another topic that interests you, and do the Examples and all the command line materials there.

Finally, go back to the beginning of the book. Do everything, from start to finish.

Rinse and repeat the above as necessary.

Refer as much as possible to the systemd materials in Chapter 2, using them as an encyclopedic source for the material you select out of Chapter 1.

Have fun!

0

"Quick Start" into Sysadmin for the Raspberry Pi OS

Objectives

To explain how to manage and maintain files and directories

To show where to get system-wide help for Raspberry Pi OS commands

To demonstrate the use of a beginner's set of utility commands

To cover the basic commands and operators

cat cd cp exit hostname -I ip login lp lpr ls man mesg mkdir more mv passwd,PATH pwd rm rmdir telnet unalias uname whatis whereis who whoami

0.1 Introduction

To start working productively with system administration on the Raspberry Pi OS, the beginner needs to have some familiarity with these sequential topics, as follows:

How to maintain and organize files in the file structure of the operating system. Creating a tree-like structure of folders (also called directories), and storing files in a logical fashion in these folders, is critical to working efficiently in the Raspberry Pi OS.

How to get help on text-based commands and their usage. With keyboard entry, in a command-based Character User Interface (CUI) environment, being able to find out, in a quick and easy way, how to use a command, its options, and arguments by typing it on the keyboard correctly is imperative to working efficiently.

How to execute a small set of essential utility commands to set up or customize your working environment. Once a beginner is familiar with the right way to construct file maintenance commands, adding a set of utility commands makes each session more productive.

DOI: 10.1201/b23405-1

To use this chapter successfully as a springboard into the remainder of the book, you should carefully read, follow, and execute the instructions and command line sessions we provide, in the order presented. Each section in this chapter, and every subsequent chapter as well, builds on the information that precedes it. They will give you the concepts, command tools, and methods that will enable you to do system administration using the Raspberry Pi OS.

Throughout this book, we illustrate everything using the following version of the Raspberry Pi OS, on the hardware listed:

System: raspberrypi Kernel: 6.1.21-v8+ aarch64 bits: 64 compiler: gcc v: 10.2.1
    Console: tty0 Distro: Debian GNU/Linux 11 (bullseye)
Machine: Type: ARM Device System: Raspberry Pi 400 Rev 1.0

In this chapter, the major commands we want to illustrate are first defined with an abbreviated syntax description, which will clarify general components of those commands. The syntax description format is as follows:

Syntax: The exact syntax of how a command, its options, and its arguments are correctly typed on the command line

Purpose: The specific purpose of the command

Output: A short description of the results of executing the command

Commonly used options/features: A listing of the most popular and useful options and option arguments

In addition, the following web link is to a site that allows you to type-in a single or multiple Raspberry Pi OS command and get a verbose explanation of the components of that command:

https://explainshell.com/

In-Chapter Exercises

1. Type the following commands on your Raspberry Pi system's command line, and note the results. Which ones are syntactically incorrect? Why? (The Bash prompt is shown as the $ character in each, and we assume that **file1** and **file2** exist)

    $ **la -ls**
    $ **cat**
    $ **more -q file1**
    $ **more file2**
    $ **time**
    $ **lsblk-a**

2. How can you differentiate a Raspberry Pi OS command from its options, option arguments, and command arguments?

3. What is the difference between a single Raspberry Pi OS command and a multiple Raspberry Pi OS command, as typed on the command line before pressing **<Enter>**?

4. If you get no error message after you enter a Raspberry Pi OS command, how do you know that it actually accomplished what you wanted it to?

0.2 File Maintenance Commands and Help on Raspberry Pi OS Command Usage

After your first-time login to a new Raspberry Pi system, one of your first actions will be to construct and organize your workspace environment, and the files that will be contained in it. The operation of organizing your files according to some logical scheme is known as *file maintenance*. A logical scheme used to organize your files might consist of creating *bins* for storing files according to the subject matter of the contents of the files or according to the dates of their creation. In the following sections, you will type file creation and maintenance commands that produce a structure similar to what is shown in Figure 0.1. Complete the operations in the following sections in the order they are presented to get a better overview of what file maintenance really is. Also, it is critical that you review what was presented in the Preface regarding the structure of a Raspberry Pi OS command, so that when you begin to type commands for file maintenance, you understand how the syntax of what you are typing conforms to the general syntax of any Raspberry Pi OS command.

0.2.1 File and Directory Structure

When you first open a terminal, or console, window, you are working in the *home directory*, or folder, of the autonomous user associated with the user-name and password you used to log into the system with. Whatever directory you are presently in is known as the *current working directory*, and there is only one current working directory active at any given time. It is helpful to visualize the structure of your files and directories using a diagram. Figure 0.1 is an example of a home directory and file structure for a user named **bob**. In this figure, directories are represented as parallelograms and plain files (e.g., files that contain text or binary instructions) are represented as rectangles. A *pathname*, or path, is simply a textual way of designating the location of a directory or file in the complete file structure of the Raspberry Pi system you are working on. For example, the path to the file **myfile?** in Figure 0.1 is **/home/**

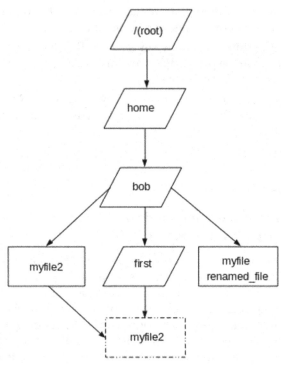

FIGURE 0.1
Example Directory Structure.

bob/myfile2. The designation of the path begins at the root (/) of the entire file system, descends to the folder named **home**, and then descends again to the home directory of the user named **bob**.

As shown in Figure 0.1, the files named **myfile, myfile2**, and **renamed_file** are stored under or in the directory **bob**. Beneath **bob** is a *subdirectory* named **first**. In the following sections, you will create these files, and the subdirectory structure, in the home directory of the username that you have logged into your Raspberry Pi system with.

In-Chapter Exercise

5. Type the following two commands on your Raspberry Pi system:
    $ **cd /**
    $ **ls**

Similar to Figure 0.1, sketch a diagram of the directories and files whose names you see listed as the output of the second command. Save this diagram for use later.

0.2.2 Viewing the Contents of Files

To begin working with files, you can easily create a new text file by using the cat command. The syntax of the cat command is as follows:

cat [options] [file-list]
Purpose: Join one or more files sequentially or display them in the console window
Output: Contents of the files in **file-list** displayed on the screen, one file at a time
Commonly used options/features:
+E Display $ at the end of each line
-n Put line numbers on the displayed lines
-- **help** Display the purpose of the command and a brief explanation of each option

The **cat** command, short for concatenate, allows you to join files. In the example, you will join what you type on the keyboard to a new file being created in the current working directory. This is achieved by the redirect character >, which takes what you type at the *standard input* (in this case the keyboard) and directs it into the file named **myfile**. You can consider the keyboard, and the stream of information it provides, as a file. As stated in the Preface, this usage is an example of a command, **cat** with no options, option arguments, or command arguments. It simply uses the command, a redirect character, and a target, or destination, named **myfile**, where the redirection will go.

This is the very simplest example of a *multiple command* typed on the command line, as opposed to a single command, as shown and briefly described in the Preface. In a multiple command, you can string together single Raspberry Pi OS commands in a chain with connecting operators, such as the redirect character shown here.

```
$ cat > myfile
This is an example of how to use the cat command to add plain text to a file
<Ctrl+D>
$
```

You can type as many lines of text, pressing **<Enter>** on the keyboard to distinguish between lines in the file, as you want. Then, on a new line, when you hold down **<Ctrl+D>**, the file is created in the current working directory, using the command you typed. You can view the contents of this file, since it is a plain text file that was created using the keyboard, by doing the following:

```
$ more myfile
This is an example of how to use the cat command to add plain text to a file
$
```

This is a simple example of the syntax of a single Raspberry Pi OS command. The general syntax of the more command is as follows:

more [options] [file-list]
Purpose: Concatenate/display the files in **file-list** on the screen, one screen at a time
Output: Contents of the files in **file-list** displayed on the screen, one page at a time
Commonly used options/features:
+E/str Start two lines before the first line containing **str**
-nN   Display N lines per screen/page
+N   Start displaying the contents of the file at line number N

The **more** command shows one screenful of a file at a time by default. If the file is several pages long, you can proceed to view subsequent pages by pressing the **<Space>** key on the keyboard, or by pressing the **Q** key on the keyboard to quit viewing the output.

In-Chapter Exercise

6. Use the **cat** command to produce another text file named testfile. Then join the contents of myfile and testfile into one text file, named myfile3, with the **cat** command.

0.2.3 Creating, Deleting, and Managing Files

To copy the contents of one file into another file, use the **cp** command. The general syntax of the **cp** command is as follows:

cp [options] file1 file2
Purpose: Copy **file1** to **file2**; if **file2** is a directory, make a copy of **file1** in this directory
Output: Copied files
Commonly used options/features:
-i   If destination exists, prompt before overwriting
-p   Preserve file access modes and modification times on copied files
-r   Recursively copy files and subdirectories

For example, to make an exact duplicate of the file named **myfile**, with the new name **myfile2**, type the following:

```
$ cp myfile myfile2
$
```

This usage of the **cp** command has two required command arguments. The first argument is the source file that already exists and which you want to copy. The second argument is the destination file or the name of the file that will be the copy. Be aware that many Raspberry Pi OS commands can take plain, ordinary, or regular files as arguments, or can take directory files as arguments. This can change the basic task accomplished by the command. It is also worth noting that not only can file names be arguments but *pathnames* as well. A pathname is the route to any particular place in the file system structure of the operating system. This changes the site or location, in the path structure of the file system, of operation of the command.

In order to change the name of a file or directory, you can use the **mv** command. The general syntax of the **mv** command is as follows:

mv [options] file1 file2
mv [options] file-list directory
Purpose: First syntax: Rename file1 to file2
Second syntax: Move all the files in file-list to directory
Output: Renamed or relocated files
Commonly used options/features:
-f   Force the move regardless of the file access modes of the destination file
-i   Prompt the user before overwriting the destination

In the following usage, the first argument to the **mv** command is the source file name, and the second argument is the destination name.

$ **mv myfile2 renamed_file**
$

It is important at this point to notice the use of spaces in Raspberry Pi OS commands. What if you obtain a file from a Windows system that has one or more spaces in one of the file names? How can you work with this file in Raspberry Pi OS? The answer is simple. Whenever you need to use that file name in a command as an argument, enclose the file name in double quotes ("). For example, you might obtain a file that you have "detached" from an e-mail message from someone on a Windows system, such as **latest revisions october.txt**.

In order to work with this file on a Raspberry Pi system – that is, to use the file name as an argument in a Raspberry Pi OS command – enclose the whole name in double quotes. The correct command to rename that file to something shorter would be:

$ **mv "latest revisions october.txt" laterevs.txt**
$

In order to delete a file, you can use the **rm** command. The general syntax of the **rm** command is as follows:

rm [options] file-list
Purpose: Removes files in **file-list** from the file structure (and disk)
Output: Deleted files
Commonly used options/features:
-f   Remove regardless of the file access modes of **file-list**
-i   Prompt the user before removing files in **file-list**
-r   Recursively remove the files in **file-list** if **file-list** is a directory; use with
        caution!

To delete the file **renamed_file** from the current working directory, type:

$ rm renamed_file
$

In-Chapter Exercise

7.   Use the **rm** command to delete the files testfile and myfile3.

The most important command you will execute to do file maintenance is the
ls command. The general syntax for the **ls** command is as follows:

ls [options] [pathname-list]
Purpose: Sends the names of the files and directories in the directory speci-
             fied by **pathname-list** to the display screen
Output: Names of the files and directories in the directory specified by
             pathname-list, or the names only if **pathname-list** contains file
             names only
Commonly used options/features:
-F   Display a slash character (/) after directory names, an asterisk (*) after
        binary executables, and an "at" character (@) after symbolic links
-a   Display names of all the files, including hidden files
-i   Display inode numbers
-l   Display long list that includes file access modes, link count, owner,
        group, file size (in bytes), and modification time

The **ls** command will list the names of files or folders in your current
working directory or folder. In addition, as with the other commands we
have used so far, if you include a complete pathname specification for the
pathname-list argument to the command, then you can list the names of files
and folders along that pathname list. To see the names of the files now in your
current working directory, type the following:

```
$ ls
Desktop Documents Downloads Dropbox Music Pictures Public Templates Videos
$
```

Please note that you will probably not get a listing of the same file names as we showed above here, because your system will have placed some files automatically in your home directory, as in the example we used, aside from the ones we created together named **myfile** and **myfile2**. Also note that this file name listing does not include the name **renamed_file**, because we deleted that file.

The next command you will execute is actually just an alternate or modified way of executing the **ls** command, one that includes the command name and options. As shown in the Preface, a Raspberry Pi OS command has options that can be typed on the command line along with the command to change the behavior of the basic command. In the case of the **ls** command, the options l and **a** produce a longer listing of all ordinary and system (dot) files, as well as providing other attendant information about the files.

Don't forget to put the space character between the **s** and the -(dash). Remember again that spaces delimit, or partition, the components of a Raspberry Pi OS command as it is typed on the command line!

Now, type the following command:

```
$ ls -la
total 30408
drwxr-xr-x   25   bob  bob   4096    May  5 07:53   .
drwxr-xr-x   5    root root  4096    Oct 20 2022    ..
drwxr-xr-x   5    bob  bob   4096    Apr 23 16:32   .audacity-data
-rw-------   1    bob  bob   36197   May  5 07:51   .bash_history
-rw-r--r--   1    bob  bob   220     Apr  4 2022    .bash_logout
-rw-r--r--   1    bob  bob   3523    Apr  4 2022    .bashrc
-rw-r--r--   1    bob  bob   47329   Sep 19 2022    Blandemic.txt
drwxr-xr-x   2    bob  bob   4096    Apr  4 2022    Bookshelf
drwxr-xr-x   15   bob  bob   4096    Apr 17 14:05   .cache
drwx------   32   bob  bob   4096    Apr 28 07:08   .config
drwx------   3    root root  4096    Jun 29 2022    .dbus
drwxr-xr-x   7    bob  bob   4096    Apr 27 05:21   Desktop
Output truncated...
```

As you see in this screen display (which shows the listing of files in our home directory and will not be the same as the listing of files in your home directory), the information about each file in the current working directory is displayed in eight columns. The first column shows the type of file, where d stands for directory, l stands for symbolic link, and – stands for ordinary or regular file. Also, in the first column, the access modes to that file for user, group, and others are shown as r, w, or x. In the second column, the number of links to that file is displayed. In the third column, the username of the owner of that file is displayed. In the fourth column, the name of the group for that file is displayed. In the fifth column, the number of bytes that the file occupies on the disk is displayed. In the sixth column, the date that the file was last modified is displayed. In the seventh column, the time that the file was last modified is displayed. In the eighth and final column, the name of the file is displayed. This way of executing the command is a good way to list more complete information about the file. Examples of using the more complete information are (1) so that you can know the byte size and be able to fit the file on some portable storage medium, or (2) to display the access modes, so that you can alter the access modes to a particular file or directory.

In-Chapter Exercise

8. Use the **ls -la** command to list all of the filenames in your home directory on your Raspberry Pi system. How does the listing you obtain compare with the listing shown above? Remember that our listing was done on a Raspberry Pi system.

You can also get a file listing for a single file in the current working directory by using another variation of the ls command, as follows:

```
$ ls -la myfile
-rw-r--r-- 1 bob bob 797 Jan 16 10:00 myfile
$
```

This variation shows you a long listing with attendant information for the specific file named **myfile**. A breakdown of what you typed on the command line is (1) **ls**, the command name, (2) **-la**, the options, and (3) **myfile**, the command argument.

What if you make a mistake in your typing, and misspell a command name or one of the other parts of a command? Type the following on the command line:

```
$ lx -la myfile
lx: not found
$
```

The lx: not found a reply from Raspberry Pi OS is an error message. There is no **lx** command in the Raspberry Pi OS, so an error message is displayed. If you had typed an option that did not exist, you would also get an error message. If you supplied a file name that was not in the current working directory, you would get an error message, too. This makes an important point about the execution of Raspberry Pi OS commands. If no error message is displayed, then the command executed correctly and the results might or might not appear on screen, depending on what the command actually does. If you get an error message displayed, you must correct the error before Raspberry Pi OS will execute the command as you type it.

NoteTypographic mistakes account for a large percentage of the errors that beginners make!

0.2.4 Creating, Deleting, and Managing Directories

Another critical aspect of file maintenance is the set of procedures, and the related Raspberry Pi OS commands you use to create, delete, and organize directories in your Raspberry Pi OS account on a computer. When moving through the file system, you are either ascending or descending to reach the directory you want to use. The directory directly above the current working directory is referred to as the *parent* of the current working directory. The directory or directories immediately under the current working directory are referred to as the *children* of the current working directory. The most common mistake for beginners is misplacing files. They cannot find the file names listed with the **ls** command because they have placed or created the files in a directory either above or below the current working directory in the file structure. When you create a file, if you have also created a logically organized set of directories beneath your own home directory, you will know where to store the file. In the following set of commands, we create a directory beneath the home directory and use that new directory to store a file.

To create a new directory beneath the current working directory, you use the **mkdir** command. The general syntax for the **mkdir** command is as follows:

mkdir [options] dirnames
Purpose: Creates directory or directories specified in **dirnames**
Output: New directory or directories
Commonly used options/features:
-m MODE Create a directory with given access modes
-p Create parent directories that don't exist in the pathnames specified in **dirnames**

To create a child, or subdirectory, named **first** under the current working directory, type the following:

```
$ mkdir first
$
```

This command has now created a new subdirectory named **first** under, or as a child of, the current working directory. Refer back to Figure 0.1 for a graphical description of the directory location of this new subdirectory.

In order to change the current working directory to this new subdirectory, you use the **cd** command. The general syntax for the **cd** command is as follows:

cd [directory]
Purpose: Change the current working directory to **directory** or return to the home directory when **directory** is omitted
Output: New current working directory

To change the current working directory to **first** by descending down the path structure to the specified directory named **first**, type the following:

```
$ cd first
$
```

You can always verify what the current working directory is by using the **pwd** command. The general syntax of the **pwd** command is as follows:

pwd
Purpose: Displays the current working directory on screen
Output: Pathname of current working directory

You can verify that **first** is now the current working directory by typing the following:

```
$ pwd
/home/bob/first
$
```

The output from the Raspberry Pi OS on the command line shows the pathname to the current working directory or folder. As previously stated, this path is a textual route through the complete file structure of the computer that Raspberry Pi OS is running on, ending in the current working directory. In this example of the output, the path starts at /, the root of the file system. Then it descends to the directory **home**, a major branch of the file system on the computer running Raspberry Pi OS. Then it descends to the directory **bob**, another branch, which is the home directory name for the user. Finally, it descends to the branch named **first**, the current working directory.

On some systems, depending on the default settings, another way of determining what the current working directory is can be done by simply looking at the command line prompt. This prompt may be prefaced with the complete path to the current working directory, ending in the current working directory.

You can ascend back up to the home directory, or the parent of the subdirectory **first**, by typing the following:

```
$ cd
$
```

An alternate way of doing this is to type the following, where the tilde character (~) resolves to, or is a substitute for, the specification of the complete path to the home directory:

```
$ cd ~
$
```

To verify that you have now ascended up to the home directory, type the following:

```
$ pwd
/home/bob
$
```

You can also ascend to a directory above your home directory, sometimes called the parent of your current working directory, by typing the following:

```
$ cd ..
$
```

In this command, the two periods (..), represent the parent, or branch above the current working directory. Don't forget to type a space character between the **d** and the first period. To verify that you have ascended to the parent of your home directory, type the following:

```
$ pwd
/home
$
```

To descend to your home directory, type the following:

```
$ cd
$
```

To verify that there are two files in the home directory that begins with the letters my, type the following command:

```
$ ls my*
myfile myfile2
$
```

The asterisk following the y on the command line is known as a *metacharacter*, or a character that represents a pattern; in this case, the pattern is any set of characters. When Raspberry Pi OS interprets the command after you press the <Enter> key on the keyboard, it searches for all files in the current working directory that begin with the letters my and end in anything else.

In-Chapter Exercise

9. Use the **cd** command to ascend to the root (/) of your Raspberry Pi OS file system, and then use it to descend down each sub-directory from the root recursively to a depth of 2 sub-directories, sketching a diagram of the component files found on your system. Make the named entries in the diagram as complete as possible, listing as many files as you think necessary. Retain this diagram as a useful map of your particular Raspberry Pi OS distribution's file system.

Another aspect of organizing your directories is the movement of files between directories, or changing the location of files in your directories. For example, you now have the file **myfile2** in your home directory, but you would like to move it into the subdirectory named **first**. See Figure 0.1 for a graphic description to change the organization of your files at this point. To accomplish this, you can use the second syntax method illustrated for the **mv file-list directory** command to move the file **myfile2** down into the subdirectory named **first**. To achieve this, type the following:

```
$ mv myfile2 first
$
```

To verify that **myfile2** is indeed in the subdirectory named first, type the following:

```
$ cd first
$ ls
myfile2
$
```

You will now ascend to the home directory and attempt to remove or delete a file with the **rm** command.

Caution: you should be very careful when using this command, because once a file has been deleted, the only way to recover it is from archival backups that you or the system administrator have made of the file system.

```
$ cd
$ rm myfile2
rm: myfile2: No such file or directory
$
```

You get the error message because, in the home directory, the file named **myfile2** does not exist. It was moved down into the subdirectory named first.

Directory organization also includes the ability to delete empty or nonempty directories. The command that accomplishes the removal of empty directories is **rmdir**. The general syntax of the **rmdir** command is as follows:

rmdir [options] dirnames
Purpose: Removes the empty directories specified in **dirnames**
Output: Removes directories
Commonly used options/features:
-p   Remove empty parent directories as well

To delete an entire directory below the current working directory, type the following:

$ rmdir first
rmdir: first: Directory not empty
$

Since the file **myfile2** is still in the subdirectory named **first, first** is not an empty directory, and you get the error message that the **rmdir** command will not delete the directory. If the directory was empty, **rmdir** would have accomplished the deletion. One way to delete a nonempty directory is by using the **rm** command with the **-r** option. The **-r** option recursively descends down into the subdirectory and deletes any files in it before actually deleting the directory itself. Be cautious with this command since you may inadvertently delete directories and files with it. To see how this command deletes a nonempty directory, type the following:

$ rm -r first
$

The directory **first** and the file **myfile2** are now removed from the file structure.

0.2.5 Obtaining Help with the man Command

A very convenient utility available on Raspberry Pi systems is the online help feature, achieved via the use of the **man** command. The general syntax of the **man** command is as follows:

man [options][-s section] command-list
man -k keyword-list
Purpose: First syntax: Display Raspberry Pi OS Reference Manual pages for
        commands in **command-list** one screen at a time
        Second syntax: Display summaries of commands related to
        keywords
                    in **keyword-list**
Output: Manual pages one screen at a time
Commonly used options/features:
-k keyword-list Search for summaries of keywords in keyword-list
                    in a database and display them
-s sec-num   Search section number sec-num for manual pages
                    and display them

To get help by using the **man** command, on usage and options of the **ls** command, for example, type the following:

$ man ls

LS(1)   User Commands   LS(1)

NAME
       ls - list directory contents

SYNOPSIS
       ls [OPTION]... [FILE]...

DESCRIPTION
       List information about the FILEs (the current directory
       by default).
       Sort entries alphabetically if none of -cftuvSUX nor –sort
       is specified.

       Mandatory arguments to long options are mandatory for
       short options too.

       -a, --all
              do not ignore entries starting with .

       -A, --almost-all
              do not list implied . and ..

       --author
Manual page ls(1) line 1 (press h for help or q to quit)

   This output from Raspberry Pi OS is a Raspberry Pi OS *manual page*, or *man page*, which gives a synopsis of the command usage showing the options, and a brief description that helps you understand how the command should be used. Typing **q** after one page has been displayed, as seen in the example, returns you to the command line prompt. Pressing the space key on the keyboard would have shown you more of the content of the manual pages, one screen at a time, related to the **ls** command.

   To get help in using all the Raspberry Pi OS commands and their options, use the **man man** command to go to the Raspberry Pi OS reference manual pages.

   The pages themselves are organized into eight sections, depending on topic described, and the topics that are applicable to the particular system. Table 0. 1 lists the sections of the manual and what they contain. Most users find the pages they need in Section 2.1. Software developers mostly use library and system calls and thus find the pages they need in Sections 2.2 and 2.3. Users who work on document preparation get the most help from Section 2.7. Administrators mostly need to refer to pages in Sections 2.1, 2.4, 2.5, and 2.8.

   The manual pages comprise multi-page, specially formatted, descriptive documentation for every command, system call, and library call in the Raspberry Pi OS. This format consists of seven general parts: name,

TABLE 0.1

Sections of the Raspberry Pi OS Manual

Section	What It Describes
1	User commands
2	System calls
3	Language library calls (C, FORTRAN, etc.)
4	Devices and network interfaces
5	File formats
6	Games and demonstrations
7	Environments, tables, and macros for troff
8	System maintenance-related commands

synopsis, description, list of files, related information, errors, warnings, and known bugs. You can use the **man** command to view the manual page for a command. Because of the name of this command, the man pages are normally referred to as Raspberry Pi OS man pages. When you display a man page on the screen, the top-left corner of the page has the command name with the section it belongs to in parentheses, as with LS(1), seen at the top of the output manual page.

The command used to display the manual page for the **passwd** command is:

$ **man passwd**

The manual page for the **passwd** command now appears on the screen, but we do not show its output. Because they are multi-page text documents, the manual pages for each topic take up more than one screen of text to display their entire contents. To see one screen of the manual page at a time, press the space bar on the keyboard. To quit viewing the manual page, press the **Q** key on the keyboard.

Now type this command:

$ **man pwd**

If more than one section of the man pages has information on the same word and you are interested in the man page for a particular section, you can use the **-S** option. The following command line, therefore, displays the man page for the read system call and not the man page for the shell command read.

$ **man -S2 read**

The command **man -S3 fopen fread strcmp** sequentially displays man pages for three C library calls: **fopen**, **fread**, and **strcmp**.

To exit from the display of these system calls, type **<Ctrl-C>**,

Using the **man** command and typing the command with the **-k** option, allows specifying a keyword that limits the search. It is equivalent to using the **apropos** command. The search then yields useful man page headers from all the man pages on the system that contain just the keyword reference. For example, the following command yields the on-screen output on our Raspberry Pi system:

```
$ man -k passwd
chgpasswd (8)              - update group passwords in batch mode
chpasswd (8)              - update passwords in batch mode
exim4_passwd (5)          - Files in use by the Debian exim4 packages
exim4_passwd_client (5)   - Files in use by the Debian exim4 packages
fgetpwent_r (3)           - get passwd file entry reentrantly
getpwent_r (3)            - get passwd file entry reentrantly
gpasswd (1)               - administer /etc/group and /etc/gshadow
openssl-passwd (1ssl)     - compute password hashes
pam_localuser (8)         - require users to be listed in /etc/passwd
passwd (1)                - change user password
passwd (1ssl)             - compute password hashes
passwd (5)                - the password file
passwd2des (3)            - RFS password encryption
update-passwd (8)         - safely update /etc/passwd, /etc/shadow and /etc/group
vncpasswd (1)             - VNC Server password utility
Output truncated...
```

0.2.6 Other Methods of Obtaining Help

To get a short description of what any particular Raspberry Pi OS command does, you can use the **whatis** command. This is similar to the command **man -f**. The general syntax of the **whatis** command is as follows:

whatis keywords

Purpose: Search the whatis database for abbreviated descriptions of each keyword

Output: Prints a one-line description of each keyword to the screen

The following is an illustration of how to use **whatis-**
The output of the two commands are truncated.

```
$ whatis man
man (7)   - macros to format man pages
man (1)   - an interface to the online
              reference manuals
$
```

You can also obtain short descriptions of more than one command by entering multiple arguments to the **whatis** command on the same command line, with spaces between each argument. The following is an illustration of this method:

$ whatis login set setenv
login (1)   - begin session on the system
login (3)   - write utmp and wtmp entries
setenv (3)   - change or add an environment variable
set: nothing appropriate.
$

The following In-Chapter Exercises ask you to use the **man** and **whatis** commands to find information about the **passwd** command. After completing the exercises, you can use what you have learned to change your login password on the Raspberry Pi system that you use.

In-Chapter Exercises

10. Use the **man** command with the **-k** option to display abbreviated help on the **passwd** command. Doing so will give you a screen display similar to that obtained with the **whatis** command, but it will show all apropos command names that contain the characters passwd.
11. Use the **whatis** command to get a brief description of the **passwd** command shown above, and then note the difference between the commands **whatis passwd** and **man -k passwd**.

0.3 Utility Commands

There are several major commands that allow the beginner to be more productive when using a Raspberry Pi system. A sampling of these kinds of utility commands is given in the following sections and is organized as system setups, general utilities, and communications commands.

0.3.1 Examining System Setups

The **whereis** command allows you to search along certain prescribed paths to locate utility programs and commands, such as shell programs. The general syntax of the **whereis** command is as follows:

whereis [options] filename
Purpose: Locate the binary, source, and man page files for a command
Output: The supplied names are first stripped of leading pathname components and extensions, then pathnames are displayed on screen
Commonly used options/features:
-b   Search only for binaries
-s   Search only for source code

For example, if you type the command **whereis bash** on the command line, you will see a list of the paths to the Bash shell program files themselves, as follows:

$ **whereis bash**
bash: /bin/bash /etc/bash.bashrc /usr/share/man/man1/bash.1.gz

Note that the paths to a "built-in," or internal, command cannot be found with the **whereis** command.

When you first log on, it is useful to be able to view a display of information about your **userid**, the computer or system you have logged on to, and the operating system on that computer. These tasks can be accomplished with the **whoami** command, which displays your **userid** on the screen. The general syntax of the **whoami** command is as follows:

whoami
Purpose: Displays the effective user id
Output: Displays your effective user id as a name on standard

The following shows how our system responded to this command when we typed it on the command line.

$ **whoami**
bob
$

The following In-Chapter Exercises give you the chance to use **whereis**, **whoami**, and two other important utility commands, **who** and **hostname** to obtain important information about your system.

To find out the IP address of the Raspberry Pi you are working on, you can use the ip command. The general syntax of the **ip** command is as follows:

ip [OPTIONS] OBJECT {COMMAND | help}
Purpose: Show/manipulate   routing,   network   devices,   interfaces,   and tunnels.
Output: Information about your LAN.

To find out the IP address of the computer you are working on, type the following command in a terminal or console window:

```
$ ip addr
1: lo: <LOOPBACK,UP,LOWER_UP> mtu 65536 qdisc noqueue state UNKNOWN group \
    default qlen 1000
    link/loopback 00:00:00:00:00:00 brd 00:00:00:00:00:00
    inet 127.0.0.1/8 scope host lo
      valid_lft forever preferred_lft forever
    inet6 ::1/128 scope host
      valid_lft forever preferred_lft forever
2: eth0: <BROADCAST,MULTICAST,UP,LOWER_UP> mtu 1500 qdisc mq state UP group \
    default qlen 1000
    link/ether dc:a6:32:ee:c6:6b brd ff:ff:ff:ff:ff:ff
    inet 192.168.1.2/24 brd 192.168.1.255 scope global dynamic noprefixroute eth0
      valid_lft 65558sec preferred_lft 54758sec
    inet6 fe80::78d9:c72e:75e2:82c/64 scope link
      valid_lft forever preferred_lft forever
3: wlan0: <BROADCAST,MULTICAST> mtu 1500 qdisc noop state DOWN group default \
    qlen 1000
    link/ether dc:a6:32:ee:c6:6c brd ff:ff:ff:ff:ff:ff
$
```

In the above output, the IP address 192.168.1.2 is the address on the LAN of this computer.

In-Chapter Exercises

12. Use the **whereis** command to locate binary files for the Korn shell, the Bourne shell, the Bourne Again shell, the C shell, and the Z shell. Are any of these shell programs not available on your system?

13. Use the **whoami** command to find your username on the system that you're using. Then use the **who** command to see how your username is listed, along with other users of the same system. What is the on-screen format of each user's listing that you obtained with the **who** command? Try to identify the information in each field on the same line as your username.

14. Use the **hostname -I** command to find out the IP address of host computer you are logged on to, on your LAN. Compares this to the output of the **ip addr** command on that same system.

0.4 Printing Commands

A very useful and common task performed by every user of a computer system is the printing of text files at a printer. This is accomplished using the configured printer(s) on the local, or a remote, system. Printers are controlled and managed with the Common UNIX Printing System (CUPS). We show this utility in detail in Chapter 1.

The common commands that perform printing on a Raspberry Pi system are **lpr** and **lp**. The general syntax of the **lpr** command is as follows:

lpr [options] filename
Purpose: Send files to the printer
Output: Files sent to the printer queue as print jobs
Commonly used options/features:
-P printer Send output to the named printer
-# copies Produce the number of copies indicated for each named file

The following **lpr** command accomplishes the printing of the file named **order.pdf** at the printer designated on our system as **spr**. Remember that no space is necessary between the option (in this case **-P**) and the option argument (in this case **spr**).

```
$ lpr -Pspr order.pdf
$
```

The following **lpr** command accomplishes the printing of the file named **memo1** at the default printer.

```
$ lpr memo1
$
```

The following multiple command combines the **man** command and the **lpr** command, and ties them together with the Raspberry Pi OS pipe (|) redirection character, to print the man pages describing the **ls** command at the printer named **hp1200**.

```
$ man ls | lpr -Php1200
$
```

The following shows how to perform printing tasks using the **lp** command. The general syntax of the **lp** command is as follows:

lp [options][option arguments] file(s)
Purpose: Submit files for printing on a designated system printer, or alter pending print jobs
Output: Printed files or altered print queue
Commonly used options/features:
-d destination Print to the specified destination
-n copies   Sets the number of copies to print.

In the first command, the file to be printed is named **file1**. In the second command, the files to be printed are named **sample** and **phones**. Note that the **-d** option is used to specify which printer to use. The option to specify the number of copies is **-n** for the **lp** command.

$ lp -d spr file1
request id is spr-983 (1 file(s))
$ lp -d spr -n 3 sample phones
request id is spr-984 (2 file(s))
$

0.5 Chapter Summary

In this introductory chapter, we covered essential Raspberry Pi OS commands, as specified in Table 0.2, that allow a system administrator to do

TABLE 0.2

Useful Commands for the Beginner

Command	What It Does
<Ctrl+D>	Terminates a process or command
alias	Allows you to create pseudonyms for commands
biff	Notifies you of new e-mail
cal	Displays a calendar on screen
cat	Allows joining of files
cd	Allows you to change the current working directory
cp	Allows you to copy files
exit	Ends a shell that you have started
hostname	Displays the name of the host computer that you are logged on to
ip	Displays IP information of the current host
login	Allows you to log on to the computer with a valid username/password pair
lpr or lp	Allows printing of text files
ls	Allows you to display names of files and directories in the current working directory
man	Allows you to view a manual page for a command or topic
mesg	Allows or disallows writing messages to the screen
mkdir	Allows you to create a new directory
more	Allows viewing of the contents of a file one screen at a time
mv	Allows you to move the path location of, or rename, files
passwd	Allows you to change your password on the computer
pg	Solaris command that displays one screen of a file at a time
pwd	Allows you to see the name of the current working directory
rm	Allows you to delete a file from the file structure
rmdir	Allows deletion of directories
talk	Allows you to send real-time messages to other users
telnet	Allows you to log on to a computer on a network or the Internet
unalias	Allows you to undefine pseudonyms for commands
uname	Displays information about the operating system running the computer
whatis	Allows you to view a brief description of a command
whereis	Displays the path(s) to commands and utilities in certain key directories
who	Allows you to find out login names of users currently on the system
whoami	Displays your username
write	Allows real-time messaging between users on the system

file maintenance and perform other useful operations. This is a mandatory set of essentials that even an ordinary, non-administrative user would need to know to work efficiently in a character, or text-based interface to the operating system. Text-based commands are the predominant means that a system administrator uses to maintain the integrity of the system. We gave examples and showed the basic format of the following commands and primitives-cat, cd, cp, exit, hostname, login, lp, lpr, ls, man, mesg, mkdir, more, mv, passwd, PATH, pwd, rm, rmdir, telnet, unalias, uname, whatis, whereis, who, whoami.

1

Basic System Administration

1.0 Objectives, Commands, and Primitives Covered

Objectives:

* To present download and installation instructions for Webmin
* To give an example of system service administration using systemd – vsftpd
* To describe the systemd target states
* To provide examples of making disk and media additions to a Raspberry Pi system
* To completely describe CUPS printing in the Raspberry Pi OS
* To detail other Linux backup facilities and commands, such as rsync
* To describe repository management for a Debian system
* To describe Linux tasks, processes, and threads
* To expand upon systemd journald messaging
* To define credentialing and various access control methods, such as DAC, MAC, and RBAC
* To describe the sudo program, command, and sudoers file
* To illustrate the uses of POSIX.1e and NFSv4 Access Control Lists (ACLs)
* To illustrate how to install an NFS server and client on Raspberry Pi OS systems
* To illustrate how to keep a Raspberry Pi system secure using the Uncomplicated Firewall (ufw)
* To show various encryption mechanisms, such as encrypting an entire hard disk
* To describe process credentialing and process capabilities
* To define and give an example of Linux namespaces
* To present a thorough overview of how systemd is the "superkernel" in the Raspberry Pi OS

Commands and Primitives Covered:

ACL addgroup adduser apt-key cat chgrp chmod chown compgen cpio CUPS DAC dd
du exec() export fdisk FileZilla fork() ftp getcap getfacl gpg id inxi journalctl kill lp
lpadmin lpc lpinfo lpmove lpoptions lpq lpr lprm lpstat MAC mdadm Mirroring mkfs.
ext4 mount nfs4_getfacl nfs4_setfacl nice ping POSIX.1e processes capabilities ps -aux
RAID1 RBAC renice setcap setfacl ssh sshd sudo sudoers file systemctl tar top touch
ufw umask umount uname vsftpd wget

1.1 Introduction – Icebreaker with inxi and FileZilla

To expand upon your beginner's knowledge of system administration topics
and commands, we present more advanced concepts, topics, commands, and
details here.

The overriding idea behind system administration of a modern,
21st-century Linux system, and for a Raspberry Pi OS in particular, is
the use of systemd to ensure that the Linux kernel works efficiently and
effectively to provide a computer system concurrency, virtualization,
and secure persistence. And this control of the kernel by a "superkernel"
(which is what systemd essentially is) must also promote the highest
level of system performance and speed, given the use cases the computer
might be put to and the perceived needs of the target user base that the
computer serves.

Certainly out of the multitude of possible topics we could have presented,
the ones you find here have been selected in somewhat of a subjective way.
That selective way was mainly guided by these concerns:

a. The secure maintenance, in terms of concurrency, virtualization, and
    persistence, of a single Raspberry Pi OS computer system that an
    ordinary novice user can install on their own personal computer.

b. How important the topics are in a perceived ranking of essential
    system administration tasks.

c. How systemd plays into the maintenance regimen chosen by that
    ordinary user.

d. The overall pedagogic integration of the selected topics presented on
    system administration.

e. How well these topics serve to prepare a beginner for entry into any
    chosen Information Technology or Computer Science profession, or
    how someone already in those professions can use this chapter to
    better their practice of that profession. In other words, for educational
    and continuing education audiences.

f. To some degree, making it possible to extrapolate these topics (for audiences in e.) from a single computer system environment to a broader and larger-scaled computing environment, such as is found on small- to medium-sized servers, or to cloud-based, virtual computing.

* Our Data Storage Model Recommendation – All Raspberry Pi models have multiple USB ports, for the attachment of additional peripherals, such as USB flash drives, or externally mounted SATA drives. We recommend that you maintain the Raspberry Pi OS on either an internal microSD card, or an externally mounted USB3 SATA or PCIe M.2 medium. We provide an example later, Example 1.5.2, that details how to boot and run the Raspberry Pi OS from a USB3 SATA SSD. We also recommend that you store all of the user data on another medium, or an array of attached media. That way, if the operating system and its bootable microSD card, USB3 SATA SSD, or PCIe M.2 medium become corrupted or unusable for some reason, *your user data is safe on separate storage media*. This technique (or storage model) dovetails very well with the most practical methods of operating system upgrades. Using it, you can then simply replace the operating system microSD card, USB3 SATA SSD, or PCIe M.2 board and reinstall either the current version of the operating system or a newer version, without significantly impacting your data storage. This will allow you to reattach the data drive(s) to the new operating system, onto whatever separate storage medium it's on. This methodology is highly valuable, not only for single-user desktop computers but also for server-class systems, such as NAS clusters that might be built using the Raspberry Pi OS and Raspberry Pi hardware as well.

The way that your data is deployed on your disks is a critical design consideration when you are building your system and is highly dependent on the particular use case that is guiding it.

The system we tested all of the following topics on, and in fact, everything from this book as well, is as follows:

System: Host: raspberrypi Kernel: 6.1.21-v8+ aarch64 bits: 64 compiler: gcc v: 10.2.1
Console: tty 0 Distro: Debian GNU/Linux 11 (bullseye)
Machine: Type: ARM Device System: Raspberry Pi 400 Rev 1.0 details: BCM2835 rev: c03130

Anything that you are required to type on the command line below is shown in **bold** type, always preceded by the shell prompt $ and always followed by pressing <Enter> on the keyboard.

1.1.1 inxi

How can you get a quick, informational snapshot of how your Raspberry Pi system is configured, particularly the hardware?

Use these two commands (when we did this on our Raspberry Pi 400, with the latest operating system version on it, we got the following output to the second command):

```
$ sudo apt install inxi
Output truncated ...
$ sudo inxi -GSCMm -t c -P -x
```

System:	Host: raspberrypi Kernel: 6.1.21-v8+ aarch64 bits: 64 compiler: gcc v: 10.2.1 Console: tty 0
Distro:	Debian GNU/Linux 11 (bullseye)
Machine:	Type: ARM Device System: Raspberry Pi 400 Rev 1.0 details: BCM2835 rev: c03130
serial:	10000000fdd89bf2
Memory:	RAM: total: 3.78 GiB used: 606.7 MiB (15.7%) gpu: 76 MiB
RAM Report:	unknown-error: Unknown dmidecode error. Unable to generate data.
CPU:	Info: Quad Core model: N/A variant: cortex-a72 bits: 64 type: MCP arch: ARMv8 rev: 3
features:	Use -f option to see features bogomips: 432
Speed:	1800 MHz min/max: 600/1800 MHz Core speeds (MHz): 1: 1800 2: 1800 3: 1800 4: 1800
Graphics:	Device-1: bcm2711-hdmi0 driver: vc4_hdmi v: N/A bus ID: N/A
Device-2:	bcm2711-hdmi1 driver: vc4_hdmi v: N/A bus ID: N/A
Device-3:	bcm2711-vc5 driver: vc4_drm v: N/A bus ID: N/A
Display:	server: X.Org 1.20.11 driver: loaded: modesetting unloaded: fbdev resolution: 1920x1080~60Hz
OpenGL:	renderer: V3D 4.2 v: 2.1 Mesa 20.3.5 direct render: Yes
Partition:	ID-1: / size: 438.79 GiB used: 10.96 GiB (2.5%) fs: ext4 dev: /dev/sda2
	ID-2: /boot size: 252 MiB used: 30.4 MiB (12.1%) fs: vfat dev: /dev/sda1
Processes:	CPU top: 5 of 220
	1: cpu: 7.5% command: xorg pid: 727 mem: 88.1 MiB (2.3%)
	2: cpu: 4.0% command: sudo pid: 2119 mem: 4.36 MiB (0.1%)
	3: cpu: 3.5% command: mutter pid: 919 mem: 79.6 MiB (2.0%)
	4: cpu: 3.0% command: packagekitd pid: 1368 mem: 20.4 MiB (0.5%)
	5: cpu: 2.4% command: init pid: 1 mem: 10.3 MiB (0.2%)

See the man page on your Raspberry Pi OS for more information about the **inxi** command.

1.1.2 FileZilla

FileZilla is nominally a graphics-based ftp client and server program that can use ssh as the tunnel or conduit between systems. It has a number of useful functions and menu choices that allow the system administrator to successfully, confidently, and efficiently backup and restore single files or directories via a network globally. It is most useful for backing up and restoring single-user files and directories.

It is not a replacement or substitute for the command-line facilities shown in the following sections. Figure 1.1 illustrates the screen display and menus available in the "client" version of FileZilla.

Both client and server, in our case, a local machine running the Raspberry Pi OS system and a remote machine running the same OS, must have ssh communications protocol enabled between them. To see more about establishing ssh between Raspberry Pi systems, see Section 1.3. You can have login access to an account on the remote server, or you can anonymously log in as well if that is enabled.

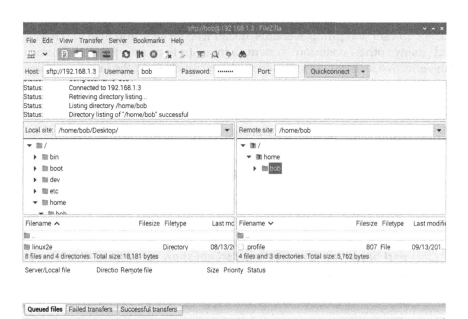

FIGURE 1.1
Filezilla Main Window.

After launching FileZilla on the client, to log in to a remote host server, you need to supply the IP address of the server, the login name and password, and the port number (22 for ssh). Once you have successfully logged in, the local machine's directory and file structure are shown on the left side of the figure. The remote machine's directory structure is shown on the right side of the figure. To transfer files or directories between machines, you simply drag and drop between the appropriate panes on the left or right. If you are overwriting previously transferred files or directories, the FileZilla default is to give you the chance to overwrite or rename the files being transferred.

There are a number of other menu choices at the top of the FileZilla screen that allows you to change preferences, set bookmarks, etc. For example, via the menu choice Manage Bookmarks and the Site Manager, you can automatically make multiple local directories and remote directories available for ssh transfer as soon as you log in to the remote server sites.

1.2 Webmin Download and Installation

This section details how to install and do a very basic configuration of Webmin on the Raspberry Pi OS. Webmin has a GUI control panel for doing many system administration tasks, and most importantly, it is a web-based interface that can be very effectively used to manage your system. Webmin can set up user and group accounts, install web servers, initialize file sharing, and many other common system administration activities. Webmin is time-effective for beginners who do not know much about the Linux command line or want a simpler, more intuitive graphical interface to the system.

Example 1.1 will lead you through the step-by-step download, installation, and initial minimal but critical configuration of Webmin on the Raspberry Pi OS. The instructions given here were executed on a Raspberry Pi 400.

Example 1.1 Webmin Installation on Raspberry Pi OS

1. Type the following on the command line to prepare your system by installing dependencies:

```
$ sudo apt-get install perl libnet-ssleay-perl openssl libauthen-pam-\
   perl libpam-runtime libio-pty-perl apt-show-versions python \
   shared-mime-info -y                              .
```

2. Type the following to download Webmin.

```
$ wget http://prdownloads.sourceforge.net/webadmin/webmin_\
   1.998_all.deb
```

At the time of the writing of this book, the version of Webmin available was version 1.998. This probably will not be the current version when you are executing these instructions, but once you have Webmin installed and running, it's very easy to upgrade to the latest version from right within the program. You can also check what the latest version of Webmin is by going to this URL and substituting the latest version number found there for webmin_1.998.

https://sourceforge.net/projects/webadmin/files/

3. Install Webmin with the following commands:

    $ sudo apt install ./webmin_1.998_all.deb

4. (Optional) If ufw is active on your system (which by default it is *not* on the Raspberry Pi OS), allow Webmin through the firewall with the following command:

    $ sudo ufw allow 10000

5. Webmin uses 10000 as its default port in the system. To access the Webmin panel using your favorite web browser from anywhere on your LAN (or, for that matter, from the same machine you installed Webmin on), type this into your URL bar on your web browser.

    https://your-ip-address:10000

    where **your-ip-address** is the IP address of the machine you just installed Webmin on.

6. A warning appears in the browser window the first time you try to access Webmin, reading

    "Your connection is not private."

    Make the Advanced choice in the dialog box that appears on the screen, and Add Exception button choice in the subsequent box. Then choose Proceed to your_ip_address (unsafe).

7. The Webmin sign-in screen appears in your browser window.

    Log in to your account on the system with your username and password pair, make sure you put an x in the box for *Remember me,* and click on Sign in.

    The Webmin System Information panel appears on the screen, showing a very extensive display of the state of your Raspberry Pi system.

8. Play with Webmin in a non-destructive way. In other words, if you encounter a Webmin function or activity that asks you to change the basic configuration of the system, do not proceed at this point. Once

you learn more about Linux configuration from the sections in this chapter, you will be better prepared to use Webmin to change them. When you are done, choose Logout from the Webmin panel on the left of your web browser display.

In the sections below in this chapter, you can go back into Webmin at any time and experiment with Webmin to find out how relatively efficient and effective Webmin is in handling the tasks we detail in those sections!

1.3 sshd and System Service Management Using systemd: vsftpd

1.3.1 Connecting via a Secure SHell (SSH) Client between Raspberry Pi OS Machines

The basic methodology, and the techniques we show below, allow a user on one Raspberry Pi OS computer to remote log in and log out of another computer using the SSH protocol. SSH is a very secure encrypted channel of communication between a client computer and a server on a LAN or the Internet. The computer you are using to log into another computer is known as the SSH *client*. The computer you want to log into with SSH is known as the *server*, or the *host* system.

Before this methodology can be used, both client and server systems must be able to talk to each other over the SSH channel. In other words, the server system must have the SSH server-side software package installed and enabled on it. This is usually not the default on most Linux systems, so you have to follow the installation and/or enabling instructions given for your particular flavor of Linux to accomplish this.

There are a few approaches to enabling SSH server-side software on the latest Raspberry Pi OS, as follows:

1. Starting from scratch, you could directly enable it when the system is flashed to the microSD card you might be running the system from. At installation, a convenient graphical dialog box allows you to do this.

2. On an already-installed system, in a terminal window, you can use the command **sudo raspi-config**, to descend through the Raspberry Pi Software Configuration Tool menu choices Interface Options>SSH, and enable it.

3. Launch the Raspberry Pi Configuration Tool from the Preferences Menu, and do the same thing as in step 2.

4. By default, the SSH server-side package was *not* installed on our Raspberry Pi OS systems, but in a terminal window, we were able to install it with the following command:

$ **sudo apt-get install openssh-server**

After the above command is executed successfully, the SSH server-side "service" is installed, started, and enabled. Being "enabled" means able to start at subsequent reboots of the Raspberry Pi OS.

The client-side SSH software is installed by default on most Linux system implementations, including on our Raspberry Pi system.

Note The user must know a valid username/password pair on the remote server system to be able to log in to the remote system!

1.3.1.1 Login and Logout Procedures

We show three possible methods that can be used in this two-way communications dialog once server-side software is installed.

First, if the user has previously already logged into the host successfully from the client before, and the authentication keys have not changed. Second, if the user has *never* logged into the host successfully before from the client. And third, if the user has logged into the host before, but the authentication key on the host has changed since the last successful login. These are practical situations one might encounter any time you use this remote login method.

What the user types in is shown in **bold** text:

Method 1. Having logged in before successfully:

$ **ssh bob@192.168.1.15**
bob@192.168.1.15's password: **www**
Linux raspberrypi 6.1.21-v8+ #1642 SMP PREEMPT Mon Apr 3 17:24:16 BST 2023 \
  aarch64

The programs included with the Debian GNU/Linux system are free software;
the exact distribution terms for each program are described in the
individual files in /usr/share/doc/*/copyright.

Debian GNU/Linux comes with ABSOLUTELY NO WARRANTY, to the extent
permitted by applicable law.
Last login: Fri May 5 07:17:44 2023 from 192.168.1.11
$ **Execute Command Line Linux Commands**
$ **logout**
Connection to 192.168.1.15 closed.
$

Method 2. Having never logged in before:

$ **ssh bob@192.168.1.15**
The authenticity of host '192.168.1.15 (192.168.1.15)' can't be established. ECDSA
    key fingerprint is SHA256:uZpqi4U6uBN5SOBVFRbqbl5HspmV3eZAw/nUvPBTS5I.
Are you sure you want to continue connecting (yes/no)? **yes**
Warning: Permanently added '192.168.1.15' (ECDSA) to the list of known hosts.
bob@192.168.1.15's password: **www**
Linux raspberrypi 6.1.21-v8+ #1642 SMP PREEMPT Mon Apr 3 17:24:16 BST 2023
    aarch64

The programs included with the Debian GNU/Linux system are free software;
the exact distribution terms for each program are described in the
individual files in /usr/share/doc/*/copyright.

Debian GNU/Linux comes with ABSOLUTELY NO WARRANTY, to the extent permitted
    by applicable law.
Last login: Fri May 5 07:17:44 2023 from 192.168.1.2
$ **Execute Command Line Linux Commands**
$ **logout**
Connection to 192.168.1.15 closed.
$

Method 3. Logged in before, but the host key has changed:

$ **ssh bob@192.168.1.15**
@@@
    @@@@@@@@@@
@ WARNING: REMOTE HOST IDENTIFICATION HAS CHANGED! @
@@@
    @@@@@@@@@@
IT IS POSSIBLE THAT SOMEONE IS DOING SOMETHING NASTY!
Someone could be eavesdropping on you right now (man-in-the-middle attack)!
It is also possible that a host key has just been changed.
The fingerprint for the ECDSA key sent by the remote host is
SHA256:hNGE725MKYvuOrAHkTX7nwLYP8GKqutPJG3pAKJmvzw.
Please contact your system administrator.
Add correct host key in /home/bob/.ssh/known_hosts to get rid of this message.
Offending ECDSA key in /home/bob/.ssh/known_hosts:2
  remove with:
  ssh-keygen -f "/home/bob/.ssh/known_hosts" -R "192.168.1.15"
ECDSA host key for 192.168.1.15 has changed and you have requested strict
    checking.
Host key verification failed.
rsync: connection unexpectedly closed (0 bytes received so far) [sender]
rsync error: unexplained error (code 255) at io.c(228) [sender=3.2.3]
$ **ssh-keygen -f "/home/bob/.ssh/known_hosts" -R "192.168.1.15"**
    Output truncated...
$ **ssh bob@192.168.1.15**
The authenticity of host '192.168.1.15 (192.168.1.15)' can't be established.
ECDSA key fingerprint is 43:e8:cf:33:d5:ed:dd:05:d9:e9:a5:9d:d3:18:1d:2b.
No matching host key fingerprint found in DNS.
Are you sure you want to continue connecting (yes/no)? **yes**

Warning: Permanently added '192.168.1.15' (ECDSA) to the list of known hosts.
bob@192.168.1.15's password: **www**
Last login: Sat Dec 24 16:54:10 2016 from 192.168.1.2
Output truncated...
$ Execute Command Line Linux Commands
$ logout
Connection to 192.168.1.15 closed.
$

In all of the three methods, the user is assumed to have an account with the same username, and possibly password, on both client and host systems.

In method 2, the keys are generated on the host and client after the user types in **yes** and presses <Enter>.

In method 3, after the first failed attempt to establish an SSH connection, the error message indicates that the authentication key has changed on the host. A very helpful component of the error message is the instruction:

Add the correct host key in /home/bob/.ssh/known_hosts to get rid of this message.

Offending ECDSA key in /usr/home/bob/.ssh/known_hosts:2

So removal of the offending key in the file **/home/bob/.ssh/known_hosts** on the client machine is done by using the command:

$ ssh-keygen -f "/home/bob/.ssh/known_hosts" -R "192.168.1.15"

Then a new key is generated, an exchange can take place, and the login can proceed.

The line in all three methods above that reads "**Execute Command Line Linux Commands**" is where the user types in any of the valid Linux commands we show in this chapter and throughout the rest of this book. Finally, after typing **logout**, the user cuts the SSH channel connection and is returned to the command-line prompt of the local client system.

Example 1.2 vsftpd

Objectives: To install, and start a system service for a secure form of ftp, using systemd

Prerequisites: Knowledge of basic Linux commands, having SSH enabled on your Raspberry Pi OS. To enable SSH on your Raspberry Pi OS, you can use the raspi-config tool from the command line or the Preferences pulldown menu and navigate to Interfacing Options to accomplish it. Or you can use the methods shown in Section 1.3.1.1. SSH will give you access to the SFTP functions of the protocol.

Background: One of the most important uses of systemd for system administration is managing essential system services. vsftpd is a secure ftp server that can be used by client machines on your network or the Internet to log into a host machine, and exchange files.

Requirements: Do the following steps, in the order presented, to meet the requirements of this example:

1. Download and install the vsftpd server with the following command:

    $ **sudo apt install vsftpd**

2. Use the systemd systemctl command to check the status of the vsftpd service using the following command:

    $ **systemctl status vsftpd.service**
    ● vsftpd.service - vsftpd FTP server
        Loaded: loaded (/lib/systemd/system/vsftpd.service; enabled; vendor
            preset>
        Active: active (running) since Sun 2022-10-02 06:35:04 PDT; 8s ago
        Process: 33498 ExecStartPre=/bin/mkdir -p /var/run/vsftpd/empty
            (code=exite>
        Main PID: 33499 (vsftpd)
         Tasks: 1 (limit: 4164)
          CPU: 13ms
        CGroup: /system.slice/vsftpd.service
               └─33499 /usr/sbin/vsftpd /etc/vsftpd.conf

    Oct 02 06:35:04 raspberrypi systemd[1]: Starting vsftpd FTP server...
    Oct 02 06:35:04 raspberrypi systemd[1]: Started vsftpd FTP server.

    Notice from the above output that the command from step 1 not only downloaded but also installed and started the vsftpd service.

3. From another host machine on your network, use the ftp command to connect to the vsftpd server on your machine. Substitute the IP address of the machine you want to ftp into for the IP 192.168.0.30 shown in this command:

    # **ftp 192.168.1.6**
    Connected to 192.168.0.36.
    220 (vsFTPd 3.0.3)
    Name (192.168.0.6:bob): bob
    331 Please specify the password.
    Password: **QQQ**
    230 Login successful.
    Remote system type is UNIX.
    Using binary mode to transfer files.

4. Get a directory listing of the files on the machine you are connected to:

    ftp> **ls**

Here is a directory listing on the machine you are connected to:

```
200 PORT command successful. Consider using PASV.
150 Here comes the directory listing.

-rw-r--r--      1 1000    1000         0 Jun 10 08:01 32m
drwxr-xr-x      2 1000    1000      4096 Jul 02 12:13 Desktop
drwxr-xr-x      2 1000    1000      4096 Jun 09 16:51 Documents
drwxr-xr-x      2 1000    1000      4096 Jun 09 16:51 Downloads
drwx------     23 1000    1000      4096 Jul 02 11:51 Dropbox
drwxr-xr-x      2 1000    1000      4096 Jun 09 16:51 Music
drwxr-xr-x      2 1000    1000      4096 Jun 09 16:51 Pictures
drwxr-xr-x      2 1000    1000      4096 Jun 09 16:51 Public
drwxr-xr-x      2 1000    1000      4096 Jun 09 16:51 Templates
drwxr-xr-x      2 1000    1000      4096 Jun 09 16:51 Videos
-rw-r--r--      1 1000    1000 134217728 Jun 10 08:14 disk1
226 Directory send OK.
```

5. Terminate the connection with the following ftp command:

```
ftp> exit
221 Goodbye.
#
```

6. In order to stop the vsftpd service, use the following command:

```
$ sudo systemctl stop vsftpd.service
$
```

7. Check the status of the vsftpd service with the following command:

```
$ systemctl status vsftpd.service
• vsftpd.service - vsftpd FTP server
  Loaded: loaded (/lib/systemd/system/vsftpd.service; enabled; vendor preset>
  Active: inactive (dead) since Sun 2022-10-02 06:44:10 PDT; 13s ago
  Process: 33498 ExecStartPre=/bin/mkdir -p /var/run/vsftpd/empty
  (code=exite>
  Process: 33499 ExecStart=/usr/sbin/vsftpd /etc/vsftpd.conf (code=killed, si>
  Main PID: 33499 (code=killed, signal=TERM)
      CPU: 203ms

Oct 02 06:35:04 raspberrypi systemd[1]: Starting vsftpd FTP server...
Oct 02 06:35:04 raspberrypi systemd[1]: Started vsftpd FTP server...
```

8. To restart the vsftpd service, use the following command:

```
$ sudo systemctl restart vsftpd.service
```

9. To make sure a service starts automatically at boot time, use the following command:

$ sudo systemctl enable vsftpd.service
Synchronizing state of vsftpd.service with SysV init with /lib/systemd/
   systemd-sysv-install...
Executing /lib/systemd/systemd-sysv-install enable vsftpd
$

10. To disable a service from starting at boot, use the following command:

$ sudo systemctl disable vsftpd.service
Synchronizing state of vsftpd.service with SysV service script with /lib/
   systemd/systemd-sysv-install.
Executing: /lib/systemd/systemd-sysv-install disable vsftpd
Removed /etc/systemd/system/multi-user.target.wants/vsftpd.service.
$

Conclusion: This example allowed you to download, install, and start a system service known as vsftpd. You could then connect to and use the computer as an ftp server. Additionally, we showed some basic systemd service management commands applied to the vsftpd service.

1.4 systemd Bootup

When the system boots, systemd on the kernel image is responsible for initializing the required file systems, services, and drivers necessary for the system's operation. With systemd, this process is split up into runtime steps whose objectives are target units. The process is done as much as possible in parallel and is non-specific, so that the order in which target units are reached is determined at runtime, with some default order.

Table 1.1 shows some critical systemd target units.

TABLE 1.1

Important systemd Targets

default.target	The target that is booted by default. Not a real target, but rather a symbolic link to another target like graphic.target.
emergency.target	Starts an emergency shell on the console. Only use it at the boot prompt as systemd.unit=emergency.target.
graphical.target	The default target in a GUI, or desktop install. Starts a system with network, multiuser support and a display manager.
halt.target	Shuts down the system.
multi-user.target	Starts a multiuser console, or terminal interface system with network.
reboot.target	Reboots the system.
rescue.target	Starts a single-user system without network.

When systemd takes over the boot process, it activates target units that are dependencies of default.target, and all other dependencies. default.target is an alias of graphical.target or multi-user.target, depending on whether the system is configured for a graphical user interface, or only for a text console.

1.5 File Systems, Connections to Persistent Media, and Adding Disks to Your System

Question: What is a computer file system?

Answer: A way of logically ordering data, so that it is persistent, can be securely and easily located very quickly, and then accessed in a consistent way for use.

Providing data persistence, which is the third primary objective of the Raspberry Pi OS itself, in large part involves establishing and maintaining connections to persistent media, such as disk drives. These drives, and the file systems found on them, can be physically connected directly inside the Raspberry Pi hardware, such as the microSD card, or externally via the USB bus. They can also be some form of remote virtual drive, such as a network-available file system on a remote drive, or remote volumes and complements of drives.

And in some cases, a file system may *not* make use of a persistent storage device or medium at all! At this higher level of abstraction, the file system can access, use, organize, and represent *any* form of data, whether it is persistent or volatile. We use the word volatile here to mean during the transient lifetime of some process or service. Of course, systemd and the Linux kernel control all processes and services running on the computer. *Pseudo* and special-purpose file systems (sometimes called *synthetic file systems*), which can be thought of as virtual file systems, have this characteristic.

There are also established protocols for connecting to and accessing either physical, virtual, or pseudo-file systems in the locations where they may reside. Two examples of access protocols that establish and maintain the connections to virtual, network-available media and file systems are the Network File System, version 4 (NFSv4), and the Internet Small Computer System Interface (iSCSI).

In this section, we first present an organizing scheme that you can use to think about types of drives and file systems. A file system may be nominally assigned according to what medium it exists on: a directly connected physical medium (such as the microSD card or a USB3 SATA SSD), a virtual medium (such as Network-Attached Storage or Storage Area Networks that use NFSv4 or iSCSI), or as a specialized pseudo-file system that is not on a persistent medium at all (such as the cgroups or proc file systems).

The following sections give examples of adding directly connected physical disks to a Raspberry Pi OS system.

Additionally, we suggest an approach, when using the recommended storage model we give in Section 1.1, to adding persistent media to your Raspberry Pi system.

That approach is a more traditional method, where you first properly connect the device to the computer with cables, partition that medium, manually add a file system to it (typically the FAT32 or ext4 file system), and then finally create directories and files in the partition(s) on the media. The following sections detail this more traditional approach.

According to our organizing scheme, a file system can be separated into three hierarchically arranged layers that perform very particular functions. These layers, arranged from farthest-to-nearest to the actual hardware of the drives or persistent media in question, are as follows:

The Logical Layer

This layer is used for interaction with user application programs and the processes they consist of via Linux system calls. It provides the application programming interface (API) for file operations, for example, system calls to OPEN, CLOSE, READ, etc., and connects with the layer below it for processing. The logical layer achieves efficient file access, logically organized directory operations, and provides user autonomy and security.

The Virtual Layer

This layer provides the interface mechanisms for maintaining multiple, simultaneously existing implementations of physical and virtual file systems on the same computer. For example, it makes it possible to mount and transparently use NFSv4, btrfs, ext3, ext4, fat32, and ZFS at the same time on the same system and operate with files from all of those implementations as if they were all of the same type.

The Linux IO (LIO) block is known as an iSCSI "target," and represents virtual layer connectivity to persistent media from various network connections. These connections traditionally use high-speed Fibre Channel technology to create a Storage Area Network (SAN), but most importantly can also be achieved using Ethernet and TCP/IP.

A more detailed architectural scheme of classifying virtual layer file systems further separates that layer into block-based, network, stackable, pseudo, and special purpose categories. Many of the different implementations of file systems, such as NFSv4, ext4, xfs, btrfs, initramfs, and the procfs, would be situated within the Virtual File Systems block. Two very contemporary and extremely important virtual file systems are the cgroups file system (cgroupsfs) used by systemd, and the userland, block-based file system, ZFS.

The Physical Layer

This layer is concerned with the physical operation of the persistent storage device. It processes physical blocks being read or written. It handles buffering and memory management and is responsible for the physical placement of blocks in specific locations on the storage medium. The physical file system interacts with the device drivers or with the channels that physical devices communicate over. At a certain level of simplification, this layer can be schematically represented by the integrated grouping of the Block Layer, SCSI Layers, and the Physical Device Layer.

Furthermore, and as a very integral part of the operation of the Linux kernel, as it exists in a transient and volatile state as we have defined it, the pseudo and special-purpose file systems can be viewed as a series of conduits through which the entire system itself "flows." Thinking along these lines, when the kernel is in the CPU and attendant RAM, the kernel code itself is organized as a file system. The kernel (or systemd superkernel) can be viewed as a file system of volatile data structures that maintains the steady state of the hardware and software using these conduits exclusively; this achieves the overarching goals of virtualization, concurrency, user-autonomy, security, and necessary archival, long-term data persistence on the file systems that are established to do so.

Over the history of Linux, various file systems have been used to provide speed, efficiency, security, and utility to the ordinary user. The most contemporary and universal of these, across the three major branches of Linux, is the Linux Extended File System (ext). The Raspberry Pi OS we show in this book uses it as the default file system.

The fourth version of ext, ext4, is the current and most robust version so far. It has several features, such as large scalability, the ability to map to very large disk array sizes, and other very critical features, such as journaling. Following is a compact listing of some of the features of ext4:

a. It can support volumes with sizes up to 1 exabyte and files with sizes up to 16 terabytes.
b. It uses an "extents" mapping scheme, which replaces block mapping used by earlier versions of ext. An extent is a range of contiguous physical blocks.
c. It is backward-compatible with ext3 and ext2. Therefore ext3 and ext2 can be mounted as ext4.
d. It delays block allocation until data is flushed to disk.
e. It has an unlimited number of subdirectories that can be created.
f. It has a multi-block allocator that can make better choices about allocating files contiguously on disk.
g. It provides timestamps measured in nanoseconds.

Most importantly, from the perspective of our recommended data storage model, adding a second hard drive, for example, allows you to keep the operating system and the user data on two different physical persistent media. That way, if the operating system fails and the system disk is corrupted and unusable, the data survives on the user data disk and can very easily be recovered.

There are many traditional, legacy methods of achieving the objective of our data storage model, using facilities such as Linux disk and file maintenance commands, utilities such as mdadm (a software RAID manager), and Linux Volume Management (LVM). But from our perspective, the modern and contemporary way of implementing the recommended data storage model is using ZFS on redundant additional persistent media. With ZFS, you get bit-level data integrity, volume management, RAID capabilities at all levels, and a failure-proof backup strategy, all rolled into one utility.

There are some very important reasons for adding persistent media to your system, aside from conforming to our recommended storage model. Your internal microSD card may be running out of space or beginning to show signs of failure.

Partitioning Schemes and Strategies
It should be evident to you that the Raspberry Pi OS organizes everything in files and uses a file system to organize those files. A disk partition can be most simply defined as a logical area of the disk that holds a file system.

Once you verify that your Raspberry Pi system can recognize the additional media, there are several reasons to adopt a particular partitioning scheme for a newly added disk drive. Creating multiple partitions on your hard drive avoids full disk problems by segregating directories into those partitions and gives the system administrator control over access to those directories and partitions. And you can maintain different file system structures simultaneously in different partitions. Even installing the system into a customized partitioning scheme allows you to install multiple operating systems on your computer.

When adding new disk drives, you can use the traditional method of partitioning with command-line utilities such as fdisk or gdisk or the option of using a GUI-based method with a utility such as Gparted. As we show in the sections below, you can implement our recommended data storage model with a traditional ext4 Linux file system scheme. We present an example detailing how to do this using the traditional ext4 scheme.

To help the administrator of a Raspberry Pi system with the task of adding persistent media, the following sections will also address these general concerns:

* The availability of software device drivers for the new hardware to be added.

* How the hardware will be recognized, configured, and deployed on the system.

As discussed in Item (1) of Section 1.5.1, our data storage model for desktop computers is capable of deploying two or more external USB2 or 3 drives, and its implementation is made possible by what we show in the following sub-sections.

The additions in the traditional ext4-based example shown below in Section 1.5.3 will be done for USB flash drives but can also be easily extended to other persistent media, such as externally mounted SSDs, spinning hard disks, or other external media, such as PCIe M.2 cards.

SATA Disks and USB Media:
Generally, when you add a persistent medium, such as USB flash drives, SSDs, or PCIe M.2 cards, some significant time after you have installed the operating system on the computer, you will want to partition it. You might even want to create a new partition table on it, create one or more partitions, and format those partitions using a standard Linux file system, such as ext4. We emphasize and encourage using the Gparted GUI-based application to do this.

When you add an external USB-bus medium, such as a flash drive or other forms of persistent storage device, it is generally already formatted to the file system type known as FAT32 (in the case of most popular commercially available USB flash drives), or to some other format depending on the media. Traditionally, you can then partition the disk using the **fdisk** command and add a file system to it with the **mkfs** command. We emphasize and encourage the use of **fdisk**, or its newer sister, **gdisk**, to do the partitioning, if that's the route you want to go on the commandline.

Note
The safe removal of USB media can be done manually in the Raspberry Pi OS. For example, using the desktop system GUI you can click on the Media Eject button on the right side from the Taskbar at the top of the screen, and safely remove attached, mounted removable media. Unmounting a USB flash drive, or other USB bus media, can also be done from the command line with the **umount** command.

When a USB flash drive or other external medium is automatically mounted on a Raspberry Pi system, the path to it is **/media/your_home_dir/id**, where **your_home_dir** is the name of your home directory on the system, and **id** is the disk id number or identifier.

For example, when we added a 2 TB Seagate USB3 externally mounted SATA disk to our Raspberry Pi 400 and created a single primary partition on it with Gparted, along with an ext4 file system automatically added to that partition at the same time, the newly mounted hard drive was accessed via the following path:

/media/bob/Seagate_Backup_Drive_Plus

1.5.1 Preliminary Considerations When Adding New Media

If you insert a USB flash drive that you know is functioning properly into your computer, and it is *not* recognized, the chances are that your Raspberry Pi system does not have a device driver available to enable communication between the computer and the flash drive.

How do you know if a new disk drive is recognized and, most importantly, is usable on your system?

There are at least three quick and easy ways to know if the new disk drive is recognized.

1. If it is a USB flash drive and it is formatted to FAT32, the Raspberry Pi OS system will auto-mount it, and an icon for it will open on the desktop (along with a file folder view of its contents).
2. In a terminal window, you can use the command **systemctl –f** and watch the screen display. It will show that a new device has been added, even though, in the case of a USB flash drive, it might be for-matted to something other than FAT32.
3. Use the before-and-after technique shown in Section 1.5.2.

The same is true when you connect a SATA hard drive properly, but the prob-ability of it not being recognized is much lower. The best and easiest thing to do in a case like this is to use another USB or SATA device. The Raspberry PiOS system has facilities to find and install device drivers on your system for a device, but this process is time-consuming and may not be fruitful for the particular device in question. Also, writing a driver for your device is possible, which is even more time-consuming. The important thing here is not that the USB flash drive is formatted to FAT32, but that a manufacturer has the device drivers available automatically when their device is inserted. This is not always true.

In many instances, it is important to know the physical device name, the instance name, and the logical device name of disk drives on your system, but practically speaking, for the Raspberry Pi OS administrator, easily finding out the logical device name of a disk drive is most important.

You may want to add an external medium to your Raspberry Pi system that has been used on another computer operating system previously. In that case, the primary and secondary examples we show can be deployed to repartition and prepare that hard disk for new use on your system.

1.5.2 Five Quick and Easy Ways to Find Out the Logical Device Names of Disks

Before attaching a new disk drive to your Raspberry Pi system, it is important to know how to determine, in a very quick and easy manner, what the currently installed logical device names of the disk drives actually attached and useable on your system are. What we mean by "attached and usable" is that the disk drive is properly connected and recognized by the system and has a device driver that the system can use to communicate with it.

Before and after: If you want to find out the logical device name of a new disk you want to add to the system, use one of the following methods to see what disks are on your system *before* you add the new disk, and then use the same method *after* the new disk has been added and note the difference. The different or new logical name that appears will be the logical device name of the new disk.

The five simple methods that follow show how to determine what disk drives are attached and usable on your system and what the logical device names of those and any others you might want to add to your system are.

Method 1 – Change your current working directory to /dev. Type **ls**. Hard drives, for example, show up in the **ls** listing as sda, sdb, etc. The full path to the first slice, or partition, on one of these disks, is specified as /dev/sda1. A USB bus device, like a flash drive, would show up in the ls listing as /dev/sdc, or whatever letter designation comes after the hard drives, and the full path to the first slice on it would be /dev/sdc1.

Method 2 – Type **df -hT** on the command line to find out the file system names and paths they are mounted at on your system. On our Raspberry Pi system, when we did this to see if a Lexar 60 Gb USB flash drive was recently successfully attached to the system, this is the output:

```
$ df -hT
Filesystem       Type       Size   Used   Avail   Use% Mounted on
/dev/root        ext4       29G    8.3G   20G     30%  /
devtmpfs         devtmpfs   1.7G   0      1.7G    0%   /dev
tmpfs            tmpfs      1.9G   0      1.9G    0%   /dev/shm
tmpfs            tmpfs      759M   1.4M   758M    1%   /run
tmpfs            tmpfs      5.0M   4.0K   5.0M    1%   /run/lock
/dev/mmcblk0p1   vfat       253M   31M    222M    13%  /boot
tmpfs            tmpfs      380M   28K    380M    1%   /run/user/1000
/dev/sdb1        vfat       120G   2.4G   117G    2%   /media/bob/Lexar
/dev/sda1        vfat       30G    27M    30G     1%   /media/bob/52DC-3D26
$
```

We address more details of the command in Section 1.16.

Method 3 – Very similar to using the **df** command, use the **lsblk -a** command. When we used this command and option on our Raspberry Pi system, after we had attached the Lexar 60 Gb USB flash drive, we got the following output:

```
$ lsblk -a
NAME        MAJ:MIN     RM    SIZE    RO        TYPE MOUNTPOINT
ram0          1:0       0     4M      0         disk
ram1          1:1       0     4M      0         disk
ram2          1:2       0     4M      0         disk
ram3          1:3       0     4M      0         disk
Output truncated . . .
sda         8:0    1    30G  0 disk
└─sda1      8:1    1    30G  0 part /media/bob/52DC-3D26
sdb         8:16   1  119.2G 0 disk
└─sdb1      8:17   1  119.2G 0 part /media/bob/Lexar
mmcblk0    179:0   0   29.7G 0 disk
├─mmcblk0p1 179:1  0    256M 0 part /boot
└─mmcblk0p2 179:2  0   29.5G 0 part /
$
```

Method 4 – Use the **findmnt** command. When we used this on our
Raspberry Pi system, we obtained the following output:

```
$ findmnt
TARGET                     SOURCE            FSTYPE        OPTIONS
/                          /dev/mmcblk0p2    ext4          rw,noatime
├─/dev                     devtmpfs          devtmpfs      rw,relatime,size=1776952k,nr_
                                                           inodes=444238,mode=755
│ ├─/dev/shm               tmpfs             tmpfs         rw,nosuid,nodev
│ ├─/dev/pts               devpts            devpts        rw,nosuid,noexec,relatime,gid=5,mode
                                                           =620,ptmxmode=000
│ └─/dev/mqueue            mqueue            mqueue        rw,nosuid,nodev,noexec,relatime
├─/proc                    proc              proc          rw,relatime
│ ├─/proc/sys/fs/binfmt_misc systemd-1       autofs        rw,relatime,fd=29,pgrp=1,timeout=0,
                                                           minproto=5,maxproto=
│ └─/proc/fs/nfsd          nfsd              nfsd          rw,relatime
├─/sys                     sysfs             sysfs         rw,nosuid,nodev,noexec,relatime
│ ├─/sys/kernel/security securityfs          securityfs    rw,nosuid,nodev,noexec,relatime
│ ├─/sys/fs/cgroup         cgroup2           cgroup2       rw,nosuid,nodev,noexec,relatime,nsdel
                                                           egate,memory_recur
│ ├─/sys/fs/pstore         pstore            pstore        rw,nosuid,nodev,noexec,relatime
│ ├─/sys/fs/bpf            bpf               bpf           rw,nosuid,nodev,noexec,relatime,m
                                                           ode=700
│ ├─/sys/kernel/tracing  tracefs             tracefs       rw,nosuid,nodev,noexec,relatime
│ ├─/sys/kernel/debug    debugfs             debugfs       rw,nosuid,nodev,noexec,relatime
│ ├─/sys/kernel/config   configfs            configfs      rw,nosuid,nodev,noexec,relatime
│ └─/sys/fs/fuse/connections fusectl         fusectl       rw,nosuid,nodev,noexec,relatime
├─/run                     tmpfs             tmpfs         rw,nosuid,nodev,size=777088k,nr_
                                                           inodes=819200,mode=755
│ ├─/run/lock              tmpfs             tmpfs         rw,nosuid,nodev,noexec,relatime,size=
                                                           5120k
│ ├─/run/rpc_pipefs        sunrpc            rpc_pipefs    rw,relatime
│ └─/run/user/1000         tmpfs             tmpfs         rw,nosuid,nodev,relatime,size=388540
                                                           k,nr_inodes=97135,m
│   └─/run/user/1000/gvfs gvfsd-fuse         fuse.gvfsd rw,nosuid,nodev,relatime,user_
                                                           id=1000,group_id=1000
├─/boot                    /dev/mmcblk0p1    vfat          rw,relatime,fmask=0022,dmask=0022,
                                                           codepage=437,iocharse
├─/media/bob/52DC-3D26 /dev/sda1            vfat          rw,nosuid,nodev,relatime,uid=1000,gi
                                                           d=1000,fmask=0022,d
└─/media/bob/Lexar         /dev/sdb1         vfat          rw,nosuid,nodev,relatime,uid=1000,gi
                                                           d=1000,fmask=0022,d
$
```

Notice that some of the file system types (FSTYPE) are shown as ext4, sysfs, tmpfs, cgroup, proc, vfat (for a Lexar USB flash drive mounted as /dev/sdb1 at /media/bob/Lexar).

Method 5 – You can also very efficiently use the GUI-Based Gparted Partition Editor, as shown in Example 1.3. With Gparted, the installation of which is indicated for the Raspberry Pi systems in Section 1.5.3, you can easily find out the logical device names of disks on your system. In addition, with Gparted, you can use graphical editing methods to affect several important characteristics of the media, such as the format and partitioning of the drives.

In-Chapter Exercise

1. Insert a USB flash drive into your computer, and mount it if necessary. What command would you use to mount it? Use the **findmnt** command to find out its logical device name. What is the logical device name for this flash drive? Along what path is it mounted on your Raspberry Pi system? What are the uses and meanings of the other file system types shown as output to the **findmnt** command? For example, are cgroup, proc, fuse.gvf, and tempfs logical, virtual, or physical file systems, and how exactly do these differ from ext4, or ZFS?

1.5.3 Examples of External Disk or Media Additions

In the following four examples, we provide an ordinary user, or appointed system administrator, with the techniques necessary to manage various methods of adding persistent external media to the system.

In Example 1.3, we install the Gnu Partition Editor(Gparted) program on a Raspberry Pi system and use it to add a new USB-connected flash drive to the system. We format that flash drive to ext-4.

In Example 1.4, we show how to boot from and run a Raspberry Pi system from a USB3-mounted SSD, a system that is recommended to conform with the data storage model we prescribed in Section 1.1.

In Example 1.5, we show how to use the **mdadm** program from the command line on a Raspberry Pi system to create two USB flash drives as a mirrored pair. This is a more traditional approach to achieve the safe and efficient archiving of our data.

In Example 1.6, we show how to use Webmin and mdadm on a Raspberry Pi system to achieve the same results as the command-line procedures from Example 1.5. This will illustrate the ease and efficiency of using modern tools on the Raspberry Pi OS to conform to our recommended data storage model prescribed in Section1.1.

Example 1.3 Using Gparted to Add a USB Flash Drive to the System

Objectives: To install the Gnu Partition Editor(Gparted) program on a Raspberry Pi OS, use it to add a new USB-connected flash drive to the system, and reformat that flash drive to ext-4.

Prerequisites: Having an adequately sized USB flash drive that will mount on the system.

Background: When writing this book, the Raspberry Pi OS automatically recognized and mounted a properly formatted USB-connected flash drive that you placed in one of the USB ports on the hardware you're running the system on. It is possible, and probable, that you want to add a USB3-connected disk, such as an SSD, mounted in an exterior enclosure, to the system. These instructions work just as well for that situation.

Requirements: Do the following steps, in the order presented, to meet the requirements of this example:

1. Install the Gparted Partition Editor software if it is not already installed on your system. This is most efficiently done using the Raspberry Pi OS **Menu>Preferences>Add/Remove Software** choice. Also, it would be very efficient to place an icon for this software on your Raspberry Pi OS desktop if you are using a GUI desktop management system.

2. Insert the USB flash drive as a new disk on the system.

3. Launch the Gparted Partition Editor, either graphically or from the command line with the command **gparted**.

4. The Gparted screen appears.

5. The current disks attached to the system appear in the menu bar at the upper right. Note all the complete paths to the current disks by clicking on the down-facing arrow shown in that menu bar in the upper right corner of the Gparted screen.

6. Scroll in that bar until you reach the disk you just added to the system. If the disk drive you just added doesn't appear automatically in the Gparted listing, you *can't* easily use that disk drive! If it does appear, continue to the next step. On our system, the new hard drive appeared as /dev/sda.

7. Pick that new disk in the menu bar. It is then shown in the main Gparted pane. Click on that disk in the main Gparted pane. You can now partition and format that new disk. In our example, it is shown as /dev/sda, a new disk we inserted in step 2. That disk might contain a single partition, /dev/sda1, that has an FAT32 file system on it, and no label, for example.

8. From the pull-down menus at the top of the Gparted window, choose Partition>Delete, or click on the red X in the icon bar. This will delete the partition information on that disk. It is now a pending operation.

9. In order to execute the pending operation, make the pull-down menu choice Edit>Apply All Operations. In the warning window, click Apply. A window shows you the progress, and hopefully successful application, of the pending operation. Click close in that window when the operation is complete.

10. The new disk should now be unallocated. Click on its listing in the main Gparted pane. Make the pull-down menu choice Device>Create Partition Table. Change the Select new partition table type: to gpt. Click Apply in the warning window. Everything on that disk will be erased! When Gparted has created a new partition table, click on that disk again in the main Gparted pane.

11. Make the pull-down menu choice Partition>New. The Create New Partition window appears on the screen. The defaults for the new partition are to take the whole disk up with this partition, create it as a primary partition, and set the file system as ext-4.

12. Add a label designation of your choice in the Label field. Leave all of the other defaults in place. Click the Add button. Make the pull-down menu choice Edit>Apply All Operations. In the warning window, click Apply. Click the Close button when the Applying pending operations appears.

13. You now have a created partition table on, partitioned and formatted, and a usable USB flash drive on the system.

14. Quit Gparted by making the pull-down menu choice Gparted>Quit.

Conclusion: You have installed the Gnu Partition Editor(Gparted) program on a Raspberry Pi OS, used it to add a new USB-connected flash drive to the system, and reformatted that flash drive to ext-4.

Example 1.4 How to Boot from and Run a Raspberry Pi OS System from a USB3-mounted SSD

Objectives: To detail how to boot from and run your Raspberry Pi system from a USB3-mounted SSD.
  Prerequisites:

a. Having your storage model conforms to the recommendation in Section 1.1,

b. Completion of Example 1.3.

Note
We do the operations in this Example on the following Raspberry Pi system:

System: Host: raspberrypi Kernel: 6.1.21-v8+ aarch64 bits: 64 compiler: gcc
            v: 10.2.1
Console: tty 0 Distro: Debian GNU/Linux 11 (bullseye)
Machine: Type: ARM Device System: Raspberry Pi 400 Rev 1.0

Background:
As recommended in our storage model in Section 1.1, the Raspberry Pi OS is
traditionally booted from and run from a microSD card mounted on the hardware. Since kernel release 5.15.X, it is possible, and highly advantageous, to
boot and run the system from a USB3-mounted SSD or other external device.
There are several advantages to doing this, chiefly among them a performance speed increase and a storage capacity increase as well.

Requirements: Do the steps below, in the order shown, to complete the
requirements for this example.

1. Update your package manager on your system using the following
    commands:

    $ **sudo apt update**
    Output truncated...
    $ **sudo apt upgrade**
    Output truncated...

2. Insert an SSD or other suitable device with a SATA-to-USB3 cable
    connection capability into a USB3 port on your Raspberry Pi hard-
    ware. On our Raspberry Pi 400, the USB3 ports had a blue-colored tab
    inside them, visible from the outside. We connected a 128 GB Silicon
    Power SSD inside an Orico SATA-to-USB tool-less enclosure. We pre-
    viously formatted the SSD in Gparted with a FAT32 partition on it.

3. The SSD mounted automatically. We then used the Accessories
    Menu> SD Card copier to copy the microSD Raspberry Pi OS to the
    USB3-mounted SSD.

Note
In the SD Card Copier, make sure that you copy the system from the microSD
card to the SSD!

4. When the copying is done, shut down the system, and remove the
    microSD card from its slot in the hardware.

5. Disconnect the power and then reconnect it to reboot the system.

6. The Raspberry Pi OS now boots from and runs on the USB3-mounted
    SSD. It is an exact clone of what was on the microSD card as you did
    the above steps.

Conclusion: At the time of the writing of this book, the Raspberry Pi OS can boot from and run from an external USB3 SSD. To gauge the performance speed advantages of using an SSD, we encourage you to use the Accessories Menu> Raspberry Pi Diagnostics program to gauge the relative performance speed advantages of an SSD over a microSD card. The log readings of SSD versus microSD card provide that information.

Example 1.5 Creating and Managing RAID Arrays Using mdadm on the Raspberry Pi OS

Objectives: To use the **mdadm** program from the command line on a Raspberry Pi OS system to create a mirrored pair on two USB flash drives.

Prerequisites:

a. Completion of Examples 1.3 and 1.4.
b. Having two identically sized USB flash drives that are recognized by your system and the available ports on your computer to accommodate them.

Special Note
Upon initial installation of mdadm on the Raspberry Pi OS, at the time of the writing of this book, mdadm was masked by systemd. It seems the **unmask** command fails when there is no existing unit file in the system other than the symlink to */dev*/null. If you mask a service, then that creates a new symlink to /dev/null in the directory */etc/systemd/system*, where systemd looks for unit files to load when the system boots up. In this instance, *there is really no unit file.*
To correct this, the general procedure is as follows:

1. Check that the unit file is a symlink to */dev*/null:

    $ file /lib/systemd/system/mdadm.service

    If the service is masked, the above command should return:
    /lib/systemd/system/mdadm: symbolic link to /dev/null

2. Delete the symlink!

    $ sudo rm /lib/systemd/system/mdadm.service

3. Because you changed a unit file, reload the systemctl daemon.:

    $ sudo systemctl daemon-reload

4.   Check the status of the mdadm:

   $ systemctl status mdadm

5.   If it still isn't loaded and running, reinstall the package:

   $ sudo apt-get install --reinstall mdadm

6.   Then, reload the daemon again:

   $ sudo systemctl daemon-reload

7.   Start the mdadm service:

   $ sudo systemctl start mdadm

A specific example of this on our Raspberry Pi OS system is as follows:

```
bob@raspberrypi:~ $ systemctl status mdadm
• mdadm.service
  Loaded: masked (Reason: Unit mdadm.service is masked.)
  Active: inactive (dead)
bob@raspberrypi:~ $ sudo rm /lib/systemd/system/mdadm.service
bob@raspberrypi:~ $ sudo systemctl daemon-reload
bob@raspberrypi:~ $ systemctl status mdadm
• mdadm.service: LSB: MD monitoring daemon
  Loaded: loaded (/etc/init.d/mdadm; generated)
  Active: inactive (dead)
  Docs: man:systemd-sysv-generator(8)
bob@raspberrypi:~ $ sudo systemctl start mdadm
bob@raspberrypi:~ $ systemctl status mdadm
• mdadm.service: LSB: MD monitoring daemon
  Loaded: loaded (/etc/init.d/mdadm; generated)
  Active: active (running) since Mon 2022-10-03 13:45:28 PDT; 4s ago
   Docs: man:systemd-sysv-generator(8)
  Process: 5292 ExecStart=/etc/init.d/mdadm start (code=exited, status=0/SUCC>
  Tasks: 1 (limit: 4164)
   CPU: 36ms
CGroup: /system.slice/mdadm.service
        └─5299 /sbin/mdadm --monitor --pid-file /run/mdadm/monitor.pid --d>

Oct 03 13:45:28 raspberrypi systemd[1]: Starting LSB: MD monitoring daemon...
Oct 03 13:45:28 raspberrypi mdadm[5292]: Starting MD monitoring service: mdadm >
Oct 03 13:45:28 raspberrypi systemd[1]: Started LSB: MD monitoring daemon.
```

Background:
Using a more traditional approach to adding disks and partitioning them in Linux involves the use of command-line tools such as **fdisk** or **gdisk**. In addition, to ensure redundancy of storage for the user data in our recommended storage model, we can create a level RAID1 mirror using two flash drives.

That way, if one of the flash drives fails, the data is retained on the other disk in the mirror.

In order to fully support redundancy in our recommended storage model, the Raspberry Pi OS makes available a Multiple Device Administration (mdadm) program to allow us to securely archive the user data component of that model. Redundant Array of Inexpensive Disks (RAID) devices are virtual devices created from two or more real block devices, like SATA disks, or USB flash drives. This allows multiple devices, typically whole disk drives but also partitions on disks, to be combined into a single logical device to hold single or multiple file systems. RAID "levels" include various degrees of redundancy to enable the data storage component to survive varying amounts of device failure.

To see a complete description of the **mdadm** command after installing the program on your system, see the man page for **mdadm**. The following is a brief description, taken from that man page, of **mdadm** syntax and use:

****

mdadm - manage MD devices or Linux Software RAID
Syntax: mdadm [mode] <raiddevice> [options] <component-devices>
where-

mode	Assemble, Build, Create, Monitor, Grow, Incremental Assembly, Manage, Misc, and Auto-detect
<raiddevice>	Name to assign to new virtual device, eg. /dev/md0
[options]	Mode-selection and other options.
<component-devices>	The physical devices to be assigned to the array, eg. /dev/sdb
Output:	New software RAID virtual device, or management of previously created one.

Common Options:

-c, --config=	Specify the config file or directory. Default is to use /etc/mdadm/mdadm.conf and /etc/mdadm/mdadm.conf.d, or if those are missing then /etc/mdadm.conf and /etc/mdadm.conf.d.
-C --create	Create a new array.
-A, --assemble	Assemble a pre-existing array.
-G, --grow	Change the size or shape of an active array.

Example: $ sudo mdadm --create /dev/md0 --level=mirror --raid-devices=2 dev/sd[b-c]1
As superuser, create the array named md0 as a mirror of the 2 first partitions on physical devices, /dev/sdb and /dev/sdc

****

Some further examples of **mdadm** syntax and use are as follows:

$ **mdadm --query /dev/name-of-device**

Find out if a given device is a RAID array, or is part of one, and will provide brief information about the device:

$ **mdadm --assemble --scan**

Assemble and start all arrays listed in the default mdadm config file. This command will typically go in a system startup file:

$ **mdadm --stop --scan**

Shut down all arrays that can be shut down (i.e., are not currently in use). Typically found in a system shutdown script:

$ **mdadm --create /dev/md0 --level=1 --raid-devices=2 /dev/sd[ac]1**

Creates /dev/md0 as a RAID1 array consisting of /dev/sda1 and /dev/ sdc1:

$ **mdadm -Ac partitions -m 0 /dev/md0**

Scan all partitions and devices listed in /proc/partitions and assemble / dev/md0 out of all such devices with a RAID superblock with a minor number of 0:

$ **mdadm --incremental --rebuild-map --run --scan**

Rebuild the array map from any current arrays, and then start any that can be started:

$ **mdadm /dev/md4 --fail detached --remove detached**

Any devices which are components of /dev/md4 will be marked as faulty and then removed from the array:

$ **mdadm --grow /dev/md4 --level=6 --backup-file=/root/backup-md4**

The array /dev/md4, which is currently a RAID5 array, will be converted to RAID6. There should normally already be a spare drive attached to the array, as a RAID6 needs one more drive than a matching RAID5:

$ **mdadm --create --help**

Provide help with the Create mode:

$ **mdadm --help**

Provide general help:

$ **mdadm --manage --help**

Provides help topics on the management commands and options of mdadm RAID.

The following set of commands, executed in sequence, allow you to replace a failed disk that is part of a RAID1 array named md0:

$ **mdadm --manage /dev/md0 --add /dev/sdd1**

Adds /dev/sdd1 to the array md0 as a spare disk:

$ **mdadm --manage /dev/md0 --fail /dev/sdb1**

Marking a RAID device, /dev/sdb1, as faulty:

$ **mdadm --manage /dev/md0 --replace /dev/sdb1 --with /dev/sdd1**

Re-add /dev/sdd1 into array /dev/md0, replacing /dev/sdb1.

Requirements: Do the steps below in the sequence presented to complete the requirements of this Example.

0. Having previously determined that the two flash drives you want to use are recognized on your system, insert them into USB ports. We used two 8 GB Kingston flash drives, which are very reliable and always auto-mount on a Raspberry Pi system. On our system, they were mounted as dev/sda and dev/sdb.

Use the following commands to unmount them:

$ **sudo umount /dev/sda1**
$ **sudo umount /dev/sdb1**

1. Install mdadm to your system if it is not there already. Read ***Special Note*** above!:

    $ **sudo apt install mdadm -y**
    Reading package lists... Done
    Building dependency tree
    Reading state information... Done
    Output truncated.
    $

2. Examine the USB flash drives with the following **mdadm** command:

    $ **sudo mdadm -E /dev/sd[a-b]**
    /dev/sda:
      MBR Magic : aa55
    Partition[0] : 15144960 sectors at   2048 (type 0b)
    /dev/sdb:
      MBR Magic : aa55
    Partition[0] : 15144960 sectors at   2048 (type 0b)

3. Use the **fdisk** command, one disk at a time, to partition the two newly
    added USB flash drives, making sure to first delete any partitions that
    are on them. For our Kingston USB flash drives, there was only one
    default partition on each one, as previously determined in step 0.

```
$ sudo fdisk /dev/sda
Welcome to fdisk (util-linux 2.36.1).
Changes will remain in memory only until you decide to write them.
Be careful before using the write command.
Command (m for help):d
1 Partition has been deleted.
Command (m for help):n
Partition type
   p   primary (0 primary, 0 extended, 4 free)
   e   extended (container for logical partitions)
Select (default p): Enter
Using default response p.
Partition number (1-4, default 1): Enter
First sector (2048-15148607, default 2048): Enter
Last sector, +sectors or +size{K,M,G,T,P} (2048-15148607, default
   15148607): Enter
Partition #1 contains a vfat signature.
Do you want to remove the signature? [Y]es/[N]o: Y
The signature will be removed by a write command.
Command (m for help): p
/dev/sda: 7.22 GiB, 7756087296 bytes, 15148608 sectors
Disk model: DataTraveler 2.0
Units: sectors of 1 * 512 = 512 bytes
Sector size (logical/physical): 512 bytes / 512 bytes
I/O size (minimum/optimal): 512 bytes / 512 bytes
Disklabel type: dos
Disk identifier: 0x01eb214b
Device    Boot Start    End Sectors    Size Id Type
/dev/sda1       2048 15148607 15146560 7.2G 83 Linux

filesystem/RAID signature on partition 1 will be wiped.
Command (m for help):

Command (m for help): l
00 Empty         24 NEC DOS        81 Minix / old Lin  bf Solaris
Output truncated...
Command (m for help): t
Selected partition 1
Hex code (type L to list all codes): FD
Changed type of partition 'Linux' to 'Linux raid autodetect'.

Command (m for help): p
Disk /dev/sda: 7.22 GiB, 7756087296 bytes, 15148608 sectors
Disk model: DataTraveler 2.0
Units: sectors of 1 * 512 = 512 bytes
Sector size (logical/physical): 512 bytes / 512 bytes
I/O size (minimum/optimal): 512 bytes / 512 bytes
Disklabel type: dos
```

Disk identifier: 0x01eb214b

Device   Boot Start   End Sectors Size Id Type
/dev/sda1   2048 15148607 15146560 7.2G fd Linux raid autodetect

Filesystem/RAID signature on partition 1 will be wiped.

Command (m for help): **w**
The partition table has been altered.
Calling ioctl() to re-read partition table.
Syncing disks.
$

Repeat Step 3. for /dev/sdc

4. Check the metadata superblock on both disks:

    $ **sudo mdadm -E /dev/sd[b-c]1**
    mdadm: No md superblock detected on /dev/sda1.
    mdadm: No md superblock detected on /dev/sdb1.
    $

Notice there are no metadata mdadm superblocks! Basically, that means that no RAID arrays have been created yet.

5. Create a RAID1 array with the two flash drives as devices:

    $ **sudo mdadm --create /dev/md0 --level=mirror --raid-devices=2 \
    /dev/sd[a-b]1**
    mdadm: Note: this array has metadata at the start and
        may not be suitable as a boot device. If you plan to
        store '/boot' on this device please ensure that
        your boot-loader understands md/v1.x metadata, or use
        --metadata=0.90
    Continue creating array? **Y**
    mdadm: Defaulting to version 1.2 metadata
    mdadm: array /dev/md0 started.

    $ **cat /proc/mdstat**
    Personalities : [raid1]
    md0 : active raid1 sdb1[1] sda1[0]
        7568128 blocks super 1.2 [2/2] [UU]
        [>...................] resync = 4.1% (314560/7568128) finish=35.1min
          speed=3442K/sec

    unused devices: <none>

    $ **sudo mdadm -E /dev/sd[a-b]1**
    dev/sda1:
            Magic : a92b4efc
          Version : 1.2
      Feature Map : 0x0
       Array UUID : 6cf34f72:c212ef04:b9126e4a:ceb653f4
             Name : raspberrypi:0 (local to host raspberrypi)

```
      Creation Time : Thu Oct  6 06:53:44 2022
         Raid Level : raid1
       Raid Devices : 2

   Avail Dev Size : 15136320 (7.22 GiB 7.75 GB)
       Array Size : 7568128 (7.22 GiB 7.75 GB)
    Used Dev Size : 15136256 (7.22 GiB 7.75 GB)
      Data Offset : 10240 sectors
     Super Offset : 8 sectors
     Unused Space : before=10160 sectors, after=64 sectors
            State : active
      Device UUID : 0b7472eb:f0f02bad:c230a8f5:26c5e890

      Update Time : Thu Oct  6 06:55:54 2022
    Bad Block Log : 512 entries available at offset 16 sectors
         Checksum : 640df1c7 - correct
           Events : 1
   Output truncated...
```

6. Check RAID device type and RAID array:

```
$ sudo mdadm --detail /dev/md0
/dev/md0:
           Version : 1.2
     Creation Time : Thu Oct  6 06:53:44 2022
        Raid Level : raid1
        Array Size : 7568128 (7.22 GiB 7.75 GB)
     Used Dev Size : 7568128 (7.22 GiB 7.75 GB)
      Raid Devices : 2
     Total Devices : 2
       Persistence : Superblock is persistent

       Update Time : Thu Oct  6 06:55:54 2022
             State : clean, resyncing
    Active Devices : 2
   Working Devices : 2
    Failed Devices : 0
     Spare Devices : 0

 Consistency Policy: resync

     Resync Status : 11% complete

              Name : raspberrypi:0  (local to host raspberrypi)
              UUID : 6cf34f72:c212ef04:b9126e4a:ceb653f4
            Events : 1

    Number   Major   Minor   RaidDevice      State
       0       8       1        0           active sync   /dev/sda1
       1       8      17        1           active sync   /dev/sdb1

$
```

7. Wait until the md0 array is totally resynced. In the output of the above command, resyncing was only 11% complete. On our Raspberry Pi system, total resyncing took approximately 35 minutes for the size of the flash drives we were dealing with. Then, when resyncing is done, create an ext4 File System on md0, and mount it at /mnt/raid1:

```
$ sudo mkfs.ext4 /dev/md0
mke2fs 1.46.2 (28-Feb-2021)
Creating file system with 1892032 4k blocks and 473280 inodes
Filesystem UUID: af6667aa-d650-4349-9581-fd49361b7b9a
Superblock backups stored on blocks:
        32768, 98304, 163840, 229376, 294912, 819200, 884736, 1605632

Allocating group tables: done
Writing inode tables: done
Creating journal (16384 blocks): done
Writing superblocks and filesystem accounting information: done
$
```

8. The following commands mount the array at /mnt/raid1 and allow you to put some data in the filesystem you created there:

```
$ sudo mkdir /mnt/raid1
$ sudo mount /dev/md0 /mnt/raid1/
$ sudo touch /mnt/raid1/raspberrypi.txt
$ sudo chmod u+x /mnt/raid1/raspberrypi.txt
$ sudo nano /mnt/raid1/raspberrypi.txt
```

Add the text-

A Raspberry Pi OS example of mirrored disks using mdadm.

Then save it, and quit nano.

In-Chapter Exercise

2. How would you ensure that /dev/md0 array is started upon every reboot of the system? Hint: See the procedures of Example 1.5.4.

9. To remove the RAID1 array and zero out the flash drives for later use, execute the following commands:

```
$ sudo umount /dev/md0
$
```

This has unmounted the file system on the array.

```
$ sudo mdadm --stop /dev/md0
mdadm: stopped /dev/md0
$
```

This has stopped the array.

Also, remove the directory /mnt/raid1 with the following command:

```
$ sudo rm -r /mnt/raid1
$
```

Delete the partitions on /dev/sdb and /dev/sdc using fdisk, gdisk, or Gparted, and then create new ones on them formatted to FAT32 if you want to continue using them as USB flash drives on your system.

Conclusion: This example illustrated the traditional method of adding persistent media to a Raspberry Pi OS system by partitioning it with fdisk, making it redundant using mdadm RAID, creating a file system on it, and mounting it at a selected location in the file system.

Example 1.6 RAID1 Using Webmin, mdadm, and the Gnome Disk Utility (Disks)

Objectives: To create a RAID-1 mirrored pair on two flash drives attached to your system, using the facilities of Webmin to accomplish the same things that the mdadm commands do. Additionally, clone your home directory on the system to the RAID-1 mirrored pair, thus segregating the system files from your user data files in order to maintain a secure level of redundancy, per our recommended data storage model.

Prerequisites:

    a.   Having two equal-sized USB flash drives available that you want to sacrifice for this example.

    b.   Having some familiarity with Webmin after doing Section 1.2.

Background: Webmin has the ability to manage RAID arrays on a Raspberry Pi system. In this example, you will use Webmin, mdadm, and the gnu disk management program in conjunction, to accomplish the mirroring of two USB flash drives in a RAID-1 configuration, and also clone your home directory onto that mirrored pair.

If you *haven't* done Example 1.5, the following ***Special Note*** is applicable to you here in this example:

Special Note

Upon installation of mdadm on the Raspberry Pi OS, at the time of the writing of this book, mdadm was masked by systemd. It seems the unmask command fails when there is no existing unit file in the system other than the symlink to /dev/null. If you mask a service, then that creates a new symlink to /dev/null in the directory /etc/systemd/system, where systemd looks for unit files to load when the system boots up. Therefore, in essence, *there is really no unit file.*

To correct this, the general procedure is as follows:

1. Check that the unit file is a symlink to /dev/null

   $ **file /lib/systemd/system/mdadm.service**

   If the service is masked, the above command should return:

   /lib/systemd/system/mdadm: symbolic link to /dev/null

2. Delete the symlink!

   $ **sudo rm /lib/systemd/system/mdadm.service**

3. Because you changed a unit file, reload the systemctl daemon.:

   $ **sudo systemctl daemon-reload**

4. Check the status of the mdadm:

   $ **systemctl status mdadm**

5. If it still isn't loaded and running, reinstall the package:

   $ **sudo apt-get install --reinstall mdadm**

6. Then, reload the daemon again:

   $ **sudo systemctl daemon-reload**

7. Start the mdadm service:

   $ **sudo systemctl start mdadm**

A specific example of this on our Raspberry Pi OS system is as follows:

```
bob@raspberrypi:~ $ systemctl status mdadm
▪ mdadm.service
  Loaded: masked (Reason: Unit mdadm.service is masked.)
  Active: inactive (dead)
bob@raspberrypi:~ $ sudo rm /lib/systemd/system/mdadm.service
bob@raspberrypi:~ $ sudo systemctl daemon-reload
bob@raspberrypi:~ $ systemctl status mdadm
▪ mdadm.service:  LSB: MD monitoring daemon
  Loaded: loaded (/etc/init.d/mdadm; generated)
  Active: inactive (dead)
  Docs: man:systemd-sysv-generator(8)
bob@raspberrypi:~ $ sudo systemctl start mdadm
bob@raspberrypi:~ $ systemctl status mdadm
```

- mdadm.service: LSB: MD monitoring daemon
  Loaded: loaded (/etc/init.d/mdadm; generated)
  Active: active (running) since Mon 2022-10-03 13:45:28 PDT; 4s ago
    Docs: man:systemd-sysv-generator(8)
  Process: 5292 ExecStart=/etc/init.d/mdadm start (code=exited, status=0/SUCC>
    Tasks: 1 (limit: 4164)
      CPU: 36ms
  CGroup: /system.slice/mdadm.service
          └─5299 /sbin/mdadm --monitor --pid-file /run/mdadm/monitor.pid --d>

Oct 03 13:45:28 raspberrypi systemd[1]: Starting LSB: MD monitoring daemon...
Oct 03 13:45:28 raspberrypi mdadm[5292]: Starting MD monitoring service: mdadm >
Oct 03 13:45:28 raspberrypi systemd[1]: Started LSB: MD monitoring daemon.

Requirements: Do the following steps in the order presented to complete the requirements of this example.

1. Install the tools necessary to setup RAID-1 Mirroring on two attached flash drives.

If you haven't already done this for Example 1.3., install Webmin:

$ sudo apt install webmin -y

If you haven't already done this for Example 1.5, install the mdadm software RAID utility:

$ sudo apt install mdadm -y

Install the gnome disk management tool:

$ sudo apt install gnome-disk-utility -y

2. Reboot:

    $ sudo reboot

The following steps allow us to use Webmin to build the RAID-1 array on the two flash drives.

3. Open the gnome disk management tool from Raspberry Pi Menu > Preferences. You can also use the command:

    $ gnome-disks

In the gnu disk management tool, choose the two flash drives, one at a time, and format both with the default formatting choices.

4. Open the web browser and enter this URL:

    https://localhost:10000

Webmin runs on localhost at port 10000. As noted in Example 1.3, since https is used and the SSL Certificate is not installed, your browser will show a warning. Click Advanced and then click Accept to take the risk and continue.

5. Login with your username/password pair.

6. In Webmin, choose Refresh Modules. Then expand the pull-down menu (the blue colored lines at the upper left of the Webmin pane onscreen) choice >Hardware, and select Linux RAID.

7. On the screen that appears, the RAID1 (Mirrored) choice will be available. At this point, you could choose other levels of RAID if so desired. Select RAID1 (Mirrored) and click the button 'Create RAID device of level:'.

8. Choose the two flash drives (which show on our Raspberry Pi OS system as SCSI devices under Partitions in RAID) by holding down the Ctrl key and clicking on them one at a time. Make a choice 'Skip initialization of devices', since this would be time-consuming even when initializing 8 GB flash drives.

The following steps allow you to choose the RAID mode in the Webmin interface.

9. Click the button 'Create' in the lower left Create RAID Device pane. Webmin should execute the selections you've made very quickly because you've skipped initialization of the disks.

You can then check more details by examining /dev/md0 in the Linux RAID screen that appears. The two disks are shown as Partitions in RAID, and the Filesystem status is 'Active, but not mounted'.

The new RAID array must be formatted before mounting it. This can be done using the gnu disk management tool .

10. Select the RAID-1 array, and make the plus sign (+) choice in the gnu disk management tool. In the gnu disk management tool dialog box that appears for this, name the array "Home Data." Select the radio button 'Internal disk for use with Linux systems only (Ext4)', and then click on the 'Create' button. Wait a minute while the gnu disk management tool does its work!

Go back to Webmin. All the disks attached to a RAID device are shown in the Webmin interface.

This array named 'Home Data' needs to be auto-mounted at every boot.

11.　In the gnu disk management tool, select the array in the Disks listing, and beneath its display in the main pane, make the meshing gears button choice. Select Edit Mount Options.

12.　Toggle 'User Session Defaults' to be in the on position (to the left), and then click on the OK button. After authentication, this process modifies the "/etc/fstab" file appropriately to auto-mount our RAID-1 array.

After every reboot of your system, the automatically mounted RAID-1 array shows up as the "Home Data" folder in the Raspberry Pi OS File Manager on your desktop.

To conform to our recommended data storage model, it would be very useful and secure to mirror our home directory, which is now stored on the microSD card that the Raspberry Pi OS resides on, to the RAID-1 array on the flash drives that we've created in the above steps of this Example.

13.　In a terminal, type the following:

$ dir /mnt
30bbf3f0-8d02-49e2-8989-b69a34d92c38

Use your mouse to copy the name of the RAID mount. On our system, it showed the mounted array as "30bbf3f0-8d02-49e2-8989-b69a34d92c38." Replace the directory name with the one shown on your system. Then use this command to clone the home directory by typing the following, substituting your directory name for the one on our system:

$ sudo rsync -av /home/* /mnt/30bbf3f0-8d02-49e2-8989-b69a34d92c38/

To make this new directory mount as /home instead of the default home directory, do the following:

$ sudo nano /etc/fstab

Use nano to go to the line /dev/disk... (probably the last line after the reboot you did in) and change mount point to "/home." Quit and save /dev/disk in nano.

Reboot the system. Your home directory is now on mirrored RAID-1 array named 'Home Data'.

14.　*Cleanup* – To remove the RAID-1 array, and zero out the flash drives for later use, execute the following:

a.　Remove the entry from step 13. in the /etc/fstab file using nano. Then reboot.

In Webmin, make the menu choice Hardware>Linux RAID, then select /dev/md0. At the bottom of the RAID Device screen, make the choice Delete RAID array. Make the red button choice 'Yes, Delete it'.

This has removed the mirrored array we created in the steps above.

b. Also remove the directories /mnt/30bbf3f0-8d02-49e2-8989-b69a34d92c38, and mnt/home with the following commands:

$ sudo rm -r /mnt/30bbf3f0-8d02-49e2-8989-b69a34d92c38
$ sudo rm -r /mnt/home

where home is the name of your home directory which was cloned onto the mirrored pair.

c. Finally, delete the partitions on /dev/sdb and /dev/sdc using the traditional commands fdisk, gdisk, or, if you so desire, Gparted. Then you'll be able to create new ones on them formatted to FAT32 if you want to continue using them as USB flash drives on your system.

Note Compare the three sub-steps in step 14 to those analogous steps found in Example 1.5..

Conclusion:
This example has used Webmin, mdadm, and the gnu disk management program to implement a secure, redundant data storage model on a Raspberry Pi system.

1.6 CUPS Printing

You can configure and manage a printer for use on your Raspberry Pi system using the three basic methods we show in this section. These methods are generally applicable to printers that are connected directly to your computer, and this most likely is via a USB connection. We also briefly mention how network-attached printers can be configured.

The three basic methods are:

1. A web-based browser CUPS interface,
2. Using the Raspberry Pi OS Menu choice Preferences > Print Settings, and
3. Using the Raspberry Pi OS command line in a terminal.

The configured printer in all three methods is controlled and managed with the Common UNIX Printing System (CUPS).

In method 1, we show a web-based browser front end to CUPS that allows you to manage printers, print jobs, and other configuration settings.

In method 2, we show the built-in graphical front end to CUPS, accessed via the Menu, which comes with the Raspberry Pi OS and achieves much of the same functionality as method 1.

In method 3., we show a completely text-based interface for controlling and managing printers from the command line.

What the Common UNIX Printing System (CUPS) Accomplishes:

Using CUPS is a standard way of printing in both Linux and Unix. Since it was developed to provide as many printer definitions as possible, it will more than likely enable you to directly connect your model of printer or connect to a print server on your LAN.

It is basically composed of two parts- a scheduler and a filtering system. The scheduler arranges jobs in print queues and sends them to the filtering system that translates the print data into device driver information for the particular printer you want your documents to print on.

1.6.1 Managing CUPS Locally with systemd

Using systemd, via the **systemctl** command, allows you to start, stop, reload, or restart the CUPS service. This is a higher level of management for your local printers via a system service.

1.6.1.1 Starting CUPS Service Using systemd

In the Raspberry Pi OS, when you attach a new printer via a USB cable to the hardware, it will generally be automatically recognized and attached via CUPS. If the CUPS service has not already been started, it will be automatically started and run when connecting the new printer. But to start the CUPS service without having any printers attached or powered on, do the following:

To start the CUPS service, and check its status, use the following commands:

```
$ sudo systemctl start cups
$ sudo systemctl status cups
• cups.service: CUPS Scheduler
  Loaded: loaded (/lib/systemd/system/cups.service; enabled; vendor preset:
    enabled)
  Active: active (running) since Thu 2022-10-06 00:00:45 PDT; 10h ago
TriggeredBy: • cups.socket
             • cups.path
  Docs: man:cupsd(8)
Main PID: 11613 (cupsd)
  Status: "Scheduler is running..."
  Tasks: 1 (limit: 4164)
    CPU: 33ms
  CGroup: /system.slice/cups.service
          └─11613 /usr/sbin/cupsd -l
```

Oct 06 00:00:45 raspberrypi systemd[1]: Starting CUPS Scheduler...
Oct 06 00:00:45 raspberrypi systemd[1]: Started CUPS Scheduler.

We see from the output that CUPS is running.

1.6.1.2 Stopping CUPS Service with systemd

The CUPS service can be stopped using the **systemctl stop cups.service** command, as follows:

$ **sudo systemctl stop cups.service**

When you check the status of the CUPS service after stopping the CUPS service, its status is inactive (dead), but still enabled.
Enabled means it will persistently start every time the system is rebooted.

1.6.1.3 Restarting, Enabling, or Disabling the CUPS Service with systemd

Restarting a service means that a service is stopped and then started again. If the service is not currently running, restarting it simply starts the service. Use the following command to restart the CUPS service:

$ **sudo systemctl restart cups.service**

You can also perform a conditional restart of a service using systemctl. A conditional restart only restarts a service if it is currently running. Any service in an inactive state is not started.

$ **sudo systemctl condrestart cups.service**

In the above command example, the CUPS service was in an inactive state before the command was executed. When the conditional restart is accomplished, no error messages appear. The cup daemon was not started because conditional restarts only affect active services.
It is always a good practice to check the status of a service after stopping, starting, or conditionally restarting it.

1.6.1.4 Configuring CUPS as a Persistent Service Using systemd

You can use the **systemctl** command to enable or disable the CUPS services on your Raspberry Pi OS system server, whether that is local or remote.
Using the **enable** option on the **systemctl** command sets a service to always start at boot (be persistent). The following shows exactly how to accomplish this:

$ **sudo systemctl enable cups.service**

Disabling a service with systemd:

You can use the disable **option** on the **systemctl** command to keep a service from starting at boot. However, it does not immediately stop the service. You need to use the stop option discussed in the "Stopping a service with systemd" section. The following example shows how to disable a currently enabled service.

$ sudo systemctl disable cups.service

1.6.2 Using Web-Based CUPS Administration

CUPS offers its own web-based administrative tool for adding, deleting, and modifying printer configurations on your computer. The CUPS print service (using the cupsd daemon) listens on port 631 to provide access to the CUPS web-based administrative interface and share printers. You can use the CUPS web browser GUI to manage your printing environment, both locally and on a LAN or the Internet, in the Raspberry Pi OS. This section describes the requirements for using the web browser interface and the administrative tasks that you can perform.

1.6.2.1 Using the Web-Based Interface to CUPS Locally

We found that if a powered-on printer has been automatically detected on your local computer, you can begin to use the web-based browser interface on that local machine. If CUPS has been enabled at system boot and is running on your computer, you can immediately use CUPS web-based administration from your web browser. A simple and easy way to test whether CUPS is running is to open a web browser on the local computer and type the following into its URL locator box:

http://localhost:631

A prompt for a valid login name and password may appear. If so, type the root login name and the root user's password, and click OK. The web-based CUPS interface Home Tab screen display should appear in your browser window. By default, web-based CUPS administration is available only from the local host.

1.6.2.2 LAN or Web-Based CUPS

To access LAN or web-based CUPS administration from another computer, do the following:

1. On your local machine, from the web-based CUPS interface Home Tab screen, select the Administration Tab. Then put check marks in the

boxes next to Allow remote administration, Share printers connected to this system, and Allow printing from the Internet.

2. Select the Change Settings button.
3. You may need to restart the CUPS service with the systemctl command before the change takes effect, as shown in Section 1.6.1.3.
4. After doing the previous steps, you can view the CUPS interface from a remote computer's web browser (and you can access CUPS locally as well as localhost:631) using the IP address of the computer you have your printer(s) connected to.

    For example, to see the web-based CUPS interface Home Tab screen in a web browser, on a machine with an IP address of 192.168.0.8, type in:

```
http://192.168.0.8:631
```

On that machine, it is *not* necessary to have a printer detected at that time, or even powered on, if those two things had been previously done.

In-Chapter Exercise

3. You have two computers on a LAN, named Pi400 and Pi4. You attach a printer, which is automatically detected and useable on Pi4 only. You use the steps shown in Section 1.6.2.2 to allow you to manage the printer from your LAN. From a web browser on Pi400, you access the CUPS web-based interface on Pi4. From Pi4, can you also use a web browser and access the web-based interface on Pi400 to manage the printer on Pi4?

1.6.3 Requirements for Using the CUPS Web Browser Interface

The web-based browser interface can be accessed from a supported browser like Firefox. Depending on the task that you are performing, you might be prompted for a username and password, or for the root username and password.

The following requirements must be met before using the web-based browser interface:

1. We found that if a printer has been automatically detected on the computer you are trying to access CUPS on, the CUPS daemon goes from the inactive to the active (running) state on that computer. Then you can begin to use the web-based browser interface.
2. The CUPS software packages must be installed on the system that you are accessing via the CUPS web-based browser interface pages. That system can be the local computer or a remote computer.

    Note These software packages were installed on our Raspberry Pi OS system by default.

3. The following CUPS packages are required:

   CUPS, cups-libs, foomatic-db, foomatic-db-engine.

4. The CUPS scheduler, svc:/application/cups/scheduler, must also be running on the system you are accessing.

To verify that the CUPS scheduler is running, open a terminal window and type the following command:

$ **sudo systemctl status cups.service**

```
▪ cups.service: CUPS Scheduler
  Loaded: loaded (/lib/systemd/system/cups.service; enabled; vendor preset:
    enabled)
  Active: active (running) since Thu 2022-10-06 12:54:09 PDT; 2h 0min ago
TriggeredBy: ▪ cups.socket
            ▪ cups.path
  Docs: man:cupsd(8)
  Main PID: 23641 (cupsd)
  Status: "Scheduler is running..."
    Tasks: 3 (limit: 4164)
      CPU: 1.382s
CGroup: /system.slice/cups.service
        ├─23641 /usr/sbin/cupsd -l
        └─23644 /usr/lib/cups/notifier/dbus dbus://

Oct 06 12:54:09 raspberrypi systemd[1]: Starting CUPS Scheduler...
Oct 06 12:54:09 raspberrypi systemd[1]: Started CUPS Scheduler.
$
```

1.6.4 Adding a Printer Using the CUPS Web Browser Interface

To configure a printer that is not automatically detected, you can add a printer from the Administration Tab as seen on the Home Tab screen display. With the Administration Tab screen displayed, you can add a printer as follows:

1. Click the Add Printer button. The Add New Printer screen appears.

2. Check the box that corresponds to the printer you want to add. Then press the Continue button.

3. In the Add Printer dialog box that appears, type a Name, Location, and Description for the printer; also choose if you want to share this printer, and click Continue.

4. Select the make of the print driver. If you don't see the manufacturer of your printer listed, choose PostScript for a PostScript printer or HP for a PCL printer. For the manufacturer you choose, you can select a specific model.

5. Choose Add Printer button to continue.

6. On the Set Printer Options page that appears, change any of the default options presented for your printer.

7. Your printer should be available. If the printer is added successfully, click the name of your printer to have the new printer page appear; from the printer page, you can select Maintenance or Administration to print a test page or modify the printer configuration.

1.6.5 Troubleshooting Issues with Accessing the CUPS Web Browser Interface

If you encounter an error while attempting to access the CUPS web browser interface, or you cannot access the interface, see Section 1.6.3 to ensure that all of the requirements have been met. In addition, verify your browser's proxy settings to determine whether a proxy server has been configured. If so, try turning off the proxy server, then re-attempt to access the CUPS web browser interface.

1.6.6 Print Administration Tasks and the Home Tab

Common print administration tasks that you can perform by using the CUPS web browser interface include the following- customizing a print server setup, assigning a print client to a common print server, setting up and managing directly attached printers and printer classes on servers, setting up and managing remote printers and printer classes on servers, and managing print jobs from print clients

When you first access the CUPS web browser interface at http://localhost:631, you see the menu choices available from the Home Tab screen. From this tab, you can access all of the print administration tasks, which are grouped by category, and the full set of CUPS documentation.

The following tabs are also displayed on the Home Tab screen display:

* Administration – Enables you to access most print administration tasks, including CUPS server configuration.

* Classes – Enables you to search printer classes. CUPS provides collections of printers, which are called printer classes. Print jobs that are sent to a class are forwarded to the first available printer in that class. Classes can be members of other classes. Therefore, you can define very large, distributed printer classes for high-availability printing.

* Help or Documentation – Enables you to access the CUPS documentation, which includes manuals, system administration documentation, FAQs, and online help.

   * Jobs – Enables you to view and manage print jobs for configured printers.
   * Printers – Enables you to view information about and modify the settings of a specific printer.

1.6.7 Using the Administration Tab

Most printing tasks can be performed from the Administration Tab.

It is important to realize that some tasks can be performed from multiple tabs.

Basic server settings can also be changed from the Administration Tab. For more information about CUPS server configuration, see the **cupsd.conf** man page on your Raspberry Pi system.

Table 1.2 describes the most important operation categories and individual tasks that can be performed from the Administration Tab.

1.6.8 Using the Printers Tab

The Printers Tab, seen on the Home Tab screen display, enables you to view and modify information for configured print queues.

From the Printers tab, you can also perform the following tasks: print a test page, stop the printer, reject a print job, move a print job, cancel all print jobs, unpublish the printer, modify a printer configuration, set printer options, delete a printer, set a specific printer as the default, and set allowed users for a printer.

1.6.9 Other Examples of Web-Based Cups Management

With the basic printer configuration done, you can now do further configuration and management of your printers. Following is a partial listing of important Home Tab screen display menu choices available:

1.   List print jobs. Click the Jobs Tab from the Home Tab screen display to see what print jobs are active from any printers you have already configured. Click Show Completed Jobs button to see information about jobs that have already been printed.

TABLE 1.2

CUPS Administration Tab Menu Choices

Operation Category	Task
Printers	Add Printer, Find New Printers, Manage Printers
Classes	Add Class, Manage Classes
Jobs	Manage Jobs
Server Edit	Configuration File, View Page Log

2. Cancel or move a print job. If you sent a print job to the wrong printer, the Move Job selection can be used to move the job to a different printer. From the Administration Tab, click Manage Jobs; then click Show Active Jobs to see what print jobs are currently in the queue for the printer. Select the Cancel Job button next to the print job you want to cancel or select Move Job to move the print job to another printer.

3. Manage Printers. You can click the Manage Printers Tab from the top of the Administration Tab screen display to view your configured printers. For each printer that appears, you can select Maintenance or Administrative tasks as follows:

   a. Under Maintenance, click Pause Printer (to stop the printer from printing but still accept print jobs for the queue),
   b. Reject Jobs (not to accept any new print jobs),
   c. Move All Jobs (to move them to another printer defined on the system),
   d. Cancel All Jobs (to delete all print jobs), or Print Test Page (to print a page)

4. Command-line Printing: Select the Command-Line Printing and Options button on the CUPS Home Tab screen display to get help with using Linux command-line methods for printing and doing print management. There is a verbose description of command-line methods shown here.

1.6.10 CUPS Print Settings GUI

CUPS support in the Raspberry Pi OS includes a Gnome-based GUI tool, **system-config-printer**. Generically, across many UNIX and Linux distributions, this tool is known as the Print Manager. It can be launched from the command line, or by making the Raspberry Pi Menu choice (at the top left of the desktop) Preferences > Print Settings. CUPS is the default print service on the Raspberry Pi OS and is managed by systemd. Detection of directly attached printers, such as our USB-connected examples in this section, is *automatic*. CUPS can also automatically discover other CUPS printers on a network if those printers have sharing enabled. As in other parts of our treatment of CUPS, we do not emphasize the network set of options in this section.

1.6.11 Starting CUPS Print Settings

To start the CUPS Print Settings GUI, use one of the following methods:
From the command line, type the following command:

```
$ system-config-printer
```

From the Raspberry Pi Menu, choose Preferences>Print Settings.

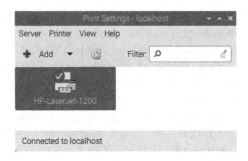

FIGURE 1.2
Print Settings GUI.

Figure 1.2 shows the window that opened when we launched the Print Settings GUI.

1.6.12 Setting Up Printers by Using CUPS Print Settings GUI

This section describes the procedures and steps that are required to set up a local printer by using CUPS Print Settings GUI. In the following sections, we give some indications about when and how you would know that the troubleshooting procedures are necessary for your installation and configuration.

1.6.12.1 How to Set Up a New Local Printer

The following example steps give a basic procedure for setting up a new locally attached printer by using the CUPS Print Settings GUI. It is possible, given the make and model of the printer you have attached to your computer, that you would only be required to do part of step 1..

Example 1.7 Local Printer Setup

1. Connect the new printer to your local hardware system, then power it on. If the printer is automatically detected by the system, a notification message appears. If the printer is not automatically detected, *there are not many things you can do*. This is very similar to adding a new USB flash drive or hard disk to the system: if it is not detected, there are not many troubleshooting steps you can easily take to get it to be recognized.

You may, at this point, *not* have to do any configuration, depending upon whether or not you can actually get a test page, or other document, to print immediately. For example, when we attached the HP-Laserjet-1200 printer to our Raspberry Pi OS on a Raspberry Pi 400, it was immediately recognized and enabled. And that model of HP printer is more than fifteen years old!

a. Start CUPS Print Settings GUI by making the Menu choice Prefer
    ences>Print Settings, or by typing the following command in a
    terminal window:

    $ **system-config-printer**

If you right-click on the newly attached printer icon display in the Main
window of the Print Settings GUI and make the menu choice Properties, the
Printer Properties dialog box appears. On it, there is a button that is labeled
Print Test Page. Click on this. The Printer State changes to Processing. If
a "good" test page comes out of your printer, game over! You could also
attempt to do some further testing by printing document types that you
would normally need to print and verify the results.

If you are adding a new printer that is *not* automatically configured
properly, or you cannot get a test page or other document to print, do the
remaining following steps:

b. Choose the Make and Model: Change... button from the Printer
    Properties window.

2. CUPS selects the USB device that is physically connected to your
    system.

3. In the Change Driver window, your printer should be highlighted.

4. Determine whether to accept the default printer driver or provide a
    PPD file.

To use the default driver, leave the Select Printer From Database option
selected.

To provide a PPD file, you can then:

a. Select the Provide PPD File option – The Select a File window is
    displayed.

b. Locate the specified PPD file on your system, then click Open to
    associate the PPD file with the new printer.

5. From the left pane of the next Choose Driver window, select a printer
    model. From the right pane, select a printer driver. Then, click Forward.
    By default, CUPS selects a "recommended" printer model and the
    appropriate driver for your printer. You can, at this point, optionally
    make another selection from the list of available drivers, if you feel
    this other driver would work better in configuring the printer.

6. To save your changes, click Apply. If prompted, type your password
    or the root password.

    After you have saved your changes, the newly configured printer is
    displayed in the CUPS Print Settings GUI window.

7. (An optional step) To set the printer as the default, right-click the printer name.

    a. Choose the Set as Default option.
    b. In the Set Default Printer window, choose one of the following options:

        Set as the system-wide default printer (default).

        Set as my personal default printer.

        Click OK to save the printer configuration.

8. Try printing a test page, or other document, at the printer. If you are not successful in printing a test page or another document at the printer, go back into the steps above to further troubleshoot your printer.

1.6.12.2 Configuring and Managing Printers by Using CUPS Print Settings GUI

This section describes how to administer printers by using CUPS Print Settings GUI. If you select the printer of interest in the main Print Settings GUI window and then select Printer > Properties, you are presented with the following choices in the Printer Properties dialog window, which allow you to modify the properties of a configured printer.

The Printer Properties dialog includes the following six sections for configuring new and existing printers:

* Settings

In the Settings section, you can configure the following properties:

Description: Descriptive text about the printer. For example, our printer description is Hewlett-Packard HP LaserJet 1200.

Location: A description of the physical location of the printer; for example, raspberrypi.

Device URI: Information about the protocol that is used to access the printer. For example, usb://HP/LaserJet%201200?serial=00CNCY043969.

Make and Model - Information about the make and model of the printer; for example, HP LaserJet 1200 pcl3 and hpcups 3.21.2.

The default settings for the above two options can be changed by clicking the Change button.

Printer State: Information about the current status of the printer; for example, Idle.

Tests and Maintenance: Contains the option to Print Test Page

* Policies

In the Policies section, you can configure the properties that control how a printer behaves.

State- Specifies the following printer states: Enabled, Accepting Requests, Shared

More than one state can be checked off at the same time!

Policies: Specifies how the printer behaves during error conditions.

Banner: Specifies whether starting or ending banner pages are printed with each print job.

* Access Control

The Allow or Deny lists determine which users can print to the printer. For our HP 1200 LaserJet, printing is allowed for everyone.

* Installable Options

For our HP LaserJet 1200, a Duplexer could be deployed to print on two sides of the same sheet of paper if desired by checking the Duplexer Installed box.

* Printer Options

In the Printer Options section, you can configure printer-specific options.

For example, for an HP LaserJet 1200, the following configurable options are displayed:

Media Size, Double-sided printing, Media Source, Output mode, Media type, and Print Quality

The number and types of Printer Options are determined by the PPD file that is associated with the specified printer.

* Job Options

Determines the options that are associated with a print job, for example, the number of copies and page orientation, as well as certain image options. The number and types of options are determined by the PPD file that is associated with the specified printer.

* Ink/Toner Levels

Only available if marker levels are reported for this printer.

1.6.12.3 *An Example of How to Modify the Properties of an Existing Configured Printer*

Example 1.8 contains steps that describe how to modify the basic configuration of an existing installed printer. It assumes that you can print from this printer normally.

Example 1.8 Modifying Printer Properties

1. Start the CUPS Print Manager GUI by making the Menu choice Preferences > Print Settings, or by typing the following command in a terminal window:

   $ **system-config-printer**

The Printer configuration main dialog window is displayed and lists all of the configured printers and any newly detected printers.

2. Right-click the name of the printer for which you want to modify the properties, then choose Properties.

The Printer Properties dialog box appears. The Properties dialog box contains six separate sections, each of which contains properties that are grouped by category. By default, the Settings section of the dialog is displayed.

3. In the Settings section, to modify the printer description or location, type any new information that you want in the corresponding text field.
4. A Uniform Resource Identifier (URI) is an addressing technology for identifying resources on the Internet or LAN. The terms URI and URL are used similarly. URIs can be used with application-level protocols, called **URI schemes**. When creating print queues for network-attached printers by using CUPS print commands or the Print Manager, you can specify the device as a *device-uri*.

To modify the device URI:

    a. As noted in Section 1.6.12.2, our device URI was listed as:

       `usb://HP/LaserJet%201200?serial=00CNCY043969`

    b. Click the Change button next to the setting.
    c. From the list of available devices, select a device, then click Apply.
    d. When prompted, type your password, or the root password. You are then returned to the Settings section.

5. To modify the printer make and model:
    a. Click the Change button next to the setting.
    b. In the Choose Driver window, select a printer make, then click Forward.
    Note: By default, CUPS uses the Select Printer From Database option and selects the appropriate printer-make for you. Alternatively, you can provide your own PPD file.
    c. From the left pane of the next Choose Driver window, select a printer model. From the right pane, select a printer driver, then click Forward.
    d. In the Existing Settings dialog, choose from the following options, then click Apply.
    Use the new PPD (Postscript Printer Description) as is.

    Try to copy the option settings over from the old PPD.

e. If prompted, type your password, or the root password. You are returned to the Settings section of the Printer Properties dialog.

6. Click OK.

1.6.12.4 *How to Rename a Printer*

It sometimes becomes necessary to rename local printers with more descriptive titles, particularly if you have more than one attached to the system. Of course, renaming network-attached printers is important so that you can keep track of where your documents are being printed.

1. Start the CUPS Print Settings GUI by making the Menu choice Preferences > Print Settings, or by typing the following command in a terminal window:

    ```
    $ system-config-printer
    ```

    The Printer configuration main dialog window is displayed, listing all the configured printers and any newly-detected printers.

2. Right-click the name of the printer that you want to rename.

3. Choose the Rename option.

4. Type a new name for the printer.

5. Type your password, or the root password when prompted, if necessary.

6. Click OK to save the changes.

1.6.12.5 *How to Duplicate a Printer Configuration*

This procedure would be necessary if you wanted to replace an old printer with an exact duplicate, or duplicate an old configuration for a similar new printer.

1. Start the CUPS Print Settings GUI by choosing the Menu Preferences > Print Settings, or by typing the following command in a terminal window:

    ```
    $ system-config-printer
    ```

    The Printer configuration dialog appears, listing all of the configured printers and any newly-detected printers.

2. Right-click the name of the printer that you want to copy the configuration.

3. Choose the Duplicate option, or type CTRL-D.

4. In the Duplicate Printer window, type a name for the printer, then click OK.
5. Type your password, or the root password when prompted, if necessary.
6. Click OK.

1.6.12.6 *How to Delete a Printer*

This procedure would be necessary when you no longer have a named printer attached to the system, or need to completely replace its configuration definition on the system before upgrading the drivers and other attendant packages related to the printer. For example, in the process of troubleshooting the HP LaserJet 1200, we needed to delete the original printer and its configuration before loading new drivers and installing the printer again.

1. Start the CUPS Print Settings GUI by choosing the Menu Preferences > Print Settings, or by typing the following command in a terminal window:

    $ system-config-printer

    The Printer configuration dialog appears, listing all of the configured printers and any newly-detected printers.
2. Right-click the name of the printer that you want to delete, then choose Delete.
3. Click Delete in the Confirm Deletion dialog.

1.6.12.7 *How to Disable or Enable a Printer*

When you configure a new printer by using the CUPS Print Settings GUI, the printer is enabled by default. This procedure describes how to disable or enable a printer.

1. Start the CUPS Print Settings GUI by choosing the Menu Preferences > Print Settings, or by typing the following command in a terminal window:

    $ **system-config-printer**

    The Printer configuration dialog appears, listing all of the configured printers and any newly-detected printers.
2. Right-click the name of the printer that you want to disable, or enable, then deselect the option.
3. Type your password, or the root password when prompted, if necessary.
4. Click OK.

1.6.12.8 How to Manage Print Jobs for a Specified Printer

This procedure is probably the most frequent and important one you will execute, especially if you are printing high volumes of documents.

1. Start the CUPS Print Settings GUI by choosing the Menu Preferences > Print Settings, or by typing the following command in a terminal window:

    $ **system-config-printer**

    The Printer configuration dialog appears, listing all of the configured printers and any newly detected printers.

2. Right-click the name of the printer for which you want to manage print jobs, then choose View Print Queue, or type CTRL-F. The Document Print Status (printer-name) window appears, listing all of the print jobs for the specified printer.

    In this window, you can view the following information:

    Job, User, Document, Printer, Size, Time submitted, and Status

3. To view information about completed jobs or printer status, select the appropriate option from the Show completed jobs menu.

4. To perform a specific action on a print job, select the print job, then select an action from the available choices on the menu bar at the top of the window. Alternatively, you can right-click the name of a print job, and from the list of available options, select an action. For example, to refresh the view of the jobs, click on the Refresh job list choice at the top of the window (the clockwise turning arrow.)

1.6.13 Configuring and Managing Printers by Using CUPS on the Command Line

This section briefly describes some of the CUPS command-line utilities on a Raspberry Pi system. It describes how to set up and administer your printers with them. We provide a range of examples of command-line control and management of printers in this section.

1.6.13.1 CUPS Command-Line Utilities

CUPS provides various commands to set up printers and make those printers accessible, both on a local machine where the printer is directly connected to it, and to systems on a LAN or the Internet. In addition, CUPS supports several printer-specific options to the command-line utilities that enable you to control printer configuration. Table 1.3 lists frequently used CUPS commands.

Some CUPS command-line names are the same as legacy command-line print commands from UNIX System-V and BSD, but the behavior of

TABLE 1.3

CUPS Command-Line Utilities

Command	Task
cancel	Cancels a print request
lpadmin	Sets up or changes a printer or class configuration
lpinfo	Shows available devices or drivers known to the CUPS server
lpmove	Moves a specified job or all jobs to a new destination
lpoptions	Displays or sets printer options and defaults
lp	Submits a print request
lpstat	Displays the status information for queues and requests

commands under CUPS management is somewhat different. You should consult the man pages on your system for all of the commands shown in Table 1.3 for further descriptions and clarification. For each sub-section below, we first provide the general form of the command-line utility, and then give a specific Example showing the actual use of the utility on our Raspberry Pi system.

1.6.13.2 *How to Set Up a Printer by Using the* lpadmin *Command*

If you have successfully attached a new printer directly to your computer, this section will allow you to view and manage the configuration for that printer.

1. After connecting the printer to the system, turn on the power to the printer.

    Consult the printer documentation for information on how to correctly setup the hardware, in terms of USB cables, switch settings on the printer itself, etc.

2. Use the **lpadmin** command with the **-p** option to add a printer to CUPS.

    Only the most commonly used options of the CUPS lpadmin command are shown here. For information about other options, see the **lpadmin** man page.

    $ **sudo lpadmin -p printer-name -E -v device -m ppd**

where

- -p specifies the name of the printer to add,
- -E enables the destination and accepts jobs,
- -v sets the device-URI attribute of the print queue,
- -m allows the designation of the PPD file for the printer, from the "model" directory, or by using one of the driver interfaces that your system provides.

3. Verify that the printer is correctly configured.

    $ **lpstat -p printer-name -l**

where

-p   the option that specifies you will be providing the name of the
                printer.

printer-name   provides the option argument, which is the actual printer name.

-l   shows a long listing of printers, classes, or jobs.

The following provides a more practical application of the lpadmin command options and their details.

   To add an HP LaserJet printer, model P1006, by using a network interface URI with the IP address 192.168.0.8, and utilizing a particular ppd, you would type the following command:

$ **sudo lpadmin -p HP_Laserjet_P1006 -E -v socket://192.168.0.8 -m laserjet.\
ppd**

1.6.13.3 Setting a Default Printer on Your System

It is very common on single-computer, and LAN-networked print server configurations, to have a default printer set so that all documents for printing go to that default. You can specify the default printer used on the system in one of the following ways:

   * By setting the LPDEST or PRINTER environment variable.

The LPDEST environment variable determines the destination of the printer. If the LPDEST variable is not set, the PRINTER variable is used. The PRINTER variable determines the output device or destination. If both the LPDEST and PRINTER variables are not set, an unspecified device is used.

   * By using the **lpoptions** command.

Use this command to display or set printer options and defaults. For more information, see the **lpoptions** man page.

The print command searches for the default printer in the following order:

1. The printer name as set by the **lp** command with the **-d** option;
2. The value of the LPDEST environment variable;
3. The value of the PRINTER environment variable.

For instructions on setting up printers by using the CUPS web browser interface, see Section 1.6.

1.6.13.4 How to Set a Default Printer at the Command Line

The default printer can be a local printer or a remote printer. Following are various methods of changing the default printer and some additional examples that show the application of those methods.

1. Set the system's default printer by using one of the following methods:

* By specifying the PRINTER variable:

$ sudo export PRINTER=printer-name

where printer-name specifies the name of the printer to be assigned as the system's default printer. If you do not specify printer-name, the system is set up with no default printer.

Note – When using the lp command with the -d option, the destination printer, which might not be the default printer, is specified. If the -d option is not specified, the print command searches for information about the printer in the PRINTER environment variable.

* By specifying the LPDEST variable:

$ sudo export LPDEST=printer-name

where **printer-name** specifies the name of the printer to be assigned as the system's default printer. If you do not specify the printer-name, the system is set up with no default printer.

Note: If both the LPDEST and the PRINTER environment variables are set, LPDEST takes precedence.

* By using the lpoptions command:

$ sudo lpoptions -d printer-name

where
-d   Specifies the destination printer.
printer-name   Specifies the name of the printer that is assigned as the system's default printer. If you do not specify printer-name, the system is set up with no default printer.

2. Verify the system's default printer.

    $ lpstat -d

3. To print to the default printer with the lp command, type the following command:

    $ lp filename

1.6.13.5 *Setting a Default Printer by Specifying the PRINTER Variable*

The following example shows how to set the printer HP_Laserjet_P1006 as the system's default printer by using the PRINTER variable.

$ export PRINTER=HP_Laserjet_P1006
$ lpstat -d

system default destination: HP_Laserjet_P1006

1.6.13.6 *Setting a Default Printer by Specifying the LPDEST Variable*

The following example shows how to set the printer HP_Laserjet_P1006 as the system's default printer by specifying the LPDEST variable.

$ sudo export LPDEST=HP_Laserjet_P1006
$ lpstat -d

system default destination: HP_Laserjet_P1006

1.6.13.7 *Setting a Default Printer by Using the* lpoptions *Command*

The following shows how to set the printer HP_Laserjet_P1006 as the system's default printer. The printer HP_Laserjet_P1006 is used as the system's default printer if the LPDEST or the PRINTER environment variable is not set. Output on our system of the **lpoptions** command is shown.

$ lpoptions -d HP_Laserjet_P1006

copies=1 cups-browsed=true device-uri=ipps://bob-PowerEdge-T110. local:631/printers/HP_LaserJet_P1006 finishings=3 job-cancel-after= 10800 job-hold-until=no-hold job-priority=50 job-sheets=none,none marker-change-time=0 number-up=1 printer-info='lpb @ Pi400' printer-is-accepting-jobs=true printer-is-shared=false printer-location=Pi400.local printer-make-and-model='Remote Printer' printer-state=3 printer-state-change-time=1478838854 printer-state-reasons=none printer-type=2097158 printer-uri-supported=ipps://Pi400:631/printers/HP_LaserJet_P1006

$ lpstat -d

system default destination: HP_LaserJet_P1006

The **lpoptions** command creates a ~/.lpoptions file that includes and entry for the default printer HP_Laserjet_P1006 in the file. By default, all print jobs are now directed to the HP_Laserjet_P1006 printer.

1.6.13.8 How to Print to a Specified Printer

If you have more than one printer defined and directly connected to your system, or you are sharing other network-enabled printers on your LAN, the following steps help you print to one of those specific printers:

1. (An optional step) Verify the status of the printer.

    $ lpstat -p printer-name

where
-p   is the option allowing you to designate a specific printer.
printer-name   is the option argument designating name of the printer you
                want to print to.

2. Give the destination printer name as an option argument to the lp command.

    $ lp -d destination-printer filename

where
-d   specifies the destination printer.
destination-printer specifies the name of the printer that you are assigning
                    as the destination printer.
filename   specifies the file name to print.

1.6.13.9 Printing to a Specified Printer by Using the lp *Command*

The following example shows how to set the printer HP_Laserjet_P1006 as the destination printer when executing the **lp** command:

$ lp -d HP_Laserjet_P1006 Proposal.doc

request id is HP_Laserjet_P1006-1 (1 file(s))

$ lpstat -d

system default destination: HP_Laserjet_P1006
   The **-d** option of the **lp** command takes precedence over the LPDEST and PRINTER environment variables.
   In the above example, the default printer is HP_Laserjet_P1006.

1.6.13.10 How to Verify the Status of Printers

The **lpstat** command displays information about accessible printers and jobs. Do the following steps to verify the status of printers on your system:

1. Log in to any system on the LAN your computer is hooked up to.
2. (An optional step) Verify the status of all printers, or a specific printer. Only the most commonly used options are shown here. For information about other options, see the **lpstat** man page.

   $ **lpstat [-d] [-p] printer-name [-l] [-t]**

where

-d	shows the system's default printer,
-p printer-name	shows whether a printer is active or idle and when the printer was enabled or disabled,
-l	shows the characteristics of printers and jobs,
-t	shows status information about CUPS, including the status of all printers, for example, whether printers are active and accepting print requests.

You can specify multiple printer names with this command. Use a space or a comma to separate printer names. If you use spaces, enclose the list of printer names in quotation marks. If you do not specify printer-name, the status of all printers is displayed.

1.6.13.11 Displaying the Status of Printers

To display the status of the printer HP_Laserjet_P1006, use the following commands:

$ **lpstat -p HP_Laserjet_P1006**

printer HP_Laserjet_P1006 is idle, enabled since Thu 10 Nov 2016 08:34:14 PM PST
   To display the system's default printer, use the following command:

$ **lpstat -d**

system default destination: HP_Laserjet_P1006
   To display the description of the printers HP-LaserJet-1200 and HP_Laserjet_P1006:

$ **lpstat -p "HP-LaserJet-P1200, HP_Laserjet_P1006" -D**

printer HP-LaserJet-1200 faulted. enabled since Jan 5 11:35 2023. available.
Description: Printer in Orange Bedroom
printer HP_Laserjet_P1006 is idle. enabled since Jan 5 11:36 2023. available.
Description: Printer in Basement.

To display the characteristics of the printer HP_Laserjet_P1006, use the following command:

$ lpstat -p HP_Laserjet_P1006 -l

printer HP_LaserJet_P1006 is idle. enabled since Jan 5 11:36 2017 PM PST

1.6.13.12 How to Print a File to the Default Printer

This sub-section is probably the most important and often-used procedure you will do with your computer and printer. Do the following steps:

1. Log in to any system on the network.
2. (Optional) Verify the status of the printer.
   $ lpstat -p printer-name
3. Issue a print request as follows:

   $ lp filename

Note: Only the basic command is shown in this procedure. For information about the other options, option arguments, and command arguments to these commands, see the **lpstat** and **lp** man pages on your system.

1.6.13.13 How to Delete a Printer and Remove Printer Access

There may come a time when you want to delete a printer and its configuration completely from the system. For example, when we first installed the HP_Laserjet_P1006 on our system, it was erroneously configured with an earlier release of the HPLIP drivers that did not allow us to print with it. So we had to delete that printer and its configuration, and reinstall some of the drivers. We were then able to re-install that printer successfully. Do the following steps to delete a printer, and remove access to it:

1. On the system that is the print client, delete information about the printer.

   $ sudo lpoptions -x printer-name

where
printer-name   Specifies the name of the printer to delete.
-x   Deletes the specified printer.

Note – The -x option only removes the default options for a specific printer and instance. The original print queue still remains until it is deleted by using the **lpadmin** command.

In-Chapter Exercise

4. Give a general example of using the **lpadmin** command to delete a print queue.

2. Delete the printer.

   $ **sudo lpadmin -x printer-name**

3. Verify that the printer has been deleted, as follows:
   a. Confirm that the printer has been deleted on the print client.

      $ **sudo lpstat -p printer-name -l**

   The command output displays a message indicating the printer does not exist.

   b. Confirm that the printer has been deleted on the print server.

      $ **sudo lpstat -p printer-name -l**

The command output displays a message indicating that the printer does not exist.

1.6.13.14 Deleting a Printer

The following command-line sequence example shows how to delete the printer HP_Laserjet_P1006 from the print client named Pi400, and then from the print server named Pi4.

   Pi400$ **sudo lpoptions -x HP_Laserjet_P1006**
   Pi400$ **sudo lpstat -p HP_Laserjet_P1006 -l**

Switch to the Pi4

   Pi4$ **sudo lpadmin -x HP_Laserjet_P1006**
   Pi4$ **sudo lpstat -p HP_Laserjet_P1006 -l**

lpstat: Invalid destination name in list "HP_Laserjet_P1006"!

In-Chapter Exercises 5. through 14

5. Why is an error generated by the command **sudo lpstat -p HP_Laserjet_P1006 -l** given on the Pi4?
6. Use the Linux Print Manager utility on your system to add a new printer named "localprinter" to your system (the printer should be

connected and powered-on to set up a print queue for the new printer). The printers setup is dependent upon the make and model you have available for your actual system.

For the next three exercises only, power off your printer first. Then use only typed command-line operations to do the three exercises.

7. Use the **lp** command to print any particular file of interest to that printer.
8. Check the print queue for that printer to see that the print job is there.
9. Remove the print job from the queue (cancel it).
10. Set up the CUPS web-browser-based interface, so other systems on your LAN can print to the printer "localprinter."
11. Check the status of "localprinter" from a web browser on another computer on your LAN.
12. Actually execute CUPS administration, using the web-browser-based interface, from one computer on your LAN to the computer that has "localprinter" connected to it.
13. Use the **systemctl** command to see the status of the cups.service.
14. Delete the "localprinter" printer from your system, using any of the methods you feel most comfortable with.

1.7 Other Linux Archiving and Backup Facilities

In addition to the traditional **tar** facility, there are several other facilities and methods a system administrator can use to archive and backup individual user accounts, files, file systems, and the entire system itself. As stated above, to get a more complete listing of the capabilities and options available for the command-line facilities shown in this, and all other sections, consult the man pages on your system for these commands. We briefly describe and give simple examples of some of the more modern and useful of these facilities and methods below.

1.7.1 cpio

As universally available as **tar** on Linux systems, the **cpio** command allows the system administrator to back up the entire system and transfer files between file systems. It may be used in conjunction with the **find** command, but not necessarily if you are backing up an entire file system. An abbreviated listing of the man page for **cpio** is as follows:

****

cpio
Purpose: Copies files to an archive, extracts files from an archive, or passes files to \
  another directory tree.
Syntax:
cpio -o [aBcv] > directory for creation of an archive, and
cpio -i [Btv] [pattern] for restoring an archive.
Output: Created or Restored archive file.
Common Options:
-o   creates the archive
-v   prints the names of the files that are archived
-i   extracts the archive
Command Arguments:
directory   A directory where the archive is found.
pattern   Source for the restored archive.

****

When creating an archive, **cpio** takes the list of files to be processed from the standard input, and then sends the archive to the standard output. A simple example of this would be as follows:

$ **ls | cpio -ov > backup.cpio**

In a more complicated example, the following commands backup selected files in the /home/bob directory to a USB flash drive, for the sake of this illustration, generically named **device**:

$ **cd /home/bob**
$ **touch level.1.cpio.timestamp**
$ **find . –newer level.0.cpio.timestamp –print \ | cpio –oacvB > device**
Output truncated...
$

A simple example of extracting a cpio archive is as follows:

$ **cpio -iv < backup.cpio**

1.7.2 dd

The **dd** facility is used to copy a single file, part of a file, a partition, or part of a partition, and can treat the data stream using, for example, compression or format conversion. An abbreviated version of the **dd** man page is as follows:

****

dd
Purpose: To copy a file (from standard input to standard output, by default) with
    possibly a changeable I/O block size, while optionally doing file conversions on it.
Syntax:
dd [options] if=device of=device bs=blocksize
Output: Modified file.
Common Options:
--help   Provides help on the dd command.
--version   Supplies the version number of the utility.
Operands and Command Arguments:
ibs=bytes   Sets the input block size in bytes. This makes dd read bytes per block.
                The default is 512 bytes.
obs=bytes   Sets the output block size to bytes. This makes dd write bytes per
                block. The default is 512 bytes.
bs=bytes   Set both input and output block sizes to bytes. This makes dd read
                and write bytes per block, overriding any 'ibs' and 'obs' settings.
device: file or pathname to object being processed.
blocksize Blocksize of copied file.

****

A multi-command example of using **dd**, used in conjunction with **ssh** and
tar, is as follows:

$ **ssh bob@192.168.0.13:/home/bob "dd if=backup.tar ibs=512" | tar --\
    extract --verbose --read-full-records --file --**

The above command extracts the remote file backup.tar file at 192.168.0.13:/
home/bob in input 512-byte blocks and streams it through **dd** to the system
you typed this command on.

1.7.3 rsync

The **rsync** command is a modern and *very* space-efficient way to backup
selected files and directories, particularly from one machine to another using
ssh across a network. Its operation can also be automated via the use of
systemd scheduling "timers." Here we provide an extensive example of the
use of **rsync**, coupled with Python, to underscore our point about the utility
of both **rsync** and Python usage in Linux.

Example 1.9 Extended Python Script Example Using rsync to Do a "Rotating" Backup

Objective: Use Python3 in conjunction with the **rsync** command to do a daily,
rotating backup of selected directories and files locally and across a network,
with a depth of five sequentially retained backups.

Prerequisites:
You should prepare to execute the Python script file by doing the following:

a. Create a file in /home/your_username/.rsync/exclude (where your_ username is your login name on your Raspberry Pi system) which contains filename matching patterns for **rsync** to ignore. You should exclude patterns such as *.tmp or *.o

b. You have a remote machine on your LAN or intranet, and know its IP address, that you can ssh into. You must have the access permissions and credentials to access directories and files on that remote machine. On our Raspberry Pi system, this IP address was 192.168.0.25.

c. You should make sure that you setup ssh on the remote machine so that you can do a login to it *without* having to type in a password. Not having done this would prevent automating the Python script with legacy cron, or a systemd timer. We provide a Project at the end of this chapter that asks you to automate this script file using a systemd timer.

We provide the Python code for the example presented in step 5 of the Requirements subsequently.

Background: As well as using the **rsync** command to achieve the objectives, it also uses the **cpio** command and the Python methods copytree and rmtree, from the shutil utility.
  Basically, there are five operations this Python script file performs:

1. Checks to see if several numbered, or versioned, backup directories exist. If they don't exist, it creates them.

2. Removes the last version, or oldest directory.

3. Hard copies directory "1" into directory "2." A hard copy makes a copy in which the two files share the same disk space, i.e., *your files take up no extra room.*

4. **rsync**'s the files you want to backup to directory "1." *rsync only overwrites changed files.* This example does this **rsync** operation first between source and local machine "backup "directories, and then between those backup directories, and their equivalent directories and files on the remote machine.

5. Also, specifically backs up designated source code, a very critical operation if you're a developer of applications.

Notice that the provided script file does *not* use OOP but uses an imperative/ procedural programming methodology.

Requirements:

1. Type in the source code for this script file exactly as shown below.
2. Read through the basic procedural steps outlined in the Background of this example above in careful conjunction with the Python code you typed in step 1 of these Requirements. Try to comprehend the sequence of the script file as it accomplishes its procedures from beginning to end. Produce a diagram or flowchart of how the program works. A graphic will always help to clarify the flow of the script file as it accomplishes its objectives.
3. **Critical** Modify the Python source code shown below using your favorite text editor, so that the lines of code under the function backupserver(), that assigns sources, localsources, localcode, target, host (the remote machine), and user are relevant and pertinent to directories, host, and your username on your Raspberry Pi system!
4. Once step 3 changes are made, execute your modified Python code.
5. Verify that the script file is doing what it is intended to do; in other words, test it on your Raspberry Pi system. That testing will include debugging and a verification regimen that is your responsibility to design and certify.

```python
#!/usr/bin/python3

# This script file does a daily, local, rotating backup to a remote machine, using rsync
#
import time
import datetime
import os
import shutil
import UserString
def backupserver():
        debug_flag = "debug"
        sources = ["/home/bob/test_dir"]
        codetarget = "/home/bob/some_code/"
        target = "/home/bob/Daily_Backups/"
        host = "192.168.0.25"
        user = "bob"
        # Target can be reached, start the rotation of the snapshot directories
        if (debug_flag == "debug"):
            print ("Date: " + str(datetime.date.today()))
            print (host +" is up, rotating snapshots.")

        # Check to see if the directories exist
        i = 1
        while i <= 5:
                temp_path = target + str(i) + "/"
                if not os.path.exists( temp_path ):
                        try:
```

```
                                os.makedirs( temp_path )
                                print ("Created " + temp_path)
                except:
                                print ("Couldn't create " + temp_path)
                i = i + 1
        # Cycle through the backups
        # First deleting the oldest one #5
        print ("Deleting oldest archive")
        shutil.rmtree( target + "5" )
        # Cycle through 2 - 4
        print "Cycle backups"
        os.rename( target + "4", target + "5")
        os.rename( target + "3", target + "4")
        os.rename( target + "2", target + "3")
        # Do hard copy of 1
        os.system('find "' + target + '1" -print | cpio -pdl ' + target +"2")
        print ("Copy first backup")
        # Copy tree does a full copy whereas cpio does hard link copies (i.e. each \
            copied file
        # takes up no extra space)
        shutil.copytree( target + "1", target + "2")
        os.system('cd "' + target + '1"; find . -print | cpio -pdl "' + target + '2"')
        print ("Rsyncing now")
        # Rsync from local directories to local backup
        for source in sources:
                print ("Local directories " + source)
                os.system('rsync -azv -e   --delete --delete-excluded ' +
                                '--exclude-from=/home/bob/.rsync/exclude "' + source +
                                '" "' + target+'1"')
        # Rsync from the server to the local backup
        for source in sources:
                print ("Downloading " + source)
                os.system('rsync -azv -e ssh --delete --delete-excluded ' +
                                '--exclude-from=/home/bob/.rsync/exclude ' + user
                                + "@" +
                                host + ':"' + source + '" "' + target+'1"')
        # Backup only the targeted programming source code
        newfolder = codetarget + str(datetime.date.today())
        # Make the new directory
        if not os.path.exists( newfolder ):
        os.makedirs( newfolder )
        # Here's the critical operation.
# Find all the source files from our rsync backup and copy them as hard links
    print ("Backing up source")
    os.system('cd "' + target + '1"; find . \( ' + " -name '*.cpp' -or -name 'Makefile'" + "-or -
                name '*.c' -or -name '*.h' -or -name '*.lex' -or -name '*.y'" + " -or -
                name '*.bat' -or -name '*.py' \) " + ' -print | cpio -pdl "' +
    newfolder +'"')
    backupserver()
```

Conclusion: Given your system administration backup requirements, this example has provided a technique you can deploy that uses a powerful strategy for fairly complex archiving of your system's persistent data.

1.8 Repository Management

Since the Raspberry Pi OS is derived from Debian Linux, a large majority of its default software, in the form of pre-configured packages, comes from those sources. The repositories are grouped into categories according to how much support is given to packages in a particular category. For example, the main Debian repository contains packages that directly have a hand in writing source code and other attendant modules. Unsupported, and to some degree, unreliable software packages are also available in the other major categories. There is always the possibility, with an "open" software operating system such as the Raspberry Pi OS, to install from source code itself. But this route has largely been co-opted by various levels and forms of pre-packaged applications.

It is possible to install from alternative software repositories in order to be able to install software not found in the default repositories. You can view the official repositories using the following commands:

```
$ cat /etc/apt/sources.list
deb http://deb.debian.org/debian bullseye main contrib non-free
deb http://security.debian.org/debian-security bullseye-security main contrib non-free
deb http://deb.debian.org/debian bullseye-updates main contrib non-free
# Uncomment deb-src lines below then 'apt-get update' to enable 'apt-get source'
#deb-src http://deb.debian.org/debian bullseye main contrib non-free
#deb-src http://security.debian.org/debian-security bullseye-security main contrib
   non-free
#deb-src http://deb.debian.org/debian bullseye-updates main contrib non-free
```

GUI-based repository management, in other words, where you get your software packages from, is normally accomplished via the Raspberry Pi OS Menu choice Preferences > Add/Remove Software. Underneath this GUI, the Advanced Packaging Tool(APT) is the primary tool for installing packages. In the following section, we use the command line to show some of the basic characteristics of package repository listings and the files that they give you access to.

1.8.1 Searching Repositories with the apt-cache Command and apt-show

Suppose a friend of yours tells you about a game that's available on Raspberry Pi systems named Seven Kingdoms. How do you find out if it's available on your system, and what its characteristics are? You can use the following commands to do that:

```
$ apt-cache search seven kingdoms
```

7kaa: Seven Kingdoms Ancient Adversaries: real-time strategy game
7kaa-data: Seven Kingdoms Ancient Adversaries - game data

$ apt-cache show 7kaa

Package: 7kaa
Version: 2.15.4p1+dfsg-1
Installed-Size: 1799
Maintainer: Debian Games Team <pkg-games-devel@lists.alioth.debian.org>
Architecture: arm64
Depends: 7kaa-data (= 2.15.4p1+dfsg-1), libc6 (>= 2.27), libcurl3-gnutls (>= 7.16.2), libenet7, libgcc-s1 (>= 3.0), libopenal1 (>= 1.14), libsdl2-2.0-0 (>= 2.0.12+dfsg1), libstdc++6 (>= 5.2), libuuid1 (>= 2.16)
Suggests: 7kaa-music (>= 2.15)
Description-en: Seven Kingdoms Ancient Adversaries: real-time strategy game
Seven Kingdoms, designed by Trevor Chan, brings a unique blend of
Real-Time Strategy with the addition of trade, diplomacy, and espionage.
.
The game enables players to compete against up to six other kingdoms allowing
players to conquer opponents by defeating them in war (with troops or
machines), capturing their buildings with spies, or offering opponents money
for their kingdom.
.
In 2009, Enlight Software released the game under the GPL license. 7kfans
project is updating the game and provides a community for fans. A free Seven
Kingdoms will help continue the legacy.
Description-md5: 37b0a07b664e6e2e6b3370a23d7a49cb
Homepage: http://www.7kfans.com/
Tag: game::strategy, interface::graphical, interface::x11, role::program,
uitoolkit::sdl, use::gameplaying, x11::application
Section: games
Priority: optional
Filename: pool/main/7/7kaa/7kaa_2.15.4p1+dfsg-1_arm64.deb
Size: 663204
MD5sum: a5fe610f90c7f86d4d534d60a0813c00
SHA256: 834c90e55492c284b5a206c4d404e4dcd4a96e188fd1334719ea680d37
4ac425

1.8.2 Basic Repository Characteristics

APT stores a list of repositories, sometimes called "software channels", in the
file /etc/apt/sources.list.

It also stores lists of repositories in any file with the suffix .list under the
directory /etc/apt/sources.list.d/

You can add new repositories to the /etc/apt/sources.list, but APT will also,
by default, look in the /etc/apt/sources.list.d/ directory for text files ending
with the .list extension. In order to take effect, the lines in these text files should
have the same format and structure as the /etc/apt/sources.list file does

Another way of adding repositories to be searched is by creating a new text file (ending in .list) for it in the directory /etc/apt/sources.list.d/. This is a cleaner and more organized way of keeping track of your repositories, and you can always remove the repository by deleting or commenting out that file. Editing these files from the command line allows a user to add, remove, or temporarily disable software repositories.

You can produce a backup of the configuration file sources.list before you edit it using the following command:

$ **sudo cp /etc/apt/sources.list /etc/apt/sources.list.backup**

1.8.3 Repository Listing Format in /etc/apt/sources.list

A typical repository line in either of these two files will look similar to the following:

deb http://deb.debian.org/debian bullseye main contrib non-free

where
deb (or deb-src), which refers to where the apt command will find binary packages (deb) or source packages (deb-src),
the actual URL, which apt will use in order to "pull" from the repository,
the codename of the release; in this case, bullseye, and
the Component named main, which references whether or not the repository contains software that is free and open source, and is supported officially.

Software packages have source code available, so if you are a developer, you are able to use this repository to fix bugs by altering the source code, and "packaging" up your changes. Software marked restricted is still supported but may have a questionable license. For example, in our repository listing shown in Section 1.8 above, the following source is given:

#deb-src http://deb.debian.org/debian bullseye main contrib non-free

In-Chapter Exercise

15. Name the parts of the entries for the following line in a /etc/apt/ sources.list file:
deb http://deb.debian.org/debian bullseye-updates main contrib non-free

1.8.4 Other Suggested Procedures for Repository Management

1. Always back up configuration files like /etc/apt/sources.list before you begin editing it! You can then reinstate your original source

listings if something goes wrong with the entries in the newly added repository.

2. If you decide to add other repositories to sources.list, make sure that the repository actually works with your release of the software. Repositories that are not designed to work with your version can introduce faults in your operating system and might force you to re-install the entire system!

3. Also, make sure that you really need to add external repositories as the software package(s) you are looking for may already have been introduced into the official repositories.

4. You may be asked to enter a security key when adding a non-Debian repository to your sources.

5. As much as possible, retrieve updated package lists by using the **sudo apt-get update** command when you have edited /etc/apt/sources. list.

1.9 Tasks, Processes, Threads, and Traditional Process Control/Monitoring

Before discussing traditional methods of process control, and how to monitor processes, it is instructive at this point to know what a "task" refers to in the Raspberry Pi OS. In particular, knowing what the difference is, if any, between a process and a thread, in the context of Linux tasks. And this is useful knowledge, especially with respect to the kernel itself. To make clear the differences between tasks, processes, and threads, consider this set of comparisons between them:

A preliminary sketch of what a Linux "task" is, relative to processes and threads, and with reference to the kernel, is as follows:

In Linux, a task and a thread are synonymous on a conceptual level.

A process at this level can be thought of as a completely independent virtual environment, which runs at least one task. A very good example is a single-thread process.

Each task is an independently executing module within the virtual environment of a process.

The main task of a process (usually called the "leading thread"), defines the Task ID (TID) number, which *is* the same as the nominal Process ID (PID) number.

Every new thread that is spawned by a process, using system calls, creates a new task within the process.

In order to identify these new tasks in the kernel, they get assigned their own individual Task ID (TID) number.

All tasks within a process share the same Thread Group ID (TGID) number. A more complete description of what the difference is between processes and threads is given by the following listing of points:

1. With respect to the Linux kernel, a task that can be run and scheduled through the CPU is called a "process."

2. Each process has a globally unique Process ID (PID) number and a Thread Group ID (TGID) number.

3. A "stand alone" process, or "single-threaded" process, has a PID that is equal to its TGID, and no other process can have this TGID value.

4. A "threaded" process has its TGID value shared by other processes: they all have the same TGID value.

5. Processes sharing the same TGID also share the same memory space, signal handlers, etc..

6. If a "threaded" process has a PID that is equal to its TGID, it can be called "the leading thread."

   In a systems program, making the system call **getpid()** from within a process will return its TGID (or "leading thread" PID).

7. From within a systems program, making the system call **gettid()** from within a process will return its PID.

8. Both a process and thread can be created with the very important Linux-specific **clone()** system call.

9. "Numbered" folders in /proc, which you can list with the ls command, are TGIDs.

10. "Numbered" folders in /proc/TGID/task contain numbers that are PIDs.

11. Even though you don't see every existing PID using the command **ls /proc**, you can still give the command **cd /proc/any_PID**, where any_ PID is the PID of a process of interest.

12. In conclusion, and with respect to the kernel, only processes exist. Each process has its own PID. A thread is just a different kind of process.

Questions: "Are all processes threads, and why?", and "Is the Linux kernel itself a process, and what are the threads created by this process?"

Answers: Since Linux is a multi-tasking, concurrent execution environment, all processes can be considered threads of execution through the system.

And at the conceptual level we are addressing here, the Linux kernel is *not* a process, but can be thought of as simply a complex interrupt handler, that controls the movement of tasks as threads through the CPU and the CPU's supportive virtualized memory system and persistent media.

1.10 Controlling and Managing CPU Consumption by Processes

The traditional way of managing the CPU consumption of a process is to use the **nice** and **renice** commands. In this sub-section, we illustrate the way you can use those commands effectively after monitoring and assessing a process's activity.

Only the root, or a user with sudo privileges, can increase a process's CPU priority by *decreasing* its nice value.

A more contemporary method of managing CPU priority is accomplished with systemd cgroups.

The following code example shows the display of the four top current processes using the most CPU resources running on the system. When we type this in on our Raspberry Pi OS system, we get the output shown:

$ ps -aux | head -5

USER	PID	% CPU	% MEM	VSZ	RSS	TTY	STAT	START	TIME	COMMAND
root	1	0.0	0.2	168300	9832	?	Ss	Oct08	0:16	/sbin/init splash
root	2	0.0	0.0	0	0	?	S	Oct08	0:01	[kthreadd]
root	3	0.0	0.0	0	0	?	I<	Oct08	0:00	[rcu_gp]
root	4	0.0	0.0	0	0	?	I<	Oct08	0:00	[rcu_par_gp]

$

The **pgrep** command displays the PIDs of running processes. Here are some examples of how to use **pgrep** to find the process IDs of the running processes and pipe those PIDs to another command to produce the output.

To search for kthreadd, run the following **ps** command:

$ ps -p `pgrep kthreadd`

```
  PID TTY        TIME    CMD
  2 ?        00:00:01   kthreadd
$
```

To search for systemd, run the following **ps** command:

$ ps -fp `pgrep systemd`

UID	PID	PPID	C	STIME	TTY	STAT	TIME	CMD
root	1	0	0	Oct08	?	Ss	0:16	/sbin/init splash
root	140	1	0	Oct08	?	Ss	0:09	/lib/systemd/systemd-journald
root	167	1	0	Oct08	?	Ss	0:08	/lib/systemd/systemd-udevd
root	486	1	0	Oct08	?	Ss	0:04	/lib/systemd/systemd-logind
bob	682	1	0	Oct08	?	Ss	0:01	/lib/systemd/systemd --user
systemd+	83391	1	0	Oct12	?	Ssl	0:01	/lib/systemd/systemd-timesyncd

$

To search for nginx and improve its priority access to the CPU (assumes you have the nginx daemon installed and running!):

```
$ sudo renice -1 `pgrep nginx`
[sudo] password for bob: QQQ
7630 (process ID) old priority 0, new priority -1
7631 (process ID) old priority 0, new priority -1
7632 (process ID) old priority 0, new priority -1
$
```

To change nginx back to priority 0:

```
$ sudo renice 0 `pgrep nginx`
7630 (process ID) old priority 1, new priority 0
7631 (process ID) old priority 1, new priority 0
7632 (process ID) old priority 1, new priority 0
```

The **nice** and **renice** commands, as seen in the previous examples, change process priorities in the CPU.

Here is an example of using a command with **nice** to change a command's **nice** value:

Run the vi text editor at a higher priority:

```
$ sudo nice -n -1 vi
```

When a process is already running, you can change the process's **nice** value using the **renice** command. Here are some examples of the **renice** command:

Renice sarwar's processes +2:

```
$ renice +2 -u sarwar
```

Renice PID 2576 by +5

```
$ renice +5 2576
```

Renice sarwar's ksmserver processes to –3:

```
$ renice -3 `pgrep -u sarwar ksmserver `
```

```
2545: old priority -1, new priority -3
2546: old priority -1, new priority -3
2547: old priority -1, new priority -3
```

The back quotes are used in the previous command lines to show that the output of the **pgrep** command (usually PIDs) should be redirected to the either the **nice** or **renice** command. The **nice** settings for your processes are displayed by default (as NI in the display later) when you run the **top** command. You can run the **top** command, with a delay of screen updates every 10 seconds, as follows:

```
$ top -d 10
top - 07:13:23 up 7 days, 18:03, 2 users,        load average: 0.18, 0.16, 0.17
Tasks:    229 total, 1 running, 228 sleeping,  0 stopped,  0 zombie
%Cpu(s): 1.5 us,     1.1 sy,     0.0 ni,     97.4 id, 0.0 wa, 0.0 hi, 0.0 si, 0.0 st
MiB Mem :  3794.4 total,  1353.8 free,   772.7 used,  1667.8 buff/cache
MiB Swap:  100.0 total,    99.5 free,     0.5 used.   2824.2 avail Mem

PID  USER    PR  NI  VIRT     RES     SHR S  %CPU  %MEM   TIME+ COMMAND
624  root    20   0  470808  255720  45488 S   4.8   6.6   228:37.97  Xorg
Output truncated...
```

Based upon the output of the **top** command, you could stop an unimportant or runaway process with the **kill** command, as follows. We previously had determined the PID of an unimportant process as 19993 (not shown in the **top** command output above). Be careful here, if you kill an important process, your system goes down!

```
$ sudo kill -9 19993
$
```

1.11 systemd Journal Log Messages

Question: What do we use the systemd journal for primarily?

Answer: To check for unauthorized entry into our system and to monitor system performance.

But it has many other uses, for example, in monitoring system performance. The journal is created and controlled by the journald daemon, which directs all of the messages produced by the kernel, initrd, services, etc., into a binary record structure. The systemd journal is a single, centralized management tool for logs, regardless of where the log messages are sent from.

One salient feature of using systemd is that log messages currently can be output using the traditional message printing APIs with the syslog function call, as well as by using the journal API function calls.

And a critical, and somewhat controversial aspect of systemd journal logging, is that the log files are stored as binary data, and can be searched by specialized database traversal techniques.

Storing the log data in a binary format, most importantly, means that the data can be displayed in useful output formats.

Access to the logs kept by the journal daemon is done using the **journalctl** command. In this section, we give you a basic overview of what can be viewed with the **journalctl** command.

1.11.1 journalctl Basics

A very simple first command to use when you want to view logs with the journalctl command, is to type that command with no options or arguments: To have a first look at the logs, just type in:

$ **journalctl**

The output you get is very similar to the traditional output when viewing system logs. With the following notable exceptions:

Lines of error priority (and higher) will be highlighted red.

Lines of notice/warning priority will be highlighted bold.

The timestamps are converted into your local time-zone.

The output is auto-paged by pressing the space bar.

This will show all available data, including rotated logs.

Between the output of each boot, we'll add a line clarifying that a new boot begins now.

By default, ordinary, unprivileged users can only watch their own logs. To add an ordinary, unprivileged user to the adm group, use the following command:

$ **sudo usermod -a -G adm somename**

where **somename** is the name you want to assign a new user.

After logging out and back in as **somename**, you have access to the full journal of the system and all users. To view logs as they grow, use the following command:

$ **journalctl -f**

This command shows the last ten Journal log lines, and then waits for changes and shows them as they take place.

To view the Journal logs of just the current boot environment (since the last reboot), use the following command:

$ **journalctl -b**

Listing all log messages with priority levels ERROR and worse, from the current boot environment, use the following command:

$ **journalctl -b -p err**

To see Journal entries in a more restricted timeframe, for example, from yesterday until now, type the following command:

$ **journalctl --since=yesterday**

All log messages from the day before at 00:00 in the morning until right now are shown on the screen.

To search for entries that were recorded in the journal on 22 October until today, use the following command:

$ journalctl --since=2022-10-25 --until=today

To see messages logged to the journal by a particular service unit, such as nginx, use the following command:

$ journalctl -u httpd --since=00:00 --until=9:30

Finally, to see journal entries for a particular device, such as the disk drive at /dev/sda, use the following command:

$ journalctl /dev/sda

1.12 Access Control Credentials: Discretionary (DAC), Mandatory (MAC), and Role-Based (RBAC)

The nomenclature we use in this section deserves some attention. When we talk about access control via security checks, here are some important terms:

Objects: The entities that are targeted, or worked on, by the processes of a program. For example, processes themselves can be objects, or the processes generated by executing instances of a program.

Files/inodes are another form of object, particularly the executable form of file objects, and the attendant data structure holding their information. Not to be confused with file system objects, which we have so far referred to as either an ordinary file or a directory.

Object Ownership: Indicates the owning user and group.

Object Context: Security checks done when objects are acted on.

Subjects: An object that is acted upon by another object. Processes are active subjects, such as those processes that are created by an **exec()** or **fork()** system call from an originating process.

Subject Context: Security checks done when an active subject performs its operations.

Action: What a subject does to an object. This includes reading, writing, creating and deleting files; forking or signaling.

Permissions: Security checks when a subject acts upon an object. Taking the subject context, the object context, and the action, and searching one or more sets of permissions to see whether the subject is granted or denied permission to act in the desired manner on the object, given those contexts. In simple terms, match subject and object permissions, and let the subject act or not on the object.

There are three basic "classes" of permissions:

1. Discretionary Access Control (DAC):

    Sometimes the object will include sets of rules as part of its description. This is an 'Access Control List' or 'ACL'. A Raspberry Pi OS file may supply more than one ACL. A traditional file, for example, includes a permissions mask that is an abbreviated ACL with three fixed classes of subject ('user' or 'owner', 'group', and 'other' or 'everyone'), each of which may be granted certain privileges ('read', 'write' and 'execute' - whatever those map to for the object in question). File permissions do not allow the arbitrary specification of subjects, however, and so are of limited use.

    A file might also support a POSIX1e ACL, or an NFSv4 ACL. This is a list of rules that grants various permissions to arbitrary subjects.

2. Mandatory access control (MAC):

    The system as a whole may have one or more sets of permissions that get applied to all subjects and objects, regardless of their source. Security Extended Linux (SELinux) is an example of this.

3. Role-Based Access Control (RBAC):

    Rather than use the user ID to determine what access rights users and groups have on the system, the Role-Based Access Control (RBAC) model grants access based on the role or roles that a user assumes. The classic RBAC example is the use of the **sudo** command to grant an unprivileged user root privileges.

These forms of access control policies determine what access action is allowed on what object, under what circumstances (DAC, MAC, or Role-Based Access Control (RBAC)), and by what subject.

A permission, for example, can be thought of as read, write, or execute privilege. A subject, for example, can be thought of as an executing process. Most importantly, an object is a process since everything is done on files, and the data in them are controlled through active processes.

On the command-line, an ordinary user, or the system administrator, is able to implement resource use restrictions and privileges by controlling process credential assignments, exercised on subject executable image files, via the **chmod** command. An ordinary unprivileged user can be given the required privileged role with the **sudo** command. Then, as root, she can issue a privileged **chmod**, **chown**, and **chgrp** to grant or modify file and directory access permissions and use the DAC, MAC, or RBAC methods as well.

1.12.1 Types of Credentials

We are concerned with the five basic types of credentials that the Linux kernel supports. These are as follows:
  * Traditional UNIX Credentials

1. Real User ID
2. Real Group ID

UID and GID are assigned to most Linux objects. These in large part define the object context of that object, with processes included in this assignment.

3. Effective (EUID), Saved (SUID), and FS (FSID) User ID
4. Effective (EGID), Saved (SGID), and FS (FSGID) Group ID
5. Supplementary groups

The additional credentials used by processes, EUID/EGID/GROUPS, are used as the subject context, and real UID/GID will be used as the object context.

1.13 sudo

The sudo program allows a single command to be run as root, or even as some other user. The system administrator utilizes a policy listing file (named sudoers) that contains commands that each user can execute. When any user needs to run a command that requires root permissions, that user types **sudo command** in a console terminal, allowing them to run **command**. Then, sudo consults its permissions list in the policy listing file. If the user has permission to run that command, it runs the command. If the user does not have permission to run the command, sudo denies execution. Running sudo does not require knowing root's password, but by default, requires the user's own password to execute successfully.

An important security access consideration, before you allow someone to execute the **sudo** command successfully, is finding out what group or groups you, or any other user for that matter, actually belong to on your system. The user you want to include in the sudoers file may already belong to a group that has adequate access privileges! For you, this can be simply done by executing the following command:

```
$ id
uid=1000(bob) gid=1000(bob) groups=1000(bob),4(adm), 20(dialout), 24(cdrom),
   27(sudo),29(audio), 44(video),46(plugdev), 60(games), 100(users), 104(input),
   106(render), 108(netdev), 117(lpadmin), 997(gpio), 998(i2c), 999(spi)
```

From the above output on our system, user bob belongs to the groups bob, adm, dialout, cdrom, sudo, audio, video, plugdev, games, users, input, render, netdev, lpadmin, gpio, i2c, and spi. Therefore, he already has access to files and directories that those groups have access to.

To find out what groups are defined on the system, you can use the following commands:

```
$ compgen -g
root
daemon
bin
sys
adm
tty
disk
Output truncated...
```

In this way, before assigning groups or users in the sudoer file "aliases", you have an idea of what groups exist on the system. We detail sudoer aliases in the following sections.

There are two aspects to sudo: the sudo program itself, and the sudoers policy file that the program uses. The sudoers policy file can only be edited by root. The sudo program includes a special tool, visudo, just for editing and validating the sudoers policy file. The path to the executable program visudo is /usr/sbin.

The sudoers policy file must only be edited with visudo, because that special editing tool has safeguards built into it. Typing **sudo visudo** on the command line of our Raspberry Pi system launches the nano text editor to allow editing of the sudoers file. The sudoers file itself is found in /etc. At this point, you should use the **sudo more** command to examine the contents of the sudoers file in /etc on your system.

The sudoers file recognizes seven types of user specification lists. They are usernames, group names (such as lxd), aliases defined within the sudoers file itself, UID numbers, GID numbers, netgroups, and non-UNIX groups. See the following section for applications of some of these seven specification lists.

The sudoers file is composed of two types of entries: aliases, and user specifications. Aliases are names that can be assigned to a variety of groups of objects, like users, hosts, etc. User specifications dictate who may run what. When multiple entries match a user, they are applied in order. Where there are multiple matches, the last match is used (which is not necessarily the most specific match). A user specification determines which commands a user may run (and as what user) on specific hosts.

By default, commands are run as root, but this can be changed on a per-command basis.

In the following two sections, we give examples of alias entries and various forms of user specification.

1.13.1 Alias Specifications and Definition in the Sudoers File

There are four kinds of aliases: User_Alias, Runas_Alias, Host_Alias, and Cmnd_Alias.

A generalized syntactic description of these alias specifications is as follows:

```
Alias = 'User_Alias'  User_Alias (':' User_Alias)* |
        'Runas_Alias' Runas_Alias (':' Runas_Alias)* |
        'Host_Alias'  Host_Alias (':' Host_Alias)* |
        'Cmnd_Alias'  Cmnd_Alias (':' Cmnd_Alias)*
```

User_Alias = NAME '=' User_List

Runas_Alias = NAME '=' Runas_List

Host_Alias = NAME '=' Host_List

Cmnd_Alias = NAME '=' Cmnd_List

NAME = [A-Z]([A-Z][0-9]_)*

An alias definition is given in the following format:

Alias_Type NAME = object1, object2, ...

where:

Alias_Type is one of User_Alias, Runas_Alias, Host_Alias, or Cmnd_Alias.
NAME is a string of uppercase letters, numbers, and underscore characters ('_').
NAME must start with an uppercase letter. To put several alias definitions of the same type on a single line, joined by a colon (':'). For example-

Alias_Type NAME = object1, object2...: NAME = object4, object5...

You cannot redefine an existing alias. But it is possible to use the same name for aliases of different types, but a name collision is possible, which would generate an error.

The following is a typical alias entry in a sudoers file, where group1 can be an alias name that includes more than one user. This alias specifies that the user group1 may run /bin/ps, /bin/nano, and /usr/sbin/vsftpd, but only as the user admin on the host named Pi400:

group1 Pi400 = (admin) /bin/ps, /bin/nano, /usr/bin/vsftpd

1.13.2 User Specifications in the Sudoers File

The user specifications in the sudoers file contain policy rules, one rule per line. Every rule uses the general format as follows:

who where = (as_whom) what

where

> *who* is the user that this rule applies to. who can also be a user specification list—for example, a group name.
>
> *where* is the hostname of the system this rule applies to.
>
> = separates the where from (as_whom) and what.
>
> *(as_whom)* designates the user specification list sudo will run the what.
>
> *what* lists the full path to each command this policy rule applies to.

You must specify full pathnames to command(s) you include in the sudoers file.

A syntactic description of the kinds of user specifications is as follows:

```
User specification
  User_Spec = User_List Host_List '=' Cmnd_Spec_List
          (':' Host_List '=' Cmnd_Spec_List)*

  Cmnd_Spec_List = Cmnd_Spec |
              Cmnd_Spec ',' Cmnd_Spec_List

  Cmnd_Spec = Runas_Spec SELinux_Spec Tag_Spec* Cmnd

  Runas_Spec = '(' Runas_List (':' Runas_List)? ')'

  SELinux_Spec := ('ROLE=role' | 'TYPE=type')

  Tag_Spec = ('EXEC:' | 'NOEXEC:' | 'FOLLOW:' | 'NOFOLLOW' |
          'LOG_INPUT:' | 'NOLOG_INPUT:' | 'LOG_OUTPUT:' |
          'NOLOG_OUTPUT:' | 'MAIL:' | 'NOMAIL:' | 'PASSWD:' |
          'NOPASSWD:' | 'SETENV:' | 'NOSETENV:')
```

The following command uses the -l option to sudo to allow you to list the permissions currently defined as policy in the sudoers file for the user typing in the command:

```
$ sudo -l
Matching Defaults entries for bob on raspberrypi:
    env_reset, mail_badpass, secure_path=/usr/local/sbin\:/usr/local/bin\:/usr/sbin\:/
    usr/bin\:/sbin\:/bin,
    env_keep+=NO_AT_BRIDGE, env_keep+="http_proxy HTTP_PROXY", env_keep+="http
    s_proxy HTTPS_PROXY",
    env_keep+="ftp_proxy FTP_PROXY", env_keep+=RSYNC_PROXY, env_keep+="no_
    proxy NO_PROXY"

User bob may run the following commands on raspberrypi:
    (ALL : ALL) ALL
    (ALL) NOPASSWD: ALL
```

We see from the above output, for example, that user bob can run all commands as root.

In the following simple user specification rule, mansoor has the permission to run any command:

mansoor ALL = ALL

The following rule allows user mansoor to run the visudo program:

mansoor ALL = /usr/sbin/visudo

Using a group name in a sudoers alias entry has the following syntax, where everyone in the group named lxd, on the system named Pi400, can run all of the commands in /etc/sbin as the user lxd:

$ lxd Pi400 = (lxd) /etc/sbin*

Using a user ID number in a sudoers alias entry has the following syntax, where the user with ID 1002 can run everything in the /usr/sbin directory:

#1002 ALL = /usr/sbin/*

Notice that the user ID number is prefaced with the pound sign character (#).

1.13.3 sudo su -

You can efficiently use the command **sudo su -** to run a login shell, unlike the default operation of the **su** command, which preserves both the environment variables, and the present working directory of the previous user.

To start a shell as a login shell, with an environment exactly like a real login, you can use the **-** (hyphen) option as follows.

bob@raspberrypi:~$ **sudo su -**
root@raspberrypi:~#

This will clear all the previous environment variables except for TERM, start new environment variables HOME, SHELL, USER, LOGNAME, and PATH, and change the current directory to the user's home directory.

Note*** To terminate the new shell, and return to the previous one, type exit on the command line.

root@raspberrypi:~#**exit**
logout
bob@raspberrypi:~ $

1.14 Raspberry Pi OS POSIX.1e Access Control Lists (ACLs)

Access Control Lists (ACLs) provide the ordinary, unprivileged user with the ability to set finer access controls on directories, and files, than the traditional UNIX and Linux permissions, whether they are used on EXT4, or NFS file systems. The root file system of the Raspberry Pi OS is an EXT4 file system. Two different basic types of ACL apply to files and directories. An ACL that defines the current access permissions of files and directories is called an *access* ACL. An ACL, which only makes sense to set on a directory, and that defines the permissions that this directory object inherits from its parent directory at the time of its creation, is called a *default* ACL. Additional basic types of ACLs are *minimal* and *extended* ACLs. ACL permissions that can be equivalent to the traditional file mode permissions are called *minimal ACLs*. Minimal ACLs have three entries, which can be the same as the traditional file permissions. ACLs with more than three entries are called extended ACLs. Extended ACLs also contain a mask entry and may contain any number of named user and named group entries. These terms, and the conditions under which they are applied, are explained in the following sections.

1.14.1 Using Access Control Lists (ACLs) in the Raspberry Pi OS

The traditional UNIX and Linux permissions model, which defines secure access to file objects like a regular file or a directory, set permissions of *read, write, and execute*. Other advanced techniques for setting permissions are setting the setuid, setgid, and sticky bit. Beyond these, the Access Control List (ACL) model gives users finer-grained control over file and directory object security. Every file object can be thought of as having associated with it an access ACL that controls the discretionary access to that object. As mentioned earlier, for a directory, this ACL is referred to as a default ACL.

Question: Why would an ordinary user, or a system administrator, want to use ACLs rather than just rely on the traditional permissions model?

Answer: To set discretionary controls on a file so that more than one group can access it. In the traditional permissions model, *any file can only belong to one group*. Therefore, to serve different collections of users, many different groups have to exist. Only administrators can create and assign group memberships. But with ACLs, a file can belong to many groups and, in addition, can be given access privileges by an ordinary user.

In-Chapter Exercise

16. Does it make any sense to set the permissions on a regular file, so that a group, user, or others have access to it, when that group, user, or others do not have permissions set to access the directory which contains the regular file?

If you have correctly answered the question posed in In-Chapter Exercise 16 above, you can see why the Examples presented in this section apply mainly to directories. ACLs provide the ordinary, unprivileged user with the ability to set finer access controls on directories and files, but with some performance costs, whether they are used on EXT4 file system objects, or even possibly on an NFS file system. Our Raspberry Pi system supports the traditional permissions model, and the ACL model (referred to here as POSIX.1e).

We cover the basics of the following topics in the sub-sections indicated:

1.14.2 Raspberry Pi OS POSIX.1e ACL Model Details
1.14.3 Examples of Setting ACLs

In order to get more help and to get more detail on ACLs on your Raspberry Pi system, we encourage you to consult the man pages for **acl**, **setfacl**, and **getfacl**.

1.14.2 Raspberry Pi OS POSIX.1e ACL Model Details

The default implementation of ACLs on the Raspberry Pi OS uses POSIX.1e syntax. These ACLs are set and displayed with the **setfacl** and **getfacl** commands.

The traditional file system object permission model defines three classes of users: owner, group, and other. Each of these classes is associated with a set of permissions. The permissions defined are read (r), write (w), and execute (x). In this model, the owner class permissions define the access privileges of the file owner, the group class permissions define the access privileges of the owning group, and the other class permissions define the access privileges of all users that are not in one of the previous two classes. The **ls -l** command displays the owner, group, and other class permissions as its output.

For example, rwxrw-r- - for some regular file, translates to read, write, and execute permission for the owner class, read and write permission for the group class, and read permission for others.

1.14.2.1 Basic Types of the POSIX.1e ACL Model

For our purposes here in this section, a "file system object" can be both a regular file or a directory. As stated above, there are two different basic types of ACL that apply to files and directories. An ACL that defines the current access permissions of files and directories is called an *access* ACL. An ACL, which can only logically be set on a directory, and that defines the permissions that a directory object inherits from its parent directory at the time of its creation, is called a *default* ACL. We give two extended examples of setting and viewing these two basic types of ACL in Section 1.14.3.

In-Chapter Exercise

> 17. Why is it logical that only directories can be associated with default ACLs?

Again, as stated above, additional basic types of ACLs are *minimal* and *extended* ACLs. ACL permissions that can be equivalent to the traditional file mode permissions are called *minimal ACLs*. Minimal ACLs have three entries, which can be the same as the traditional file permissions. An example of a minimal ACL, obtained on the command line with the **getfacl** command, is as follows:

```
$ getfacl acltest
# file: acltest
# owner: bob
# group: bob
user::rw-
group::r--
other::r--
```

Note that the last three lines of output are the same as traditional permissions.

As noted above, ACLs with more than three entries are called *extended* ACLs. Extended ACLs also contain a mask entry and may contain any number of named user and named group entries. An example of the extended ACL type, obtained on the command line with the **getfacl** command, is as follows:

```
$ getfacl acltest2
# file: acltest
# owner: bob
# group: bob
user::rwx
user:mansoor:rwx
group::rwx
mask::rwx
other::---
```

1.14.2.2 How Permissions Map to the Basic ACL Types

An ACL, whether it is access, default, simple, or extended, as defined above, draws its permission classes from those shown in Table 1.4. Each of the three traditional file permission classes (owner, group, and others) is represented by an ACL entry. The only other classes that are added in an extended ACL are permissions for additional users or additional groups. This is very critical to understanding POSIX.1e ACLs, because this feature allows a file object to have its permissions controlled by and associated with different users and groups: the very objective gained by using POSIX.1e ACLs in the first place.

Table 1.4 shows the allowed Entry Types and their text formats, as opposed to their numerical forms. Each Text Format in the table consists of a type, a

TABLE 1.4

Allowed Types of POSIX.1e ACL Entries

Entry Type	Text Format
Owner	user::rwx
Named user	user:name:rwx
Owning group	group::rwx
Named group	group:name:rwx
Mask	mask::rwx
Others	other::rwx

TABLE 1.5

ACL Entries in Extended BNF

ACL Entry	Description
u[ser]::perms	File owner permissions.
g[roup]::perms	File group permissions.
o[ther]:perms	Permissions for users other than the file owner or members of file group.
m[ask]:perms	The ACL mask. The mask entry indicates the maximum permissions allowed for users (other than the owner) and for groups. The mask is a quick way to change permissions on all the users and groups. For example, the mask:r-- mask entry indicates that users and groups cannot have more than read permissions, even though they might have write/execute permissions.
u[ser]:uid:perms	Permissions for a specific user. For uid, you can specify either a user name or a numeric UID.
g[roup]:gid:perms	Permissions for a specific group. For gid, you can specify either a group name or a numeric GID.

qualifier that specifies to which user or group the entry applies, and a set of permissions.

Table 1.5 shows ACL entries and their descriptions.

Table 1.6 shows default ACL entries and their descriptions.

In-Chapter Exercise

18. What undefined qualifiers do not require a specification of qualification, as seen in Table 1.4? Why?

1.14.2.3 The Meaning of the "Mask" Entry

The extended classes, "Named group" and "Named user", assign permissions to the group class, which already contains the owning group entry. In minimal ACLs, the group class permissions are the same as the owning group permissions. In an extended ACL, the group class contains

TABLE 1.6

ACL Default Entries in Extended BNF

Default ACL Entry	Description
d[efault]:u[ser]::perms	Default file owner permissions.
d[efault]:g[roup]::perms	Default file group permissions.
d[efault]:o[ther]:perms	Default permissions for users other than the file owner or members of the file group.
d[efault]:m[ask]:perms	Default ACL mask.
d[efault]:u[ser]:uid:perms	Default permissions for a specific user. For uid, you can specify either a user name or a numeric UID.
d[efault]:g[roup]:gid:perms	Default permissions for a specific group. For gid, you can specify either a group name or a numeric GID.

ACL entries with different permission sets than the group class. That is the meaning of "extended." The group class permissions can possibly contain conflicting permission sets, given that they now have several competing specifications included in them. This raises the possibility of inconsistency. For example, the results of using the **getfacl** command on the directory file object named acltest_dir, after adding an extended ACL specification of r - - for the already-existing group named "development", yields the following:

```
$ getfacl acltest_dir
# file: acltest
# owner: bob
# group: bob
user::rwx
user:manny:rwx
group:development:r--
group::rwx
mask::rwx
other::---
```

As found in the example above, with extended ACLs, the Owning group (bob) class permissions (rwx) are mapped to what is known as the "mask", or masking entry, with its attendant permissions. The Owning group (bob) entries (rwx) still define the owning group permissions. The group class permissions for the Owning group bob, as shown (rwx) are more "inclusive", that is, they include more permissions. They represent the widest, most inclusive set of the permissions that any entry in the Owning group class will grant. On the file object acltest_dir, to handle the "inconsistency" of differences in Named group and Owning group permissions, the "masking" permissions are used and are specified, as shown in the example, as the mask entry. This means that permissions in entries that are a member of the group class are also present in the mask entry and are effective.

Take note that permissions that are absent in the mask entry are *masked* and do not take effect.

In-Chapter Exercise

19. Construct a hypothetical extended ACL on paper that shows how a named user manny, with an rw- set of permissions, sets the mask of the Owning group class, even though the Owning group permissions are set to r--.

So what do the mask entries actually mean and achieve? Following, we show some specific explanatory examples of mask entry use. The first example shows what the extended ACLs would look like after making a change to the users traditional permissions with the **chmod** command. Notice it has no effect on the ACL mask entries:

```
$ chmod u-w acltest
$ getfacl acltest
# file: acltest
# owner: bob
# group: bob
user::r-x
user:manny:rwx
group::rwx
group:development:r--
mask::rwx
other::---
```

When the **chmod** command changes any of the traditional permissions, for the owner, group, or other class, the ACL entry changes as well. And when the Owner class ACL entry permissions change, via use of the **setfacl** command and its option, the traditional permissions of the Owner class change also.

But if you change the group traditional permissions with **chmod**, notice the effect on the ACL mask entries:

```
$ chmod g-w acltest
$ getfacl acltest
# file: acltest
# owner: bob
# group: bob
user::r-x
user:manny:rwx                #effective:r-x
group::rwx                    #effective:r-x
group:development:r--
mask::r-x
other::---
```

If an ACL entry contains permissions that are disabled by the mask entry, such as user manny's write access, and the Owning groups' write access, the

getfacl display shows a comment next to each that signifies the "effective" set of permissions that are given by that entry.

After executing the **chmod** command to remove the write permission from the group class, the mask permissions have changed. Now write permission is limited to the owner of the directory acltest_dir. This output includes a comment for all those entries in which the effective permissions do not correspond to the original permissions *because they are modified by the mask entry*.

In-Chapter Exercise

10. How can you restore the original group write permission on the acltest_dir directory?

In conclusion, with extended ACLs, masking permissions do the following: permissions in entries that are a member of the group class also in the mask entry, are effective. Permissions that are not in the mask entry are masked and do not take effect. The owner and other entries are not in the group class. Their permissions are always effective and not masked.

1.14.2.4 Drawbacks and Alternatives to the POSIX.1e ACL Model

Some of the drawbacks of the POSIX.1e ACL model are as follows:

Unfortunately, at the time of the writing of this book, the Raspberry Pi OS and the POSIX.1e ACL model that it supports does not easily allow for the interoperability, in terms of Network File System, version 4 (NFSv4) ACLs, between Linux and non-Linux servers and clients.

For example, if a Linux user were to mount an NFSv4 ACL-compliant file system as an NFS shared resource, the default POSIX.1e implementation on Linux would not be able to take advantage of the NFSv4 ACL model of that file system. As noted above, that restriction is true even if a user were to install a special tool, nfs4-acl-tools, in addition to enabling NFS server facilities on the remote system and client facilities on her Linux system. Since that is necessarily a more advanced application of ACLs, we briefly cover the particular situation of interoperabilty between POSIX.1e and NFSv4 ACLs in Section 1.15.

Another very practical limitation in this respect is virtualization with LXC/ LXD containers. If you create LXC/LXD containers, on the Linux host for those containers, the NFSv4 ACLs could not be used on LXD container file objects.

Additionally, ACLs are *not* retained by the **tar** command.

1.14.2.5 Command Syntax for Setting and Viewing POSIX.1e ACLs

To set or modify ACLs, use the **setfacl** command. To see the results of using **setfacl**, use the **getfacl** command. Following is an abbreviated syntax description of those two commands, taken from the man pages for those commands, with common and allowable POSIX.1e ACL options shown:

****

setfacl - set file access control lists
Syntax: setfacl [-bkndRLPvh] [{-m|-x} acl_spec] [{-M|-X} acl_file] file ...
       setfacl --restore=file
Purpose:
   The **setfacl** utility sets discretionary access control information on the
   specified file(s).
Output: Modified ACL specifications.
Common Options and Option Arguments:
   -b   Remove all ACL entries except for base ACL entries owner, group, others.
   -m   [entries]
        Modify the ACL on the specified file. New entries will be added,
        and existing entries will be modified according to the entries
        argument. For NFSv4 ACLs, you can also use the -a and -x
        options instead.
  -M file
        Modify the ACL entries on the specified files by adding new ACL
        entries and modifying existing ACL entries with the ACL entries
        specified in the file file.
  -x entries
        If entries is specified, remove the ACL entries specified there
        from the access or default ACL of the specified files.

****

****

getfacl - get file access control lists
Syntax: getfacl [-aceEsRLPtpndvh] file ...
      getfacl [-aceEsRLPtpndvh] -
Purpose:
The **getfacl** utility writes discretionary access control information associated with
   the specified file(s) to standard output
Output: Indicated file ACL settings on stdout.
        The complete output format of an example getfacl command, and of which
        we show many example cases in the sub-sections below, is as follows:
        1: # file: filename
        2: # owner: bob
        3: # group: admin
        4: # flags: -s-
        5: user::rwx
        6: user:mansoor:rwx   #effective:r-x
        7: group::rwx   #effective:r-x
        8: group:developers:r-x
        9: mask::r-x
        10: other::r-x
        11: default:user::rwx
        12: default:user:mansoor:rwx   #effective:r-x
        13: default:group::r-x
        14: default:mask::r-x
        15: default:other::---

Common Options:
- -a   Display the file access control list.
- -d   Display the default access control list.
- -n   Display numeric user and group IDs .

****

1.14.3 ACL Examples

Example 1.10 provides the ordinary user with the ability to set and view POSIX.1e ACL attributes on files and directories.

Example 1.10 Setting and Viewing Access ACLs

Objectives: Using the **getfacl** and **setfacl** commands on the command line to set and view ACLs on files.

Prerequisites: Reading and understanding all of the material and exercises presented above. Additionally, and perhaps most importantly, review material related to umask, particularly the way umask is set depending upon whether or not you are working in a login or non-login terminal. The premise of this example is that you are giving the following commands and working in a non-login terminal.

Background: The commands presented here allow an ordinary user to change the ACLs of files and directories. For more information on the commands, see the man pages for getfacl and setfacl on your Linux system.

Requirements: Do the steps presented, in the order shown, to fulfill the requirements for this example.

1. Before creating a directory, check the default umask setting, then use the **umask** command to define which access permissions should be masked each time a file object is created. The command **umask 007** sets the default permissions by giving the owner the full range of permissions (0), giving the group the full range of permissions (0), and giving other users no permissions at all (7). **umask** "masks" the permission bits, effectively turning them off. For a complete description of how this masking takes place, look at the **umask** man page on your system.

Then, create a directory and check its traditional permissions with the **ls -la** command.

```
$ umask
0022
$ umask 007
$ mkdir acltest
$ ls -la acltest
total 8
drwxrwx--- 2 bob bob 4096 Oct  6 09:56 .
drwxr-xr-x 44 bob bob 4096 Oct  6 09:56 ..
$
```

2. These traditional permissions have an equivalent representation of ACL access permissions. Display the ACLs of the same directory using the **getfacl** command:

```
$ getfacl acltest
# file: acltest
# owner: bob
# group: bob
user::rwx
group::rwx
other::---
```

The first three output lines display the name, owner, and owning group of the directory. The next three lines contain the three ACL entries for owner, owning group, and other. This output is an example of a "minimum" ACL listing, as opposed to an "extended" ACL listing. The **getfacl** command produces the same information as **ls -la command from step 1**.

3. Give read, write, and execute access to user Mansoor in addition to the existing permissions. For that, the -m (modify) option of **setfacl** is used. Shown is the access ACL using the **getfacl** command.

```
$ setfacl -m user:mansoor:rwx acltest
$ getfacl acltest
# file: acltest
# owner: bob
# group: bob
user::rwx
user:mansoor:rwx
group::rwx
mask::rwx
other::---
```

Two additional entries have been added to the ACL: one is for user mansoor, and the other for the mask entry.

The "mask" entry is applied by the **setfacl** command and is governed by the group class permissions. It is composed of whatever is in the group class permission set, the logical "union" of all group class permissions.

4.   Use the **ls -la** command to show changes to the traditional permissions of the directory.

```
$ ls -la acltest
total 8
drwxrwx---+ 2 bob bob 4096 Oct  6 09:56 .
drwxr-xr-x 44 bob bob 4096 Oct  6 09:56 ..
```

An additional "+" character is displayed after the traditional permissions of all files that have extended ACLs.

The permissions of the group class permissions include read and write access. Traditionally such file permission bits would indicate read and write access for the owning group. With ACLs, the effective permissions of the owning group are defined as the intersection of the permissions of the owning group and mask entries. The effective permissions of the owning group in the example are rwx, the same permissions as before creating additional ACL entries as done in step 3.

According to the output of the **ls -la** command in this step, the permissions for the mask entry include read and write access. Traditionally, such permissions would mean that the owning group also has write access to the directory. The access permissions for the owning group are the "union" of the owning group permissions and the mask permissions, which is rwx in our example.

5.   The group class permissions are modified using the **setfacl** or **chmod** command. If we remove write access from the group class using the **chmod** command for example, we can use **ls -la** and **getfacl** to see how the traditional permissions and ACLs have been changed.

```
$ chmod g-w acltest
$ ls -la acltest
total 8
drwxr-x---+ 2 bob bob 4096 Oct  6 09:56 .
drwxr-xr-x 44 bob bob 4096 Oct  6 09:56 ..
$ getfacl --omit-header acltest
user::rwx
user:mansoor:rwx         #effective:r-x
group::rwx               #effective:r-x
mask::r-x
other::---
```

If an ACL entry contains permissions that are disabled by the mask entry, **getfacl** adds a comment that shows the effective set of permissions granted by that entry. If the owning group entry had written access, there would have been a similar comment for that entry.

After executing the **chmod** command to remove the write permission from the group class permissions, the output of the **ls** command shows us that the mask permissions have changed accordingly: write permission is now limited to the owner of the directory acltest. The output of the **getfacl** confirms this. This output includes a comment for all those entries in which the effective permission bits do not correspond to the original permissions because they are reset according to the mask entry. The original permissions can be restored at any time with **chmod g+w**, as is done in the next step.

6. Give write access to the group class again, and view the traditional and ACL access permissions.

    ```
    $ chmod g+w acltest
    $ ls -la acltest
    total 8
    drwxrwx---+  2 bob bob 4096 Oct  6 09:56 .
    drwxr-xr-x 44 bob bob 4096 Oct  6 09:56 ..
    $ getfacl --omit-header acltest
    user::rwx
    user:mansoor:rwx
    group::rwx
    mask::rwx
    other::---
    ```

Conclusion:

An important thing to notice here is that after adding the write permission back to the group class, the access ACL defines the same permissions as before taking the permission away.

Example 1.11   Setting and Viewing Default ACLs

Objectives: To give some simple cases of setting and viewing default ACLs.

Prerequisites: Completion of Example 1.10. Additionally, and perhaps most importantly, review material related to umask, particularly the way umask is set depending upon whether or not you are working in a login or non-login terminal. The premise of this example is that you are giving the following commands and working in a non-login terminal.

Background: Directories can have a default ACL, which is a special kind of ACL defining the access permissions that objects in the directory inherit when they are created. A default ACL affects both sub-directories and files.

There are two ways in which the permissions of a directory's default ACL are passed to files and sub-directories: a sub-directory inherits the default ACL of the parent directory both as its default ACL and as its ACL, or a file inherits the default ACL as its ACL.

If the parent directory does not have a default ACL, the permissions defined by the umask are subtracted from the permissions that are given by the system call file access mode parameter. If a default ACL exists for the parent directory, the permission bits assigned to the new object correspond to the overlapping portion or logical "intersection" of the permissions of the system call-set mode parameter, discussed below, and those that are defined in the default ACL.

The previous example examined ACLs that define access permissions of file system objects. This example examines default ACLs.

It is important to note that only directories can be associated with default ACLs. Regular files do not have default ACLs because no file system objects can be created "inside" of regular files.

When a sub-directory is created, the new sub-directory *inherits* the parent directory's default ACL, both as its access ACL and default ACL. Regular files inherit the default ACL of the directory they are created in as an access ACL.

System calls for accessing and changing file attributes include the following:

access(), chmod(), chown(), rename(), umask(), and utime().

The permissions of inherited access ACLs are modified by the file access mode parameter that each system call that creates the file system object exercises. The file access mode parameter established by these system calls contains the traditional nine permission bits that are the permissions of the owner, group, and other class permissions. The effective permissions of each class are set to the logical "intersection" of the permissions defined for any class in the ACL and specified in the system call file access mode parameter.

The umask setting has no effect if a default ACL exists.

Requirements: Do the steps presented, in the order shown, to fulfill the requirements for this example.

1. Create a group named development on your system, with the **addgroup** command.

   ```
   $ sudo addgroup development
   [sudo] password for bob: QQQ
   Adding group `development' (GID 1002) ...
   Done.
   ```

2. Add a default ACL to the directory acltest you created in the first example, which gives read and execute privileges to members of the development group on the directory acltest. Finally, use the **getfacl** command to view the ACLs on that directory.

   ```
   $ setfacl -d -m group:development:r-x acltest
   $ getfacl --omit-header acltest
   user::rwx
   user:mansoor:rwx
   group::rwx
   mask::rwx
   other::---
   default:user::rwx
   default:group::rwx
   default:group:development:r-x
   default:mask::rwx
   default:other::---
   ```

Following the access ACL, the default ACL is printed with each entry prefixed with "default:". This output format is an extension to POSIX.1e which is typically available on all Linux systems.

We have only specified an ACL entry for the development group in the **setfacl** command. The other entries required for a complete ACL have been copied from the access ACL to the default ACL.

The default ACL contains no entry for mansoor, so mansoor will not have access (except possibly through group membership or the other class permissions). **getfacl** returns both the ACL and the default ACL. The default ACL is formed by all lines that start with 'default'. Although we executed the **setfacl** command with an entry for the 'development' group for the default ACL, **setfacl** automatically used all other entries from the ACL to create a default ACL. Default ACLs do not have an immediate effect on access permissions. They only are effective when directory file system objects are created. These new objects inherit permissions only from the default ACL of their parent directory.

3. This step will show that a subdirectory inherits ACLs, as shown next. Unless otherwise specified, the **mkdir** command uses a value of 0777 as the mode parameter to the **mkdir** system call, which it uses for creating the new directory. Observe that both the access and the default ACL contain the same entries.

```
$ mkdir acltest/acltest2
$ getfacl --omit-header acltest/acltest2
user::rwx
group::rwx
group:development:r-x
mask::rwx
other::---
default:user::rwx
default:group::rwx
default:group:development:r-x
default:mask::rwx
default:other::---
```

As expected, the newly created subdirectory named acltest2 has the permissions from the default ACL of the parent directory. The ACL of the sub-directory acltest2 is an exact reflection of the default ACL of its parent directory, acltest. And, most importantly, the default ACLs that this directory will pass to objects created in it are also the same.

4. In this step, we will create a file with the text editor vi, inside the directory acltest, and show how it inherits permissions.

```
$ cd acltest
~/acltest $ vi testfile1
In your favorite text editor, create and save a sample file named testfile1. We used vi.
~/acltest $
~/acltest $ ls -la testfile1
-rw-rw----+ 1 bob bob 21 Oct  6 13:07 testfile1
~/acltest $
~/acltest $ getfacl --omit-header testfile1
user::rw-
group::rwx                       #effective:rw-
group:development:r-x            #effective:r--
mask::rw-
other::---
```

Conclusion:

In this example, we have given some simple cases of setting and viewing default ACLs and have explained mask and effective ACLs.

In-Chapter Exercise

11. To get practical experience with setting and viewing ACLs, execute all of the steps of Examples 1.10 and 1.11, and verify that the output of each is the same on your Raspberry Pi system.

1.15 Raspberry Pi OS NFS Server and Client Install and Setting NFSv4 ACLs on the Client

The NFSv4 ACL model is very similar to the Windows NT ACL model. The major differences between NFSv4 and the POSIX.1e ACLs, as they were illustrated in the sections above, are as follows:

1. NFSv4 ACLs provide finer-grained permissions than the rwx model.
2. NFSv4 ACLs allow for both Allow and Deny entries.
3. NFSv4 ACLs provide more complete and extensive inheritance syntax and contents. POSIX.1e ACLs also have inheritance, but with the NFSv4 model, as far as directories are concerned, you can specify whether inheritance is applied to the directory itself, to just one level of subdirectories below that, or is propagated downward to all the subdirectories of the upper-level directory.
4. NFSv4 ACLs enable administrators to designate the order in which ACL entries are verified. With POSIX.1e ACLs, the file system itself reorders ACL entries into a definite, strict access checking order.

5. There is some interoperability and translation between NFSv4 ACLs and POSIX.1e ACLs.

Note

Permissions can be specified in three different ACL formats: verbose, compact, or positional. The verbose format uses descriptive words to indicate the permissions, which are separated with a forward slash (/) character. Compact format uses the applicable permission letters in ACL permission assignment. Positional format, similar to compact format, uses the hyphen character(-) to identify that there are no applicable permissions positionally in the listing of assigned permission.

In this section, we create an NFSv4 server and client and view and manipulate ACLs on the client Raspberry Pi OS machine using the NFSv4 ACL protocol.

1.15.1 ACLs Have Two Basic Forms

1. Trivial (Minimal) ACL contains only entries for traditional UNIX user categories that are represented as owner@, group@, and everyone@.

For a newly created file, the default ACL has the following entries, shown in positional format:

```
# file: acl_default_for_file
# owner: bob
# group: bob
        owner@:rw-p--aARWcCos:------:allow
        group@:r-----a-R-c--s:------:allow
        everyone@:r-----a-R-c--s:------:allow
```

For a newly created directory, the default ACL has the following entries, shown in positional format:

```
# file: acl_default_for_directories
# owner: bob
# group: bob
        owner@:rwxp--aARWcCos:------:allow
        group@:r-x---a-R-c--s:------:allow
        everyone@:r-x---a-R-c--s:------:allow
```

2. Nontrivial (Extended) ACL contains entries for added user categories. The entries might also include inheritance flags or be ordered in a nontraditional way. A nontrivial entry might look like the following example, where permissions are specifically granted to user **mansoor,** shown in verbose format:

    0:user:mansoor:read_data/write_data:file_inherit:allow

1.15.1.1 ACL Entry Descriptions: Components of NFSv4 ACL Command Entry Descriptions

The following describes the "positional," or abbreviated format, of the syntactic components, both general and specific, of the **setfacl** command applied to files and directories. We also show the general form of the output from the **getfacl** command after the example is executed:

```
            Command To Whom    Permissions         To What
Files       setfacl –a 0 user:bob:rwx-----------:------:allow filename
            a    b c  d    e      f            g    h      i
```

```
Directories setfacl –a 0 user:bob:r------------:fd----:allow dirname
            a    b c  d    e      f            g    h      i
```

key-
a-command
b-option
c-position option argument starting at 0, cannot be a number at the end!
d- ACL tag
e- ACL qualifier, in these cases user
f- 14 permissions, in short form, the hyphens(-) optional
g- 6 inheritance flags, for directories only, the hyphens(-) optional
h- ACL type, either allow or deny
i- command argument, a filename or directory name specification

Format of getfacl output for the preceding file's command:

%getfacl filename
```
#file        filename
#owner       owner name
#group       group name
position 0          user:bob:rwx-----------:------:allow filename
position 1          owner@ ----------------------------------------
position 2          group@ ----------------------------------------
position 3          everyone@ ----------------------------------------
```

An example of a "verbose" format display is as follows, *on a system capable of displaying NFSv4 ACLs(in our case, a Solaris 11.4 UNIX system):*

$ ls -v file.1
```
-rw-r--r-- 1 root    root    206663 Aug 31 11:53 file.1
  0:owner@:execute:deny
  1:owner@:read_data/write_data/append_data/write_xattr/write_attributes
    /write_acl/write_owner:allow
  2:group@:write_data/append_data/execute:deny
  3:group@:read_data:allow
  4:everyone@:write_data/append_data/write_xattr/execute/write_attributes
    /write_acl/write_owner:deny
  5:everyone@:read_data/read_xattr/read_attributes/read_acl/synchronize
    :allow
```

An example of a compact format display of ACLs is as follows:

```
A::OWNER@:rwatTnNcCy
A::john@nfsdomain.org:rxtncy
A::bobby@nfsdomain.org:rwadtTnNcCy
A:g:GROUP@:rtncy
D:g:GROUP@:waxTC
A::EVERYONE@:rtncy
D::EVERYONE@:waxTC
```

It would be very beneficial for you to use the following additional sample entry as a reference to the elements that comprise an ACL entry. These elements apply to both trivial and nontrivial ACLs,

user:mansoor:read_data/write_data:file_inherit:allow

where:

ACL tag and qualifier: The user category. In trivial ACLs, only entries for owner@, group@, and everyone@ are set. In nontrivial ACLs, user:username and group:groupname are added. In the example, the entry tag and qualifier are **user:mansoor**.

Access privileges: Permissions that are granted or denied to the entry type. In the example, user mansoor's permissions are shown in long form as read_data and write_data.

Inheritance flags: An optional list of ACL flags that control how permissions are propagated in a directory structure. In the sample entry, file_inherit is also granted to **user:mansoor**.

ACL type (permission control): Determines whether the permissions in an entry are allowed or denied. In the example, the permissions for **mansoor** are allowed.

Table 1.7 describes each ACL entry type more fully.
Table 1.8 describes ACL access privileges more fully.

TABLE 1.7

ACL Entry Types

ACL Entry Type	Description
owner@	Specifies the access granted to the owner of the object
group@	Specifies the access granted to the owning group of the object
everyone@	Specifies the access granted to any user or group that does not match any other ACL entry
user	With a user name, specifies the access granted to an additional user of the object
group	With a group name, specifies the access granted to an additional group of the object

TABLE 1.8

ACL Access Privileges

Access Privilege	Compact Access Privilege	Description
add_file	w	Permission to add a new file to a directory
add_subdirectory	p	On a directory, permission to create a subdirectory
append_data	p	Permission to modify a file but only beginning from the EOF
delete	d	Permission to delete a file
delete_child	D	Permission to delete a file or directory within a directory
execute	x	Permission to execute a file or search the contents of a directory
list_directory	r	Permission to list the contents of a directory
read_acl	c	Permission to read the ACL (ls)
read_attributes	a	Permission to read basic attributes (non-ACLs) of a file
read_data	r	Permission to read the contents of the file
read_xattr	R	Permission to read the extended attributes of a file
synchronize	s	Permission to access a file locally at the server with synchronized read and write operations
write_xattr	W	Permission to create extended attributes or write to the extended attributes directory
write_data	w	Permission to modify or replace the contents of a file
write_attributes	A	Permission to change the times associated with a file or directory to an arbitrary value
write_acl	C	Permission to write the ACL or the ability to modify the ACL by using the chmod command
write_owner	o	Permission to change the file's owner or group, or the ability to execute the chown or chgrp commands on the file

Table 1.9 provides additional details about ACL delete and delete_child behavior.

1.15.2 Installing and Configuring the NFS Server and Clients and Setting NFSv4 ACLs on the Client

In the procedures, we illustrate how to create an NFS share on a client Raspberry Pi OS machine and share an NFS file system from an NFS server on the same network. Additionally, we show how to interrogate and set NFSv4 ACLs on the client system.

On our Raspberry Pi OS systems, the following is true in the code below:

The IP address of the server on the LAN is 192.168.1.33

The IP address of the client on the LAN is 192.168.1.24

The user on the server and client is bob, with **sudo** privilege on both machines.

Why would you want to share user data using the Network File System (NFS)? Traditionally NFS has the great utility of allowing users on multiple "client" systems to easily and securely share diverse file system types and

TABLE 1.9

ACL Delete and Delete_Child

Parent Directory Permissions	Target Object Permissions		
" " (empty)	ACL Allows Delete	ACL Denies Delete	Delete Permission Unspecified
ACL allows delete_child	Permit	Permit	Permit
ACL denies delete_child	Permit	Deny	Deny
ACL allows only write and execute	Permit	Permit	Permit
ACL denies write and execute	Permit	Deny	Deny

their data that are contained on a "server" machine. We extend this model by showing you how to achieve the same sharing in a simple manner. The NFS protocol was developed by Sun Microsystems in the early 1980s. It was designed to allow a client computer to access files over a network. The NFS protocol is an "open" standard defined in an official Request for Comments(RFC), and anyone can install it easily on a variety of hardware architectures and operating systems. It is primarily used by network administrators setting up Network Attached Storage (NAS) systems, or ordinary people at home constructing media servers.

It would be very useful to get some exposure to the NFSv4 ACL model, for two important reasons. First, that model allows an ordinary user to exercise a much wider range of permission controls than the default POSIX.1e ACL model on the Raspberry Pi OS. Second, in anticipation of the NFSv4 models' complete adoption in Linux, you can experiment with the NFSv4 commands and options and gain some familiarity with the details of it.

Procedure I Installing the NFS Server and Client

On the Server

Install the NFS server software.

$ sudo apt install nfs-kernel-server
Output truncated...

Create the folder that will be shared.

$ sudo mkdir -p /mnt/sharedfolder

Change the ownership and group of that folder to an anonymous user.

$ sudo chown nobody:nogroup /mnt/sharedfolder

Adjust the traditional permissions on that folder.

$ sudo chmod 777 /mnt/sharedfolder

Modify the export file so you can share the folder, and anyone can gain access to it. The file */etc/exports* contain a table of local physical file systems on an NFS server that are accessible to NFS clients. The contents of the file are maintained by the server's system administrator.

Each file system in this table has a list of options and an access control list. The table is used by exportfs(8) to give information to mountd(8).

The file format is similar to the SunOS *exports* file. Each line contains an export point and a whitespace-separated list of clients allowed to mount the file system at that point. Each listed client may be immediately followed by a parenthesized, comma-separated list of export options for that client. No whitespace is permitted between a client and its options list.

$ **sudo nano /etc/exports**

Add the following line at the end of the file:

/mnt/sharedfolder 192.168.1.24(rw,sync,no_subtree_check,no_root_squash)

Save and quit.
Execute the export with this command:

$ **sudo exportfs -a**

Restart the NFS server.

$ **sudo systemctl restart nfs-kernel-server**

Check the firewall.

$ **sudo ufw status**
Staus:inactive
$

If it were active, and you wanted to inactivate it, the easiest way to do that is with the Gufw graphical firewall manager, accessible from the Raspberry Pi OS Menu> Preferences> Firewall Configuration.

On the Client
You need to install the NFS software on the client system, if it's not already installed, as follows:

$ **sudo apt-get install nfs-common**
Reading package lists... Done
Building dependency tree... Done
Reading state information... Done
...

You also need to install the nfs4-acl-tools on the client in order to interrogate or set NFSv4 ACLs on that system:

```
$ sudo apt-get install nfs4-acl-tools
Reading package lists... Done
Building dependency tree... Done
Reading state information... Done
...
```

Create a directory that will hold the share from the server:

$ sudo mkdir -p /mnt/sharedfolder_client

Mount the share on the client with the following command:

$ sudo mount 192.168.1.33:/mnt/sharedfolder /mnt/sharedfolder_client

Procedure II- Applying and Testing NFSv4 ACLs on Client Files and \ Directories

Note
NFSv4 ACLs can only be interrogated or applied on NFS-mounted file systems!

The file system we are sharing is an EXT4 file system as it exists on the server, but as mounted on the client, it is an NFS file system! So you can only interrogate, or apply NFSv4 ACLs using the nfs4-acl-tools if you're working on the client system.

In order for you to apply NFSv4 ACLs on a Raspberry Pi system, we provide complete information on the **nfs4_setfacl** command from the man page for nfs4_setfacl(1) on a Raspberry Pi OS as follows:

****

SYNOPSIS
      nfs4_setfacl [OPTIONS] COMMAND file...
      nfs4_editfacl [OPTIONS] file...

DESCRIPTION
      nfs4_setfacl manipulates the NFSv4 Access Control List (ACL) of one or more files (or directories), provided they are on a mounted NFSv4 file system which supports ACLs.

      nfs4_editfacl is equivalent to nfs4_setfacl -e.

      Refer to the nfs4_acl(5) manpage for information about NFSv4 ACL terminology and syntax.

COMMANDS
      -a acl_spec [index]
            add the ACEs from acl_spec to file's ACL. ACEs are inserted starting at the indexth posi tion (DEFAULT: 1) of file's ACL.

      -A acl_file [index]
            add the ACEs from the acl_spec in acl_file to file's ACL. ACEs are inserted starting at the indexth position (DEFAULT: 1) of file's ACL.

-x acl_spec | index
> delete ACEs matched from acl_spec - or delete the indexth ACE - from file's ACL. Note that the ordering of the ACEs in acl_spec does not matter.

-X acl_file
> delete ACEs matched from the acl_spec in acl_file from file's ACL. Note that the ordering of the ACEs in the acl_spec does not matter.

-s acl_spec
> set file's ACL to acl_spec.

-S acl_file
> set file's ACL to the acl_spec in acl_file.

-e, --edit
> edit file's ACL in the editor defined in the EDITOR environment variable (DEFAULT: vi(1)) and set the resulting ACL upon a clean exit, assuming changes made in the editor were saved. Note that if multiple files are specified, the editor will be serially invoked once per file.

-m from_ace to_ace
> modify file's ACL in-place by replacing from_ace with to_ace.

-?, -h, --help
> display help text and exit.

--version
> display this program's version and exit.

NOTE: if '-' is given as the acl_file with the -A/-X/-S flags, the acl_spec will be read from stdin.

OPTIONS
-R, --recursive
> recursively apply to a directory's files and subdirectories. Similar to setfacl(1), the default behavior is to follow symlinks given on the command line and to skip symlinks encountered while recursing through directories.

-L, --logical
> in conjunction with -R/--recursive, a logical walk follows all symbolic links.

-P, --physical
> in conjunction with -R/--recursive, a physical walk skips all symbolic links.

--test
> display results of COMMAND, but do not save changes.

PERMISSIONS ALIASES
> With nfs4_setfacl, one can use simple abbreviations ("aliases") to express generic "read" (R), generic "write" (W), and generic "execute" (X) permissions, familiar from the POSIX mode bits used by, e.g., chmod(1). To use these aliases, one can put them in the permissions field of an NFSv4 ACE and nfs4_setfacl will convert them: an R is expanded to rntcy, a W is expanded to watTNcCy (with D added to directory ACEs), and an X is expanded to xtcy.

Please refer to the nfs4_acl(5) manpage (above) for information on specific NFSv4 ACE permissions.

For example, if one wanted to grant generic "read" and "write" access on a file, the NFSv4 permissions field would normally contain something like rwatTnNcCy. Instead, one might use aliases to accomplish the same goal with RW.

The two permissions not included in any of the aliases are d (delete) and o (write-owner). However, they can still be used: e.g., a permissions field consisting of Wdo expresses generic "write" access as well as the ability to delete and change ownership.

EXAMPLES

Assume that the file `foo' has the following NFSv4 ACL for the following examples:

```
A::OWNER@:rwatTnNcCy
D::OWNER@:x
A:g:GROUP@:rtncy
D:g:GROUP@:waxTC
A::EVERYONE@:rtncy
D::EVERYONE@:waxTC
```

- add ACE granting `alice@nfsdomain.org' generic "read" and "execute" access (defaults to prepending ACE to ACL):
  $ nfs4_setfacl -a A::alice@nfsdomain.org:rxtncy foo

- add the same ACE as above, but using aliases:
  $ nfs4_setfacl -a A::alice@nfsdomain.org:RX foo

- edit existing ACL in a text editor and set modified ACL on clean save/exit:
  $ nfs4_setfacl -e foo

- set ACL (overwrites original) to contents of a spec_file named `newacl.txt':
  $ nfs4_setfacl -S newacl.txt foo

- recursively set the ACLs of all files and subdirectories in the current directory, skipping all symlinks encountered, to the ACL contained in the spec_file named `newacl.txt':
  $ nfs4_setfacl -R -P -S newacl.txt *

- delete the first ACE, but only print the resulting ACL (does not save changes):
  $ nfs4_setfacl --test -x 1 foo

- delete the last two ACEs above:
  $ nfs4_setfacl -x "A::EVERYONE@rtncy, D::EVERYONE@:waxTC" foo

- modify (in-place) the second ACE above:
  $ nfs4_setfacl -m D::OWNER@:x D::OWNER@:xo foo

- set ACLs of `bar' and `frobaz' to ACL of `foo':
  $ nfs4_getfacl foo | nfs4_setfacl -S - bar frobaz

****

To test the interrogation, setting, and translation of NFSv4 ACLs between server and client, do the following on both server and client:
On the Server:

```
$ cd /mnt/sharedfolder
/mnt/sharedfolder$ ls
/mnt/sharedfolder$ touch test0
/mnt/sharedfolder$ ls -la
total 3
drwxrwxrwx 2 nobody nogroup 3 Oct 21 13:22 .
drwxr-xr-x 3 root   root    3 Oct 21 13:02 ..
-rw-rw-r-- 1 bob    bob     0 Oct 21 13:22 test0
/mnt/sharedfolder$
```

On the Client:

```
$ cd /mnt/sharedfolder_client
/mnt/sharedfolder_client $ ls
test0
/mnt/sharedfolder_client $ ls -la
total 6
drwxrwxrwx 2    nobody nogroup    3 Oct 21 13:22 .
drwxr-xr-x 3    root   root    4096 Oct 21 13:11 ..
-rw-rw-r-- 1    bob    bob        0 Oct 21 13:22 test0
```

```
/mnt/sharedfolder_client $ nfs4_getfacl test0
A::OWNER@:rwatTcCy
A::GROUP@:rwatcy
A::EVERYONE@:rtcy
/mnt/sharedfolder_client $
```

On the Server:
Since the file system on the server for the directory /mnt/sharedfolder is an ext4 file system, you cannot set NFSv4 ACLs on files and directories on the server. So to change permissions on those entities, you have to use the traditional UNIX file permission command, **chmod**.

```
/mnt/sharedfolder$ chmod u+x,g+x,o+wx test0
/mnt/sharedfolder$
```

On the Client:

```
/mnt/sharedfolder_client $ ls -la
total 6
drwxrwxrwx 2    nobody nogroup    3 Oct 21 13:22 .
drwxr-xr-x 3    root   root    4096 Oct 21 13:11 ..
-rwxrwxrwx 1    bob    bob        0 Oct 21 13:22 test0
```

```
/mnt/sharedfolder_client $ nfs4_getfacl test0
A::OWNER@:rwaxtTcCy
A::GROUP@:rwaxtcy
A::EVERYONE@:rwaxtcy
```

Notice the change in the ACL specs for Owner@, Group@, and Everyone@ from what it was previously.

```
/mnt/sharedfolder_client $ chmod g-x test0
/mnt/sharedfolder_client $ nfs4_getfacl test0
A::OWNER@:rwaxtTcCy
A::GROUP@:rwatcy
D::GROUP@:x
A::EVERYONE@:rwaxtcy
/mnt/sharedfolder_client $ df -hT
```

file system	Type	Size	Used	Avail	Use%	Mounted on
/dev/root	ext4	29G	3.4G	25G	13%	/
devtmpfs	devtmpfs	325M	0	325M	0%	/dev
tmpfs	tmpfs	455M	0	455M	0%	/dev/shm
tmpfs	tmpfs	182M	1.1M	181M	1%	/run
tmpfs	tmpfs	5.0M	4.0K	5.0M	1%	/run/lock
/dev/mmcblk0p1	vfat	255M	31M	225M	12%	/boot
tmpfs	tmpfs	91M	20K	91M	1%	/run/user/1000
192.168.1.33: /mnt/sharedfolder	nfs4	47G	3.1G	44G	7%	/mnt/sharedfolder_ client

Notice that in the next **nfs4_setfacl** command, we specify the principal as 1000, the uid of bob on this client system.

```
/mnt/sharedfolder_client $ nfs4_setfacl -a A::1000:W test0
/mnt/sharedfolder_client $ nfs4_getfacl test0
A::OWNER@:rwaxtTcCy
D::1000:x
A::1000:rwatcy
A::GROUP@:rwatcy
D::GROUP@:x
A::EVERYONE@:rwaxtcy
/mnt/sharedfolder_client $
```

On the Server:

To create a sub-directory on the server, and put a file in it, to test how the client will respond to that creation.

```
/mnt/sharedfolder$ mkdir test_dir
/mnt/sharedfolder$ cd test_dir
/mnt/sharedfolder/test_dir$ touch test1
/mnt/sharedfolder/test_dir$ ls -la
total 3
drwxrwxr-x 2    bob     bob      3 Oct 22 05:25 .
drwxrwxrwx 3    nobody nogroup  4 Oct 22 05:24 ..
-rw-rw-r-- 1    bob     bob      0 Oct 22 05:25 test1
/mnt/sharedfolder/test_dir$
```

On the Client:
/mnt/sharedfolder_client $ **cd test_dir**
/mnt/sharedfolder_client/test_dir $ **nfs4_getfacl test1**
A::OWNER@:rwatTcCy
A::GROUP@:rwatcy
A::EVERYONE@:rtcy
/mnt/sharedfolder_client/test_dir $

Note

A very critical point here, you should note the translations of permissions from what they are set to on the server, and what they resolve to in terms of NFSv4 ACLs on the client! This is particularly true if the two operating systems are different, i.e., Raspberry Pi OS and Solaris 11.4, for example.

Procedure III – Applying and Testing NFSv4 ACLs on Client Files and Directories Shared from a Solaris 11.4 Server

This Procedure aims to show how NFSv4 ACLs are translated between a server and a client, where the server is a UNIX machine, and the client is a Raspberry Pi OS machine. This procedure is also an illustration of how NFSv4 ACLs are inherited by sub-directories on a file system on the server.

It's assumed in this Procedure that you have access to a Solaris 11 server on your LAN (our representative UNIX system illustrated here is Solaris 11.4) and that you have root privileges on that server. Additionally

1. we had an external USB flash drive mounted on the Solaris 11 system, with a file system mounted at /test4 on that flash drive,
2. there is a file named file1, and a directory named test2.dir, in the mounted file system on the flash drive.

On the Solaris 11 Server:

The first step is to change the file inheritance mode to "allow" for newly created subdirectories.

chmod A+user:bob:read_data:file_inherit:allow /test4/test2.dir
#

Next, enable the NFS server software, and see if it's running.

```
# svcadm enable network/nfs/server
# svcs -a | grep -i nfs
disabled    3:40:07 svc:/network/nfs/cbd:default
disabled    3:40:07 svc:/network/nfs/client:default
online      3:40:28 svc:/network/nfs/fedfs-client:default
online      3:40:31 svc:/network/nfs/cleanup-upgrade:default
Output truncated ...
#
```

Mount the NFS directory.

```
# share -F nfs -o rw,root /test4
#
```

Check that it's mounted.

```
# share -F nfs
test4   /test4  sec=sys,root,rw
#
```

Change to the mounted directory.

```
# cd /test4
#
```

List the files and directories in it.

```
# ls
file1      test2.dir
#
```

Make the subdirectory test2.dir the current working directory.

```
# cd test2.dir
#
```

Create a file named 'file2' in this subdirectory.

```
# touch file2
#
```

List the files in that subdirectory.

```
# ls
file2
#
```

Interrogate the NFSv4 ACL settings on the file named 'file2' in that directory. Notice in Solaris 11, the **ls** command and its pertinent options are used to accomplish this, similar to the **nfs4_getfacl** command in the Raspberry Pi OS nfs4-acl-tools suite.

```
# ls -V file2
-rw-r--r--+ 1 root     root       0 Oct 24 00:35 file2
        user:bob:r-------------:------:I:allow
        owner@:rw-p--aARWcCos:-------:allow
        group@:r-----a-R-c--s:--------:allow
        everyone@:r-----a-R-c--s:-------:allow
#
```

Also notice that for the user bob, the **file_inherit** option of the **chmod** command above set the inherit flag on file2, and that that **chmod** command also added the read_data ACL on 'file2'.

On the Raspberry Pi OS Client:
Mount the Solaris 11 directory on the Raspberry Pi OS client. In this procedure, the IP address of the Solaris 11.4 server is 192.168.1.31.

```
$ sudo mount -t nfs 192.168.1.31:/test4 /mnt
$
```

Change the working directory to /mnt.

```
$ cd /mnt
$
```

Notice that there are two entities in that shared folder on our system, a file and a subdirectory:

```
$ ls
file1  test2.dir
$
```

Descend into the subdirectory

```
$ cd test2.dir
$
```

The file created on the server is in that share.

```
$ ls
file2
$
```

Check the NFSv4 ACLs on that file.

```
$ nfs4_getfacl file2
A::100:r
A::OWNER@:rwatTnNcCoy
A:g:GROUP@:rtncy
A::EVERYONE@:rtncy
$
```

It's, again very important to notice the ACE translations from what the NFSv4 ACLs assigned to that file on the Solaris server are to what they are shown as via the nfs4-acl-tools on the Raspberry Pi OS. As in Procedure II. above, the first ACL is for the id of user 100 on the Solaris system, which is bob.

1.16 ufw and Netfilter Interface in the Raspberry Pi OS

The Raspberry Pi OS uses the Uncomplicated Firewall (ufw) to protect your system. By default, the firewall is configured to allow all outgoing connections but to deny all incoming connection requests. The default configuration file for its rules is located in /etc/ufw/ufw.conf. If you want to know more about text-based modifications to firewall rules, see the **ufw** man page on your Linux system.

It is not absolutely necessary to change the firewall rules, and the basic details of using the command-line method of doing this are shown here.

Note
Be very careful when adding custom rules or modifying the firewall, it may endanger your system's security!

1.16.1 ufw Defaults

The default firewall configuration utility for the Raspberry Pi OS is ufw. Unlike the iptables firewall configuration utility, ufw is a much easier way to create an IPv4 or IPv6 host-based firewall. It is a rule-based system, which means that you create rules to control network connection access to your system. By default, ufw is disabled for example. But once enabled, it has a minimal set of rules, as part of its profile, that go into effect. ufw's most basic application is to allow or deny access on ports or from specific IP addresses.

ufw is based upon the Netfilter interface to the Linux kernel, particularly the filter table operations and protocols found in that interface. The rule format is also similar to the Packet Filter (PF) syntax in OpenBSD UNIX.

There is a GUI front end for ufw, known as gufw. gufw can easily be installed on your system from the Raspberry Pi OS Menu> Preferences> Add/Remove Software. In the Questions and Problems section at the end of this chapter, in Problem 27., we pose a scenario of firewall creation that uses gufw.

1.16.2 Basic Syntax, Use Case, and Rules Examples

An abbreviated listing of the **ufw** man page is as follows:

```
**********************************************************************
ufw
Purpose:
    ufw is used to manage a Linux firewall, and provides an easy to use interface
    for the creation of firewall rules. The rules use a basic syntax as shown below.
Syntax:
    ufw [option[s]] [command] [rule[s]]
Output: New, modified, or deleted firewall rules to/from ports/ IP addresses, or
    devices.
```

Common Options:

--version	show program's version number and exit
-h, --help	show help message and exit
--dry-run	don't modify anything, just show the changes

Common Commands:

enable	reloads firewall and enables firewall on boot.
disable	unloads firewall and disables firewall on boot
reload	reloads firewall rules
default	change the default connection policy
logging	toggle and affect logging to journalctl
reset	disables and resets firewall to defaults
status	show status of firewall and rules
allow	add a valid allow rule
deny	add a valid deny rule
reject	add a valid reject rule
limit	add a valid limit rule
delete	deletes a valid by specification
insert	inserts a valid rule as a numbered rule

Common Rules:

ufw allow 22   allow tcp and udp port 22 to any IP address on a valid NIC

ufw deny proto tcp to any port 80   deny all connectons to tcp port 80

ufw allow in on enp2s0 to 192.168.0.6 proto tcp allow tcp connections through enp2s0 nic to IP address 192.168.0.6

ufw limit ssh/tcp   allow rate limiting on ssh to prevent brute-force attacks

ufw delete deny 80/tcp   delete the rule denying tcp connections on port 80

ufw delete 3   delete rule 3, number determined with the status command

****

When you turn ufw on, it uses a default set of rules (profile) for the average home user. By default, all "incoming" connections are denied. Following is a listing of the simple syntactic forms.

Use Case and Rules Examples:

To Check the Status, Enable, and Disable ufw:

Use Case 1.
To turn ufw on with the default set of rules:

```
$ sudo ufw enable
Firewall is active and enabled on system startup
$
```

Use Case 2.
To check the status of UFW:

```
$ sudo ufw status verbose
Status: active
Logging: on (low)
Default: deny (incoming), allow (outgoing), disabled (routed)
New profiles: skip
$
```

Note carefully that by default, deny is being applied to incoming connections.

Use Case 3.

```
$ sudo ufw show raw
Verbose output truncated...
```

You can also read the rules files in /etc/ufw (the files whose names end with .rules).
   To Disable ufw Use.

Use Case 4.
To disable ufw use:

```
$ sudo ufw disable
Firewall stopped and disabled on system startup
$
```

To Allow and Deny Connections by Creating Rules:
   The allow command rule syntax is as follows:

sudo ufw allow <port>/<optional: protocol>

Use Case 5.
To allow incoming tcp and udp packet on ephemeral port 32000

```
$ sudo ufw allow 32000
$
```

Use Case 6.
To allow incoming tcp packets on port 22

```
$ sudo ufw allow 22/tcp
$
```

Use Case 7.
To allow incoming udp packets on ephemeral port 16000

```
$ sudo ufw allow 16000/udp
```

The deny syntax is as follows:

sudo ufw deny <port>/<optional: protocol>

Use Case 8.
To deny tcp and udp packets on port 23

```
$ sudo ufw deny 23
$
```

Use Case 9.
To deny incoming tcp packets on port 23

```
$ sudo ufw deny 23/tcp
$
```

Use Case 10.
To deny incoming udp packets on port 23

```
$ sudo ufw deny 23/udp
$
```

Deleting an Existing Rule:
  To delete a rule, prefix the original rule with delete. For example, if the original rule was:
  ufw deny 8080/tcp, then to delete it, use:

Use Case 11.

```
$ sudo ufw delete deny 8080/tcp
$
```

To Allow by Service Name:

The allow syntax is as follows:

```
sudo ufw allow <service name>
```

Use Case 12.
To allow ssh by name

```
$ sudo ufw allow ssh
$
```

Rule added
Rule added (v6)

Check the status of rules after the above command:

$ sudo ufw status
Status: active
To   Action   From
--   ------   ----
22   ALLOW   Anywhere
22 (v6)   ALLOW   Anywhere (v6)
$

Deny by Service Name:
The deny syntax is as follows:

sudo ufw deny <service name>

Use Case 13.
To deny ssh by name

$ sudo ufw deny ssh
$

ufw Logging
   System logs can record events that impact ufw, as well as the effects network connections and traffic have on other components of the system.

Use Case 14.
To enable logging use:

$ sudo ufw logging on
$

Use Case 15.
To disable logging use:

$ sudo ufw logging off
$

In-Chapter Exercise

   12. What is the biggest advantage of logging ufw events?

1.16.3 Advanced ufw Syntax

The advanced syntax, or long-form syntax, can contain more command arguments. These can specify objects like source and destination addresses, ports, and protocols.

Allow Access
This section shows how to allow specific access.

Allow by Specific IP
The allow syntax is as follows:

sudo ufw allow from <ip address>

Use Case 16.
To allow packets from 192.168.0.8:

$ sudo ufw allow from 192.168.0.8
$

To Add a Rule to Allow by Subnet

Use Case 17.
You may use a subnet mask as follows:

$ sudo ufw allow from 192.168.1.0/24
$

To Add a Rule to Allow by specific port and IP address:
The general syntax for adding an allow rule is as follows:

sudo ufw allow from <target> to <destination> port <port number>

Use Case 18.
Allow IP address 192.168.0.4 access to port 22 for all protocols-

$ sudo ufw allow from 192.168.0.4 to any port 22
$

Use Case 19.
To add a range of ports into a rule, then the following command example will do that:

$ sudo ufw allow 32000:32500/tcp
$

To allow to a specific port, IP address, and using a specific protocol:
The general syntax for specific ports, IP addresses, and protocols is:

sudo ufw allow from <target> to <destination> port <port number> proto <protocol name>

Use Case 20.
To allow IP address 192.168.0.4 access to port 22 using TCP

$ sudo ufw allow from 192.168.0.4 to any port 22 proto tcp
$

Deny Access
To deny connections by designating a specific IP address

The general format for denying to a specific IP address is:

sudo ufw deny from <ip address>

Use Case 21.
To block connections from 192.168.0.12:

```
$ sudo ufw deny from 192.168.0.12
$
```

To deny by a specific port and IP address:
The general syntax for denying is:

sudo ufw deny from <ip address> to <protocol> port <port number>

Use Case 22.
To deny a connection from IP address 192.168.0.7 to port 22 for all protocols

```
$ sudo ufw deny from 192.168.0.7 to any port 22
$
```

Specification by Numbered Rules
Listing rules with a reference number:

Use Case 23.
Use the status numbered rule construct to show the order and id number of existing rules:

```
$ sudo ufw status numbered
Status: active
     To              Action      From
     --              ------      ----
[ 1] 65000          DENY IN    16000
[ 2] 65000 (v6)     DENY IN    16000 (v6)
$
```

To delete a numbered rule

Use Case 24.
After executing the command in Use Case 23., you can delete rules using the numbers found at the left margin of the output. The following will delete the first rule, and the remaining rules will shift up in numbering to fill in the list.

```
$ sudo ufw delete 1
$
```

1.16.4 An Extended Example of Applying ufw Rules

The following example applies some of the previous Use Case commands in an extended and more complex arrangement. Basically, it applies some user-defined rules in the first two steps, and then shows a means of changing those rules. For a further description of rule syntax and interaction, we refer you on to the existing documentation for the Netfilter interface.

Example 1.12

1. Deny connection from the IP address 192.168.0.8 for ssh:

```
$ sudo ufw deny from 192.168.0.8 to any port 22
Rule added
$
```

2. Allow ssh connections from all other IP addresses on our LAN, using the tcp protocol:

```
$ sudo ufw allow from 192.168.0.0/24 to any port 22 proto tcp
Rule added
```

3. Check the status of ufw rules:

```
$ sudo ufw status
Status: active
To              Action      From
--              ------      ----
22              DENY        192.168.0.8
22/tcp          ALLOW       192.168.0.0/24
$
```

4. To test the above rules, first login from the machine with the IP address of 192.168.0.8 on your LAN:

```
$ ssh bob@192.168.0.6
ssh: connect to host 192.168.0.6 port 22: Connection timed out
$
```

To further test, you can login from a machine on your LAN that is not 192.168.0.8. You should be able to ssh login from any other machine on your LAN within the range specified.

5. Add an additional deny rule to deny an ssh connection from 192.168.0.31. Since the rules are evaluated in order, from 1 to n, an addition of a deny rule at this point would make it rule #3. Therefore, according to the precedents of chain and rule evaluation designated in the Netfilter protocols, it is *not* evaluated. The following steps are one way of moving a rule into the chain of evaluation.

So first delete rule #2, the allow rule for all IP addresses on the LAN:

```
$ sudo ufw delete allow from 192.168.0.0/24 to any port 22 proto tcp
Rule deleted
$
```

Check the status of rules:

```
$ sudo ufw status
Status: active
To                Action     From
--                ------     ----
22                DENY       192.168.0.8
$
```

6. Add in the rule denying ssh connections from 192.168.0.31, using tcp protocol:

```
$ sudo ufw deny from 192.168.0.31 to any port 22
Rule added
$
```

7. Add back the rule allowing ssh from all other IP addresses on the LAN, at the end of the chain:

```
$ sudo ufw allow from 192.168.0.0/24 to any port 22 proto tcp
Rule added
$
```

8. Check the status of rules:

```
$ sudo ufw status
Status: active
To                Action     From
--                ------     ----
22                DENY       192.168.0.8
22                DENY       192.168.0.31
22/tcp            ALLOW      192.168.0.0/24
$
```

9. Test from 192.168.0.8 and 31 and from some other IP on the LAN to verify the effectiveness of the rules.

In-Chapter Exercises

13. What ufw rule could have been used at step 5 that would have the same effect as steps 6 through 8?
14. Give all the ufw commands that would erase all the rules established here.

1.16.5 Interpreting ufw Log Entries in the systemd Journal

Question: Why would you want to look at log entries generated by ufw?

Answer: Someone is trying to crack into your machine from your LAN or the Internet, and you want to have information about their method of attack.

This section details an example procedure for generating ufw-blocked messages in the log kept by the systemd Journal. We then give brief descriptions of the details of the components of the log entry. The Journal, and the journalctl command in particular, allows you to view consolidated log messages from a variety of sources on your system, all using one command. We give details of the systemd Journal, and the journalctl command, in Section 1.11.

Example 1.13 ufw Log Entries

1. You have to set up a deny rule that blocks connections. In this example, to set up a rule that blocks connections from 192.168.0.8 on our LAN, we give the following ufw rule:

```
$ sudo ufw deny in log-all from 192.168.0.8
Rule added
$
```

The log-all parameter turns on full ufw logging. Since this parameter generates quite a bit of log entry data, it would be advisable to turn logging off promptly, as shown in step 5.

2. When we view ufw's verbose status, it gives us this output:

```
$ sudo ufw status verbose
Status: active
Logging: off
Default: deny (incoming), allow (outgoing), disabled (routed)
New profiles: skip
To                 Action    From
--                 ------    ----
Anywhere           DENY      IN    192.168.0.8          (log-all)
$
```

3. Attempt to log in to the current machine that you set up the rule on in step 1, from some other place on your LAN or possibly from the Internet. We attempted an ssh login from another machine on our LAN with an IP address of 192.168.0.8. Of course, this login attempt assumes that sshd is running on the system you created the ufw rule on in step 1. In the Questions and Problems section at the end of this chapter, we pose a problem where you use different forms of remote login and note the differences in log entries for those types of attempted connections.

4. Immediately examine the Journal log, using the **journalctl –f** command. The –f option of the journalctl command shows you log entries generated in real time. This yields log entries similar to the one in the next step. This is the contemporary method of examining system logging.

5. Turn ufw logging off with the following command:

   $ sudo ufw logging off
   Logging disabled
   $

6. Here is a sample of one of the log entries we got by using **journalctl -f**. Following it, we will comment on some of the items in it that would be useful for a system administrator to use when analyzing the entry.

Log Entry
Nov 01 11:23:33 raspberry pi kernel: [UFW BLOCK] IN=enp2s0 OUT= MAC=ff:ff:ff:ff:ff: ff:b8:ac:6f:9a:80:dc:08:00 SRC=192.168.0.8 DST=192.168.0.6 LEN=194 TOS=0x00 PREC=0x00 TTL=64 ID=53133 DF PROTO=TCP SPT=17500 DPT=17500 LEN=174

An explanation of the components of this entry is as follows:

Date - Nov 01 11:23:33
Places entries in time order, so you can see the progress of what connections have been done, or most importantly, what connections have been attempted. Since this log entry in the Journal was generated and viewed in real time using the journalctl –f command, it is a very recent excerpt from the real time display of the Journal log.

Hostname – raspberry pi kernel
The server's hostname is useful to identify the machine you are reading the Journal on if you are dealing with several remote machines and are monitoring their Journal entries.

Event - [UFW BLOCK]

A short description of the logged event; depending on the level of error generated, this could be just an Audit.

IN - enp2s0

Incoming connection at the NIC enp2s0. Useful if the machine you are monitoring the log entry on has several NIC's, connected to different branches on your network.

OUT- blank

IN our log entry, blank because it is not an outgoing connection attempt.

MAC- ff:ff:ff:ff:ff:ff:b8:ac:6f:9a:80:dc:08:00

A 14-byte combination of the Destination MAC, Source MAC, and EtherType fields, following Ethernet protocol.

SRC - 192.168.0.8

The source IP, in our case the IP address of the machine on the LAN we attempted to connect from. If this source is an IPV4 address, it can tell you how to apply an additional set of filtering rules to prevent unwanted connections.

DST - 192.168.0.6

This indicates the destination IP. In this case, the IP address of the system we created the deny rule on.

LEN - 194

This indicates the length in bytes of the packet. Can tell you about what type of entry connection has been attempted.

  The next five entry components are not important in basic log interpretation:

TOS - 0x00
PREC -0x00
TTL - 64
ID – 53133
DF
PROTO - TCP

The protocol of the packet - TCP or UDP. TCP in our case, because it was an ssh connection.

SPT - 17500

The port the source sent the packet through from. Interesting here that the ssh client on 192.168.0.8 used an ephemeral port to attempt the connection on.

DPT - 17500

The port on the destination the packet was sent to. Again, interesting that the packet was routed to this ephemeral port on the destination system, and ufw blocked it.

LEN - 174

Not important in basic log interpretation.

1.17 Encrypting Directories and Files Using tar and gpg

The Raspberry Pi OS has several utilities that allow you to archive your files and directories in a single file, and the **tar** command is the most popular, widely used, and traditional method that allows you to achieve this. But in the 21st century, one has to wonder why these traditional commands are still used, with the ubiquity and prevalence of cheap and plentiful archival storage media available, such as large gigabyte capacity flash drives, SSDs, NAS, and cloud storage? When was the last time any ordinary user of the Raspberry Pi reverted to using a tape drive? This section offers a rational for the continued use of these traditional archiving methods.

Contemporary tar on Linux is the Gnu version.
The tar (short for *tape archive*) utility was originally designed to save file systems on tape as a backup, so that files could be recovered in the event of a system crash. It is primarily used now to pack a directory hierarchy as an ordinary disk file. That disk file can then be either saved for system backup purposes locally or remotely, or transmitted to someone via the Internet. It is also used commonly with a compression utility, such as gzip, via a command-line option. Doing so saves disk space and transmission time. The saving in disk space results primarily from the fact that empty space within a cluster is not wasted. A brief description of the tar utility follows.

The GNU version of **tar** has some important functional features, and incorporates a more friendly syntax, than traditional UNIX **tar**. Therefore, for beginners, we only show the "long form" of the Gnu-style syntax because it is more intuitive and easy to understand. Once you get more familiar with **tar**, you may switch to the UNIX-style short form at your discretion.

System administrators normally use a cost-effective archival medium for archiving complete file system structures as backups so that, when a system crashes for some reason, files can be recovered. Linux-based computer systems normally crash for reasons beyond the operating system's control, such as a disk head crash because of a power surge. Linux rarely causes a system to crash because it is a well-designed, coded, and tested operating system. In a typical commercial server installation, backup is done every day during off hours (late night or early morning) when the system is not normally in use.

1.17.1 The tar Command General Syntax

The general syntax of the tar command, shown with Gnu-style syntax as opposed to traditional UNIX-style syntax, is as follows:

tar
Syntax: tar [operation mode] [operation mode options] [FILE...]

Purpose: Archive (copy in a particular format) files to or, restore files from, an archival medium (which can be an ordinary file). Directories are by default archived and restored recursively.

Output: Archived or restored files or directory structures.

Main Operations and Operation Options in Gnu-Style Usage:

--append	Append files to the end of an archive.
--concatenate	Append an archive to the end of another archive.
--compare	Find differences between archive and file system.
--create	Create a new tape and record archive files on it
--delete	Delete from the archive.
--extract	Extract files from an archive.
--help	Display a short option summary.
--list	List the contents of an archive.
--show-defaults	Show built-in defaults for options.
--test-label	Test the archive volume label and then exit.
--update	Append files which are newer than the versions in an archive.
--usage	Display a list of available options.
--version	Display program version and copyright information.

Common Options:

--preserve-permissions	Extract information about traditional file permissions.
--acls	Enable POSIX.1e ACL support.
--gzip	Filter the archive through gzip.
--verbose	Verbosely list files processed.
--file ARCHIVE.tar	Send archive to file named ARCHIVE.tar.

Command Arguments:
FILE... Target, either an archive file, or file object to be archived.

1.17.2 Directory Encryption

The objective of this section is to illustrate not only encryption and compression of an entire directory but also to further show use of the **tar** command to preserve the directory structure.

Example 1.14 Directory Encryption

Objectives: To take a directory, and treat it with **tar** and **gpg,** to both compress and encrypt it.

Prerequisites: Having a directory, containing files you want to protect with encryption using gpg.

Requirements: Do the following steps in the order presented to fulfill the requirements of this example.

1. While in your home directory, use the following command to tar/ compress and encrypt a directory of your choice. In our case the directory was named 18_C:

```
$ tar --gzip --create --verbose --file - 18_C | gpg -c > 18_C.tar.gz.gpg
18_C/
18_C/THE ARCADES PROJECT.pdf
gpg: directory '/home/bob/.gnupg' created
gpg: keybox '/home/bob/.gnupg/pubring.kbx' created
18_C/beautiful-flower-3447424_1280.jpg
18_C/rs_1024x759-200729103613-1024-The-Lost-Boys-cast-photo-3-ch-
    072920.jpg
18_C/640px-Seattle_-_Showbox_marquee_01.jpg
18_C/Canguilhem_Georges_The_Normal_and_the_Pathologic_1991.pdf
18_C/allfiles_final.zip
18_C/20220425154705.pdf
18_C/thumb16.jpg
18_C/TextToSpeech.m4a
$
```

On our Raspberry Pi system, a graphical dialog box opened on screen, asking to enter a password and confirm it. Remember to write down the passphrase so you can decrypt the directory! The tarred, compressed, and encrypted directory is named 18_C.tar.gz.gpg.

2. This step decrypts and "untars" and uncompresses the encrypted directory and all its files.

```
$ gpg --decrypt 18_C.tar.gz.gpg | tar --extract --gunzip --verbose --file -
gpg: AES256.CFB encrypted data
gpg: encrypted with 1 passphrase
18_C/
18_C/THE ARCADES PROJECT.pdf
18_C/beautiful-flower-3447424_1280.jpg
18_C/rs_1024x759-200729103613-1024-The-Lost-Boys-cast-photo-3-ch-
    072920.jpg
18_C/640px-Seattle_-_Showbox_marquee_01.jpg
18_C/Canguilhem_Georges_The_Normal_and_the_Pathologic_1991.pdf
18_C/allfiles_final.zip
18_C/20220425154705.pdf
18_C/thumb16.jpg
18_C/TextToSpeech.m4a
$
```

In-Chapter Exercise

15. Use the methods of Example 1.14 to encrypt, but not compress, an important directory under your home directory on your system. Then, decrypt that directory using **gpg**. Where are the decrypted files placed, for example, is the original directory you encrypt overwritten?

1.17.3 Encrypting a User File

There are times when an ordinary user might want to keep one or more files secure by encrypting them. This might be true when you want to archive the files using a USB flash drive or other removable medium, and want to avoid loss of privacy if you lose the flash drive. The following example illustrates the use of **gpg** to encrypt a single important file.

Example 1.15 Encryption of a Single File

Objective: To encrypt an important file in your home directory.

Prerequisites: Doing Example 1.14, and having a file in your home directory you want to encrypt.

Requirements: Do the following steps in the order presented to fulfill the requirements of this example.

1. Create a file with nano, that contains the string "This is a test file for encryption."

    $ nano newfile

Or use some existing file.

2. Use **gpg** to encrypt the file. Make sure to enter a passphrase you can remember, or even write down the passphrase!

    $ gpg --symmetric --cipher-algo AES256 newfile
    On our Raspberry Pi OS system, a graphical dialog box opened on screen, asking to enter a password and confirm it. Remember to write down the passphrase so you can decrypt the directory!
    $

You can replace the AES56 with many other alogrithms, such as IDEA, 4DES, CAST5, BLOWFISH, AES, etc..

3. Examine the contents of newfile. It's unreadable.

    $ more newfile.gpg
    ```
    # ##h   D=     (  `  \#
    33       v  #K  Y+  m#  v  (7  -
      #  Ym    '&g@\  #  4  8H          q#G1{zG#    H  #  $+    <  j# l  d
    /#  w  OA
    ```

4. Delete the original, unencrypted file.

    $ rm newfile

5. Decrypt the file we encrypted in step 2..

   $ gpg newfile.gpg
   gpg: WARNING: no command supplied. Trying to guess what you mean ...
   gpg: AES256.CFB encrypted data
   gpg: encrypted with 1 passphrase

6. Examine what is in your current working directory.

   $ ls

Notice both the newly decrypted file and the encrypted file are both there.

7. Examine the contents of the newly decrypted file.

   $ more newfile
   This is a test file for encryption.
   $

Notice its contents are the same as the original.

In-Chapter Exercise

16. Use the methods of Example 1.15 to encrypt an important file in your home directory on your system. Then, decrypt that file using gpg. Where is the decrypted file placed, for example, is the original file you encrypted overwritten?

1.17.4 Encrypting a USB Flash Drive

Since USB removable media are easily subject to loss of privacy issues, we present this method of encrypting an entire USB flash drive. An important aspect of this method is that it may be applied to other partitions, which may be on other persistent media attached to your system.

Example 1.16 How to Encrypt a USB Flash Drive

Objectives: To encrypt an entire single-partition USB flash drive.

Prerequisites: Having a blank, automatically mounted USB flash drive for use on your system.

Background: The facilities that allow this procedure to be done are the cryptsetup utility, which is available by default on the Raspberry Pi OS, and the Disks utility. A properly single-partitioned and formatted USB flash drive, which is usable on your Raspberry Pi system, automounts, and an icon for it appears on the desktop when it is inserted into a USB port. This example allows you to encrypt that flash drive, so that in case it is lost, the private data you subsequently put on it is not compromised. Also, if you insert it in another computer, you can type in the encryption passphrase, and it will be unlocked and usable on that second computer as well. This feature allows you to safely transport the flash drive between computer sites.

Requirements: Do the following steps, in the order presented, to fulfill the requirements of this example.

1. Insert your USB flash drive into a USB port, and then Launch the Disks utility from the Raspberry Pi OS Menu> Accessories. In the left side of the Disk utility window, your disk drives will be shown.

2. Click on the USB flash drive in the left side window. On the right side of the window, information about your USB flash drive will be shown. In the little black square under the block showing the flash drive partition, make a choice "unmount selected partition" by clicking on the black square.

3. Click on the black gearbox square under the block showing the flash drive partition, and make the choice Format Partition. In the Format Volume window that opens on the screen,
    a. Next to Type, select the radio button 'Internal disk for use with Linux systems only (Ext4)'
    b. Check the box Password protect volume (LUKS)
    c. Give the volume a name of your choice in the Volume Name field.
    d. Click the Next block at the top of the Format Volume window.
    e. Type in a Passphrase, and Confirm Passphrase. Make sure you can remember the passphrase
    f. Click Next
    g. Click on the red Format... button in the upper-right of the Format Volume window
    e. Wait until the file system is built, then quit the Disk utility.

4. Withdraw the USB flash drive from the computer, and reinsert it. A window appears on screen, asking you to "Enter a passphrase to unlock the volume." In the password field, enter the passphrase you typed-in in step 3.e. above. If you always want the passphrase to be remembered whenever you plug this USB flash drive into the computer, check off the Remember forever choice. Then click on the connect button. The USB flash drive will be mounted, and a file window will open into it.

5. You are now free to add directories and files to the flash drive. Notice that on the Raspberry Pi desktop, the icon for the USB flash drive appears with an unlocked u-lock figure shown on it.

6. To eject the USB flash drive, right-click on the gray arrow plus bar in the upper-right corner of the desktop, and choose that flash drive.

7. When mounting this USB flash drive on another computer, you will be asked for the passphrase before it can be unlocked on the other computer.

In-Chapter Exercise

17. Use the methods of Example 1.16 to encrypt a USB flash drive you attach to your system. Then, detach the flash drive, mount it on another Raspberry Pi OS computer, and use the passphrase to unlock it on that computer.

1.18 How a Process Gets Its Credentials

Each Linux Raspberry Pi OS process, or task, has a number of data structure identifiers that are created by the relevant system calls to maintain that process's autonomy and the steady state of the multi-programming model. These identifiers are critical to authentication checks on processes. As examples, a child process created by the fork system call inherits its parent's session ID and process group ID. A process's session and group ID are maintained across an execve system call. These identifiers include objects such as Process ID (PID), Parent Process ID (PPID), Process Group ID and Session ID, and User and Group Identifiers. All of these identifiers, and the data structures associated with them, play directly into the Raspberry Pi OS security model. Most important to our notion of security are User and Group Identifiers.

In terms of process authentication checks, User and Group Identifiers are listed as real user and group ID, effective user and group ID, the saved set-user-ID and set-group-id, the specific file system user and group ID, and supplementary group IDs.

The interaction of assignments of these identifiers is complex but can be prioritized as follows:

* Privileged processes (with UID=0) have access to everything.
* The effective UID is the same as the owner's UID; access is given by the owner's permissions on a file object.
* The effective GID, or supplementary process GID's match the owning group GID, permission is given by the owning group permissions on the file object.
* Finally, access permissions are given by the "other" permission on the file object.

Additionally, a process's user IDs are applied in other ways, such as:

1. When determining the permissions for sending signals, such as the kill signal.

2. When determining the permissions for setting process scheduling, such as setting the nice value.

3. When checking resource limits and the number of inotify instances possible for the process.

For more information on credentials, see the man page for credentials on your Raspberry Pi OS system.

1.18.1 Process Capabilities

There is also a way to assign credentials to processes through a scheme known as "capabilities." Capabilities use a finer-grained technique to limit, or grant credentials to processes you want to give privileges to. This is in contrast to the traditional RBAC method of using sudo to give coarse-grained privileges to a process or set of processes initiated by an unprivileged user.

For a more complete discussion of Linux Capabilities, see the man page for capabilities on your system. The scope of capabilities generally follows this outline:

1. Set of permitted capabilities
2. Set of inheritable capabilities
3. Set of effective capabilities
4. Capability bounding set

These make the most sense when they apply to processes, which are the active element in system operation. They are privileged permissions exercised in a "finer-grained" context. Finer-grained is used here to mean a more specific, targeted privilege, such as those shown in Table 1.10. These are applied to a process or processes that ordinarily, via the traditional model, could only be granted a blanket, all-or-none tableau of privileges. Including a user in the sudoers file is an example of this traditional model's application.

Capabilities are controlled by changes in the traditional Linux permissions but can also be set more finely and viewed directly by the capset and getcap system calls.

It is possible to use Bash to assign and view process capabilities using the **setcap** and **getcap** commands. Essentially, a program and its processes have individualized and custom high-level privileges, rather than a blanket or generalized high-level privilege, such as a user ID of 0 (root). We show an example of this technique in Example 1.17.

You can also assign capabilities from within system programs using the appropriate system calls from the libcap API.

For each process, the kernel maintains three capability sets that contain any of the capabilities specified in Table 1.10 *if they are enabled*. At the same time, if

TABLE 1.10

Linux Capabilities

Capability	What It Applies To
CAP_AUDIT_CONTROL	Enable and disable kernel auditing
CAP_AUDIT_READ	Allow reading the audit log via a multicast netlink socket.
CAP_AUDIT_WRITE	Write records to kernel auditing log.
CAP_BLOCK_SUSPEND	Employ features that can block system suspend.
CAP_CHOWN	Make arbitrary changes to file UIDs and GIDs (see chown(2)).
CAP_DAC_OVERRIDE	Bypass file read, write, and execute permission checks.
CAP_DAC_READ_SEARCH	Bypass file read permission checks and directory read and execute permission checks;
CAP_FOWNER	Bypass permission checks on operations that normally require the file system UID of the process to match the UID of the file.
CAP_FSETID	Don't clear set-user-ID and set-group-ID mode bits when a file is modified; set the set-group-ID bit for a file whose GID does not match the file system or any of the supplementary GIDs of the calling process.
CAP_IPC_LOCK	Lock memory (mlock(2), mlockall(2), mmap(2), shmctl(2)).
CAP_IPC_OWNER	Bypass permission checks for operations on System V IPC objects.
CAP_KILL	Bypass permission checks for sending signals (see kill(2)).
CAP_LEASE	Establish leases on arbitrary files (see fcntl(2)).
CAP_LINUX_IMMUTABLE	Set the FS_APPEND_FL and FS_IMMUTABLE_FL inode flags .
CAP_MAC_ADMIN	Override Mandatory Access Control (MAC).
CAP_MAC_OVERRIDE	Allow MAC configuration or state changes.
CAP_MKNOD	Create special files using mknod(2).
CAP_NET_ADMIN	Perform various network-related operations.
CAP_NET_BIND_SERVICE	Bind a socket to Internet domain privileged ports (port numbers less than 1024).
CAP_NET_BROADCAST	(Unused) Make socket broadcasts, and listen to multicasts.
CAP_NET_RAW	Use RAW and PACKET sockets.
CAP_SETGID	Make arbitrary manipulations of process GIDs and supplementary GID list.
CAP_SETFCAP	Set file capabilities.
CAP_SETPCAP	If file capabilities are not supported: grant or remove any capability in the caller's permitted capability set to or from any other process.
CAP_SETUID	Make arbitrary manipulations of process UIDs.
CAP_SYS_ADMIN	Perform a range of system administration operations.
CAP_SYS_BOOT	Use reboot(2) and kexec_load(2).
CAP_SYS_CHROOT	Use chroot(2).
CAP_SYS_MODULE	Load and unload kernel modules.
CAP_SYS_NICE	Raise process nice value (nice(2), setpriority(2)) and change the nice value for arbitrary processes.
CAP_SYS_PACCT	Use acct(2).
CAP_SYS_PTRACE	Trace arbitrary processes using ptrace(2).
CAP_SYS_RAWIO	Perform I/O port operations (iopl(2) and ioperm(2)).
CAP_SYS_RESOURCE	Use reserved space on ext2 file systems, and other resource limits.
CAP_SYS_TIME	Set system clock.
CAP_SYS_TTY_CONFIG	Use vhangup(2); employ various privileged ioctl(2) operations on virtual terminals.
CAP_SYSLOG	Perform privileged syslog(2) operations.
CAP_WAKE_ALARM	Trigger something that will wake up the system.

a file has associated capability sets, then these sets are used to determine the capabilities that are given to a process if it uses the exec() system call on that file. The three sets for process and file, arranged in order from least to most inclusive, are:

Inheritable: These are capabilities that can be passed on to the permitted set when a process uses the exec() system call when accessing a file.

Effective: These are the capabilities used to perform privilege checking for the process.

Permitted: These are the maximum capabilities, formed from effective and inherited capabilities, that a process can actually use.

The possible file capability set and its contents give executable file process capabilities.

It assigns a group of capabilities that are given to the process's permitted capability set during a system call to exec() made by the process.

Think of the process and file sets as the raised ridges on a house key (the process set) and as tumblers in the lock on the front door (the file set). If the key ridges match the tumbler settings, you are granted access and can open the door lock with the key. The process can be authenticated via its capability set checked against the capability set on any file it wants to use exec() on .

The simplified syntax of the **setcap** command is as follows:

setcap [-options] (capabilities) filename

The simplified syntax of the **getcap** command is as follows:

getcap [-options] filename

See the man pages on your system for more details about the **setcap** and **getcap** commands.

Example 1.17 Setting Capabilities on the Command Line

Objectives: To set and view a process capability using the **setcap** and **getcap** commands.

Prerequisites: Having a root-privileged account, and also having created a standard, non-privileged account (which we named lowly, with a password low) that is *not* a member of the root, or sudoers group. In the steps below, when you are required to use the privileged account, that account should be a part of the sudoers group to execute the **sudo** command as shown.

Background: We modify a copy of the Bash external command **/bin/ping program**, so that when it is used from an unprivileged account, it can execute without setting the SUID permission bit.

To quickly and easily switch between privileged and unprivileged accounts, you can make use of the virtual terminals available in Linux with the **<Ctrl>+<Alt>+Function key(s)**. On our Raspberry Pi system, **<Ctrl>+<Alt>+F2** enabled us to log into the unprivileged account in a virtual, text-only terminal. To return to the default tty, and into the privileged account was available by using **<Ctrl>+<Alt>+F7**.

Requirements: Do the following steps in the order presented to meet the requirements of this example.

0. If you haven't added an unprivileged user to your Raspberry Pi OS system, use the following command:

    ```
    $ sudo adduser lowly
    Adding user `lowly' ...
    Adding new group `lowly' (1001) ...
    Adding new user `lowly' (1001) with group `lowly' ...
    Creating home directory `/home/lowly' ...
    Copying files from `/etc/skel' ...
    New password: QQQ
    Retype new password: QQQ
    passwd: password updated successfully
    Changing the user information for lowly
    Enter the new value, or press ENTER for the default
            Full Name []: low
            Room Number []:
            Work Phone []:
            Home Phone []:
            Other []:
    Is the information correct? [Y/n] Y
    $
    ```

1. Use **<Ctrl>+<Alt>+F2** to login to the unprivileged account, and use the **ls –la** command to see the permission bits set on the system-wide /bin/ping executable program. Then test ping, by executing the ping command to connect to localhost:

    ```
    $ ls -la /bin/ping
    -rwsr-xr-x 1 root root 44168 May  7  2014 /bin/ping
    $ /bin/ping localhost
    PING localhost (127.0.0.1) 56(84) bytes of data.
    64 bytes from localhost (127.0.0.1): icmp_seq=1 ttl=64 time=0.048 ms
    64 bytes from localhost (127.0.0.1): icmp_seq=2 ttl=64 time=0.053 ms
    64 bytes from localhost (127.0.0.1): icmp_seq=3 ttl=64 time=0.053 ms
    <Ctrl>+C
    --- localhost ping statistics ---
    3 packets transmitted, 3 received, 0% packet loss, time 1998ms
    rtt min/avg/max/mdev = 0.048/0.051/0.053/0.006 ms
    ```

The "s" bit of the file's permission mode is the setuid-executable bit, and as an unprivileged user, you are able to use ping because of this.

2. While still in the unprivileged account, copy the /bin/ping file to the unprivileged user home directory. As the command below shows, ping loses its privilege and no longer works, as shown by the following commands:

```
$ cp /bin/ping .
$ ls -la ping
-rwxr-xr-x 1 lowly lowly 44168 Dec 25 15:16 ping
$ ./ping localhost
ping: icmp open socket: Operation not permitted
$
```

ping requires privilege to write the network packets that are used to probe the network. The Linux kernel checks to see whether this copy of ping in the unprivileged account is capable(CAP_NET_RAW), which means cap_ effective (pE) for the current process includes CAP_NET_RAW. By default, root gets all effective capabilities, so it defaults to having more-than-enough privilege to successfully use ping. Similarly, when setuid-root, the /bin/ping version is also overly privileged. If some attacker were to discover a new buffer-overflow or more subtle bug in the ping application, then they might be able to exploit it to invoke a shell with root privilege. File system capability support adds the ability to bestow just-enough privilege to the ping application.

3. To give the unprivileged ping just enough privilege to execute the ping command in it's home directory, switch to the privileged account by using the key combination **<Ctrl>+<Alt>+F7**. Use the utilities from libcap to do the following:

```
$ sudo setcap cap_net_raw=ep /home/lowly/ping
$ sudo getcap /home/lowly/ping
ping = cap_net_raw+ep
$
```

What the first command does is add a limited permitted (the p argument) capability for CAP_NET_RAW, and also sets the effective bit (e), to automatically raise this effective bit in the unprivileged ping process at the time the ping command is executed.

4. Switch back to the unprivileged account using **<Ctrl>+<Alt>+F2**, and then use the following command to test the local ping command:

```
$ .ping localhost
PING localhost(localhost (::1)) 56 data bytes
64 bytes from localhost (::1): icmp_seq=1 ttl=64 time=0.256 ms
64 bytes from localhost (::1): icmp_seq=2 ttl=64 time=0.226 ms
64 bytes from localhost (::1): icmp_seq=3 ttl=64 time=0.232 ms
64 bytes from localhost (::1): icmp_seq=4 ttl=64 time=0.257 ms
64 bytes from localhost (::1): icmp_seq=5 ttl=64 time=0.234 ms
64 bytes from localhost (::1): icmp_seq=6 ttl=64 time=0.233 ms
<Ctrl>+C
--- localhost ping statistics ---
6 packets transmitted, 6 received, 0% packet loss, time 5112ms
rtt min/avg/max/mdev = 0.226/0.239/0.257/0.012 ms
$
```

Unlike setting the setuid-root permission bit, the ping in the unprivileged account after step 3 is not given blanket privileges, such as any privilege to modify a file that is not owned by the calling user, or to deploy a kernel module in some way. There is no direct way to subvert this localized ping program.

Conclusion: Instead of giving a process blanket root privileges, Linux capabilities allow you to only give an application and its processes just enough privilege to accomplish its objectives.

In-Chapter Exercise

18. Following the general procedure of Example 1.17, give an unprivileged user the capability of changing both owner and group of any file on your system. Utilize the information found in Table 1.10.

1.19 Namespaces and User Namespaces

These are security-related features built into the Raspberry Pi OS kernel that differentiate it from UNIX kernels, particularly FreeBSD and Solaris. They are methods of creating a virtual environment for a group of processes. The kinds of resources that can be 'virtualized' in these environments for groups of processes are currently process IDs, hostnames, user IDs, network access, interprocess communication, and file systems. Namespaces are a fundamental component of the container virtualization technique, for systems like Docker, or LXD/LXC.

User namespaces isolate security-related identifiers and attributes of processes, in particular, user IDs and group IDs, the root directory, keys, and very importantly capabilities (as seen in Section 1.18). A very distinctive characteristic useful in isolating, or "sandboxing" processes, is that a process's user and group IDs can be different inside and outside a user namespace. In particular, a process can be unprivileged outside a user namespace but inside have a user ID of 0; in other words, the process has full privileges to utilize system resources *inside* the user namespace but cannot have full privileges on system resources *outside* the namespace. These isolated processes can share the global resources within a locally scoped, privileged environment.

The details of the namespaces and cgroups APIs are beyond what we can reasonably cover in this book. But we do provide an example, which can be found in it's entirety in the Example sub-section of the user_namespaces man page on your system. We encourage you to refer to the **namespaces**, and **user_namespaces** man pages on your Raspberry Pi OS system for a more complete and detailed description of these two kernel features.

Example 1.18 Namespaces

Objectives: To allow experimentation with establishing various forms of namespaces, using a system program illustrated and pre-built into the **user_namespaces** man page.

Prerequisites: Using the **man user_namespaces** command, copy the sample program from the EXAMPLES sub-section, called userns_child_exec.c, into a text editor of your choice. Save the file as example_1_18.c, and compile it with the command

gcc -w example_1_18_1.c -o example_1_18

Background: The program example_1_18.c is designed to allow experimenting with user namespaces, as well as other types of namespaces. It creates namespaces as specified by command-line options and then executes operations inside those namespaces. Of course, if you are already familiar with the namespaces API, the comments and functions inside the program source code provide a basic explanation of the program.

The following Bash session demonstrates its use.

Requirements: Do the steps below, in the order presented, to complete the requirements for this example.

1. Examine the version of the kernel, to verify the level of namespace functionality available on your system. You need to have at least kernel level 3.8 or higher:

```
$ uname -rs
Linux 6.1.21-v8+
$
```

2. Examine your user and group ID numbers, so that you can supply them as subsequent command-line arguments:

```
$ id -u
1000
$ id -g
1000
$
```

3. Create a new user namespace with a new shell(bash), a new user (-U), mount (-m), PID (-p), with user ID (-M) and group ID (-G) 1000 (as found in step 2.), and indexed to PID 0 inside the new namespace. Use the following command:

```
$ ./example_1_18 -p -m -U -M '0 1000 1' -G '0 1000 1' bash
#
```

You now have a bash shell in the new namespace, as indicated by the new shell pronpt (#).

4. To see the real and effective user and group id's in the new namespace, repeat the two commands from step 2.:

```
# id -u
0
# id -g
0
```

You are now a privileged user in this new namespace, since you designated this mapping in the command in step 3. with -M '0 1000 1' and -G '0 1000 1'.

5. The shell in this new namespace is PID 1, as you can see by typing the following command:

```
# echo $$
1
```

6. Mount a new /proc file system, and list all of the processes visible in the new namespace. This shows that the shell is isolated from any processes outside the namespace:

```
# mount -t proc proc /proc
# ps ax
PID   TTY     STAT    TIME  COMMAND
1     pts/0   S       0:00  bash
38    pts/0   R+      0:00  ps -ax
```

7. Inside the user namespace, the shell has user and group ID's of 0. This is shown by the following command:

```
namespaces # cat /proc/$$/status | egrep '^[UG]id'
Uid:    0     0     0     0
Gid:    0     0     0     0
```

8. Since we have used the clone() system call in the program example_
    1_18 to clone the user and process ID spaces, any program you run
    inside the new namespace has a PID assigned inside the namespace.
    To verify this, open another terminal and use the ps -ax command to
    find the PID's of the example_1_18 process, and its bash shell. Then
    compare these PID's to those inside the new namespace.

9. To terminate the isolated process, type the exit command.

```
# exit
$
```

1.20 Chapter Summary

This chapter presented the core of the system administrator commands and
procedures that are the foundation of this volume, which provide computer
system concurrency, virtualization, and secure persistence for the Raspberry
Pi hardware and software. We covered the following: ACL addgroup adduser
apt-key cat chgrp chmod chown compgen cpio CUPS DAC dd du exec() export
fdisk FileZilla fork() ftp getcap getfacl gpg id inxi journalctl kill lp lpadmin
lpc lpinfo lpmove lpoptions lpq lpr lprm lpstat MAC mdadm Mirroring
mkfs.ext4 mount nfs4_getfacl nfs4_setfacl nice ping POSIX.1e processes capabilities ps -aux RAID1 RBAC renice setcap setfacl ssh sshd sudo sudoers file
systemctl tar top touch ufw umask umount uname vsftpd wget.

2

Applications of systemd for the Beginner

2.0 Objectives, Commands, and Primitives Covered

Objectives:

* Describe the systemd "superkernel," sub-commands, and applications
* Expose and emphasize the importance of systemd units and unit files
* Dissect the anatomy of a unit file, with a specific example
* Show how to create instance units from unit template files
* Describe systemd targets, their variety, and their utility
* Give a specific systemd target example – running a clock-time-based script
* Add to the repertoire of unit management commands
* Provide much additional practice with target units to the novice user
* Illustrate how to switch the system between important target states
* Expand our coverage of Linux cgroups, in the context of a systemd environment
* Briefly mention the Linux kernel namespace concept
* Define and expound upon the systemd journal daemon, journald
* How to view system logs with the journalctl command
* How to maintain the journal, and execute varieties of boot process querying
* Give further examples of systemd-controlled timers
* Illustrate the activation behavior of "new-style" daemons

To cover the Commands and primitives:

id -u, journalctl, ncat, nmap, systemctl, systemd-activate, systemd-cgls, systemd-socket-activate, who -r

DOI: 10.1201/b23405-3

2.1 Introduction – Applications of systemd for the Beginner

In this chapter, we give a novice user a brief, but useful, introduction to the Linux "superkernel" known as systemd. Unless that novice user, or even a more seasoned system professional, has not only a basic, but also a more complete knowledge of how systemd controls and oversees every process operation of a modern Linux system, they will never be able to master administrating and implementing the kind of functionality that their use case(s) might ultimately require. Particularly for the user base on the system, and the demands that the user base makes.

Everything illustrated in this chapter, in the specific form (and the syntax of commands) found here, is explicitly applicable to the Raspberry Pi OS.

The selective choices of subject matter are made according to the pedagogic needs of a beginner, as it follows from the system administration materials that precede it in the last chapter.

Anything that you are required to type on the command line is shown in **bold** type, always followed by pressing <Enter> on the keyboard.

2.2 Bootup in the Initial RAM Disk (initrd)

The initial RAM disk implementation (initrd) can also be set up using systemd, and follows a prescribed structure. initrd is a scheme for loading a root file system, from a variety of possible sources, into memory, and it is used as part of the Raspberry Pi OS startup process.

2.2.1 Querying the Boot Process

As shown in Section 2.6.2.6 Boot Process Querying, the systemd journald daemon and journal give you the ability to view log records of how the system boots. In particular, it allows you to look at a log record of the current boot process, and past boot processes, with some specific command line tools, options, and their arguments. We refer you to Section 2.6.2.6 for a more complete treatment of the systemd journal, and its capabilities with respect to booting logs.

2.3 systemd Units and Unit Files

Systemd unit files are one of the most critical and ubiquitous features of systemd that a beginner needs to understand. In this section, we discuss more of the lower-level functionality and application of systemd Units and Unit Files.

2.3.1 Introduction to Units and Unit Files

In systemd, a unit refers to an object that changes the characteristics of the steady state of the Raspberry Pi OS, or its normal operating condition. Units, and unit files, are the primary objects that systemd creates and manipulates, with user commands such as **systemctl**. These objects are configured with files called unit files. We will introduce you to the different units that systemd can handle. We will also be covering some of the many "directives" that can be put in unit files in order to configure the way these objects handle resources on your system.

2.3.2 Roles systemd Units Play

Units and unit files take on a very standardized format, which we describe in detail because they are the primary instrument of user functionality and control in systemd. They enable you to manage system resources, using the daemons, services, and utility commands shown in Figure 2.1. They are

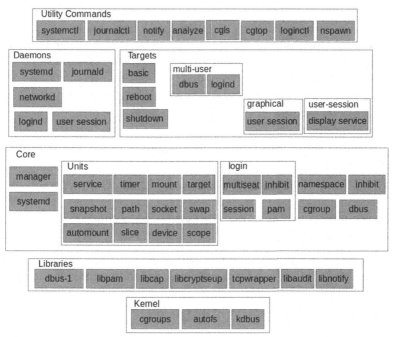

FIGURE 2.1
systemd Architecture.

found schematically on the first two top levels of that figure. We provide that figure for your reference as follows.

A unit works with and affects traditional system services, network resources, devices, file system mounts, resource pools known as Control Groups, and even very transient tasks such as single Linux commands.

Some of the key advantageous features that units have are:

1. socket-based activation: The delay of the start of service until activation of its socket(s). This feature is very crucial in making the system run faster and the startup process itself much faster.

2. D-bus-based activation: Units can be started when an associated bus is published.

3. path-based activation: A unit can be started based on activity on, or the availability of, certain file system paths.

4. udev device-based activation: The start of units can also be delayed until the first time a piece of hardware becomes available. This feature is also very crucial in making the system run faster, and startup much faster.

5. implicit dependency mapping: Most of the dependence between units, during their start time, can be built by systemd itself, although by editing and changing the dependencies between units, this can be modified by the user.

6. instances and templates: Template unit files can be used to create multiple instances of the same general unit. This is very critical and efficient in operating system virtualization via containers and virtual machines!

7. security: Units can implement security features, via the use of directives in the unit file.

8. drop-ins and snippets extensibility: Units can easily be extended by providing modifiers that will override parts of the system's unit file.

We address many of the above features in the following sections.

2.3.3 Unit File Locations in the File System and Editing or Modifying Them

Unit files are located in basically three different, very standardized locations in the Raspberry Pi OS file system structure, depending upon how important the unit file is.

Table 2.1 lists these default locations and gives a brief description of their utility.

Adding, or modifying a unit by editing it to modify the way that the unit functions, should be done by creating it in the /etc/systemd/system

TABLE 2.1

Unit File Locations

/etc/systemd/system	Place where unit files used to override default ones are stored.
/run/systemd/system	Middle-priority unit file location, the systemd process itself uses this location for dynamically created unit files created at runtime.
/lib/systemd/system	System copy where software using the unit file is installed. Also locates the default controlling unit file for the software.

directory. Unit files found in this directory location take precedence over any of the other locations.

If you need to modify the system's copy of a unit file, putting a replacement in this directory is the most reliable, safest, and flexible way to do this.

To override specific directives from the system's generic unit file, you create unit file "snippets", i.e., smaller versions, within a very standard and specific subdirectory. This will add to or modify the directives of the system's copy, allowing you to specify only the behavior of the unit you want to change. These systemd directives are what specify explicitly how the unit behaves.

To do this, you create a directory named after the unit file with .d appended to the name. For a unit called example.service, you create a subdirectory called example.service.d. Within this directory, a file ending with .conf can be used to override or add to the directives of the system's default unit file.

2.3.3.1 Editing Unit Files

Editing unit files is secondarily important to actually creating one from scratch, for a service that you want to create and run on the Raspberry Pi OS. We show how to create a unit file below. The premier systemd command, **systemctl**, provides options for editing and modifying unit files if you need to make adjustments. The **systemctl edit** command, by default, will open a unit file snippet for the unit in question.

For example, to further customize an nginx webserver service, which has a unit file automatically created by the Aptitude package manager when it is installed on the Raspberry Pi OS, you can use the following command:

$ **sudo systemctl edit nginx.service**

This will be a blank file that can be used to override or add directives on top of the existing service unit definition. A directory will be created within the /etc/systemd/system directory, which contains the name of the unit with .d appended. For instance, for the nginx.service, a directory called nginx. service.d will be created.

Within this directory, a snippet will be created called override.conf. When the unit is loaded, systemd will merge the override snippet with the full unit file. The snippet's directives will take precedence over those found in the original unit file.

To edit the full unit file, instead of creating a snippet, use the --full option:

$ **sudo systemctl edit --full nginx.service**

This will load the current unit file into the default editor, where it can be changed. When you exit the editor, the changed file will be written to /etc/systemd/system, which will take precedence over the system's unit definition found in /lib/systemd/system.

To remove any additions you have made, either delete the unit's .d configuration directory, or the modified service file from /etc/systemd/system. To remove a snippet, use the following command:

$ **sudo rm -r /etc/systemd/system/nginx.service.d**

To remove a full modified unit file, type:

$ **sudo rm /etc/systemd/system/nginx.service**

After deleting the file or directory, you should reload the systemd process so that it no longer attempts to reference these files and reverts back to using the system default copies.

You can do this with the following *very ubiquitous and critical command*:

$ **sudo systemctl daemon-reload**

In-Chapter Exercise

1. When you install the nginx Webserver, where does the installer locate the default copy of the service unit file? How did you find this out? If you haven't done the installation of nginx, either do that now, or answer this exercise with another service that you have installed.

2.3.4 Types of Units

systemd units, and the files that define them, are the primary mechanism that systemd uses to keep in control of system state. If you look at the suffix attached to a unit file, you can determine which of the twelve types of unit it is. The following list describes the types of units available to systemd:

1. service: A service unit, which we detail most extensively below, describes how to manage a service or application on the system. Important things like path to executable code, how the service starts or stops, when and how it should be automatically started, and dependencies and 'order-of-starting' information. These are also part of cgroup categories, as we detail in Section 2.6.1.

2. socket: This defines network, IPC socket, or a FIFO buffer, that are used for a socket-based activation, which we give examples of below. Socket-based activation means starting a service when the socket it's attached to sees traffic. This allows the starting of services in parallel, a very critical speedup procedure different from what has traditionally been available to init systems.

3. device: Describes a device that requires systemd management by udev, or the sysfs file system. Udev is a device manager for the Linux kernel, and manages device nodes in the /dev directory. Udev also manages user space events, and hardware devices that are added into the system or removed from it.

4. .mount: Defines mountpoints on the system. These are assigned names after the mount path, with slashes changed to dashes in those names.

5. .automount: Defines a mountpoint that is automatically assigned. These must be named after the mount point they refer to, and have a matching .mount unit to define the actual details of the mount.

6. swap: Defines swap space on the Raspberry Pi OS. The name of these units comes from the device name or file pathname of the swap space.

7. target: Provides a way of coordinating other units operations, when the system starts up, or when there are changes in the system's state. A good example, that we describe in Section 2.5.3, is going from the multi-user.target state to the graphical.target state, and vice versa. We cover much of what can be done with targets in this chapter.

8. path: Defines a path that can be used for path-based activation. Path-based activation allows the operating system to take action if a particular file, group of files, or directory gets modified or changed somehow.

9. .timer: We illustrate these in detail in Section 2.6.3. They define timing controls that systemd uses when controlling system state.

10. snapshot: Created automatically by the **systemctl snapshot** command. There is no unit file associated with snapshots. It allows you to reconstruct portions of the current state of the system after making changes. It is important to note that snapshots do *not* survive across reboots or restarts of the system and are used essentially to roll back to temporary system states during the current boot.

11. slice: Defined by Linux cgroup nodes, allowing system resources to be given to any processes associated with the named slice. These are also a crucial cgroup feature, detailed in Section 2.6.1.

12. scope: Created automatically by systemd, using information from its bus interfaces. These are also a crucial cgroup feature, detailed in Section 2.6.1.

We will mainly be focusing on .service unit files, and their editing and creation, for the ordinary user of a Raspberry Pi system. This is due to the fact that they are most useful for an ordinary user, and the use cases she might put the system to. We will also detail, to some extent, their use by an appointed system administrator to manage the state of the system in general. Aside from .service unit files, all of the other unit file types are basically coordinating and synchronization tools, that link services to hardware, cgroups, IPC sockets, timing constraints, etc. This coordination and synchronization is the hallmark and greatest advantage systemd has, and its major advantage over any older UNIX or Linux init system(s).

2.3.5 Anatomy of a Unit File

The internal structure of unit files is segregated into sections. Sections are delimited by a pair of square brackets "[" and "]", with the section name enclosed in the brackets. Each section extends until the beginning of the next section or until the end of the file.

2.3.5.1 An Example Service Unit File – ssh.service

It would be very instructive at this point to show the structure, and the exact contents of a typical service unit file. Figure 2.2 shows the contents of the ssh unit file on our Raspberry Pi system, found in /lib/systemd/system. You should carefully look at this figure while reading an actual service unit file (perhaps the ssh service file on your system) for comparison.

2.3.5.2 The General Format of Unit Files

As seen in Figure 2.2, the sample file is divided into sections. Section names are case-sensitive, and enclosed in square brackets []. Within each section, the way the unit works and stores data is done using standard, simple directives, with allowed values assigned as follows:

```
In any section:
[Section]
Directive=value
Directive=value
```

If you use an override file, as is explained when editing the unit file in Section 2.3.3, directives are reset by assigning them to an empty string or null string. For example, the system's copy of a unit file could have a directive set to a value as follows:

```
Directive=default_value
```

```
[Unit]
Description=OpenBSD Secure Shell server
Documentation=man:sshd(8) man:sshd_config(5)
After=network.target auditd.service
ConditionPathExists=!/etc/ssh/sshd_not_to_be_run

[Service]
EnvironmentFile=-/etc/default/ssh
ExecStartPre=/usr/sbin/sshd -t
ExecStart=/usr/sbin/sshd -D $SSHD_OPTS
ExecReload=/usr/sbin/sshd -t
ExecReload=/bin/kill -HUP $MAINPID
KillMode=process
Restart=on-failure
RestartPreventExitStatus=255
Type=notify
RuntimeDirectory=sshd
RuntimeDirectoryMode=0755

[Install]
WantedBy=multi-user.target
Alias=sshd.service
```

FIGURE 2.2

ssh Unit File Example.

The default_value can be eliminated in an override file by referencing the directive without a value, like this:

Directive=

2.3.5.3 ssh Example Unit, Service, and Install Sections Directives

This section details the specific directives for the three sections of the ssh example unit file shown in Figure 2.2.

[Unit] Section Directives

The first section found in the ssh.service unit file is the [Unit] section. This is generally used for defining metadata for the unit and configuring the relationship of the unit to other units.

Although section order does not matter to systemd when reading the file, this section is traditionally placed at the top because it provides an overview of the unit. The particular directives that are in the [Unit] section are:

1. Description=**OpenBSD Secure Shell server**
   Describes the name and basic functioning of the unit. It's used by various systemd tools.

1.a. Documentation=**man:sshd(8) man:sshd_config(5)**
This directive names existing man pages that describe **ssh**, and the **sshd** daemon.

2. After=network.target auditd.service
Units Ithat will will be started <u>before</u> starting the current unit.

3. ConditionPathExists=**!/etc/ssh/sshd_not_to_be_run**
This can be used to provide a generic unit file that will only be run on appropriate systems. If the condition is not met, the unit is skipped.

[Service] Section Directives
The [Service] section provides a configuration that is only applicable for services.

The basic thing that should be specified in the [Service] section is the Type= of the service. This categorizes services by their process and behavior as a daemon. This is important because it tells systemd how to correctly manage the service and find out its state.

1.   EnvironmentFile=**-/etc/default/ssh**
Reads the environment variables for the unit from a text file. The text file should contain new-line-separated variable assignments. Lines without a "=" separator, or lines starting with; or # will be ignored as comments. A line ending with a backslash will be continued on the following one.

2.a. ExecStartPre=**/usr/sbin/sshd -t**
Additional commands that are executed before or after the command in ExecStart=, respectively. Syntax is the same as for ExecStart=, except that multiple command lines are allowed, and the commands are executed one after the other, serially.

2.b. ExecStart=**/usr/bin/sshd –D $SSHD_OPTS**
Probably the most critical directive! It designates the full path and the possible arguments of the command to be executed to start the process. This may only be specified once (except for "oneshot" services).

3.   ExecReload=**/bin/kill –HUP $MAINPID**
This optional directive indicates the command necessary to reload the configuration of the service if available. One additional, special environment variable is set: if known, $MAINPID is set to the main process of the daemon, and may be used for command lines.

4.   KillMode=**process**
Designates how processes associated with this unit shall be killed.

5. Restart=**on-failure**

Indicates how systemd will attempt to automatically restart the service. Allowable values are "always", "on-success", "on-failure", "on-abnormal", "on-abort", or "on-watchdog".

6. RestartPreventExitStatus=**255**

Lists exit status definitions, when returned by the main service process, prevent automatic service restarts, no matter what the restart setting configured, with Restart=. Exit status definitions are numeric exit codes, or termination signal names, separated by spaces.

7. Type=**notify**

Establishes the process start-up type for this service unit, within certain constraints. That type can be: simple, forking, oneshot, dbus, notify, or idle.

8. RuntimeDirectory=**sshd**

Take as argument(s) a space character-separated list of directory names. The directory names are relative, and may not include the designation of parent directory (..).

9. RuntimeDirectoryMode=**0755**

Designates the access mode of the directories specified in RuntimeDirectory=, StateDirectory=,

CacheDirectory=, LogsDirectory=, or ConfigurationDirectory=, as an octal number. Defaults to 0755.

[Install] Section Directives

The last section found in the ssh.service unit file is the [Install] section. This section is optional. It is used to configure extra features of a unit that will either enable or disable it. *A unit can be automatically started at boot with directives in this section.*

1. WantedBy=**multi-user.target**

The WantedBy= directive is the most common way to specify how a unit is enabled. It is similar to the Wants= directive in the [Unit] section. When a unit with this directive is enabled, a directory is created within /etc/systemd/system named after the specified unit with **.wants** appended to the name. A symbolic link to the current unit is created, creating the dependency. If the current unit has WantedBy=multi-user.target, a directory called multi-user.target.wants is created within /etc/systemd/system (if it's not already there), and a symbolic link to the current unit is placed within that directory. Disabling this unit removes the link and removes the dependency . relationship.

2.   Alias=**sshd.service**

Allows the unit to be enabled under another name, or alias.

2.3.5.4 Additional Unit File Sections and Their Unit-Specific Section Directives

As can be seen in our ssh service unit file example in Section 2.3.5.2, the Service Section is found between the Unit Section and the Install Section.

In a more complex unit file, the following sections are found between the Unit and Install Sections. Note that among the 12 unit types, most contain directives that only apply to their type.

The following brief listings provide references for additional critical values assigned to directives in those sections:

The [Socket] Section
Socket unit files are configured because, as seen in many sections and problems we present below, many services implement socket-based activation to achieve system parallelization and speed.

Note that each socket unit must have a matching service unit that will be activated when the socket receives activity.

Perhaps the hallmark of systemd control, the methods of socket control simplify and enhance an administrator's ability to oversee everything that is happening on the computer. By default, the socket name will attempt to start the service of the same name upon receiving a connection. When the service is initialized, the socket will be passed to it, allowing it to begin processing any requests.

To specify the actual socket, the premier directive is ListenStream=,which defines an address for a stream socket, and which supports socket IPC communication. Services that use TCP generally use this unit type.

The [Timer] Section
This section is used to schedule system events. At some specific time, either measured on a clock, on the calendar, or after a certain delay. This unit file type is meant to replace the traditional function of the cron daemon. A unit file, such as a service unit, must be created, to be activated when the timer is "triggers"!

The [Timer] section of a unit file contains the directive "Unit=", which specifies the unit that should be activated when the timer signals the event.

2.3.6 Creating Instance Units from Template Unit Files

For an ordinary user, template unit files let you reproduce a unit file several times, to get multiple copies of it (which you can slightly modify for each copy).

The primary commercial reason for using template unit files, and their mechanisms, is to run multiple containers on a server.
For example, when you want to have many services listen on many sockets or ports at the same time, you could run multiple instances of the service as separate isolated virtual machines or container environments, each with a different name, and each using different ephemeral ports they are listening on.

You must map these virtual machine or container's ports to network-facing IP addresses.

These could be public-facing network addresses assigned by a DHCP server, rather than private addresses, as is used primarily by container software such as Docker.

2.3.6.1 Template and Instance Unit Names for Services

A template unit file contains an @ symbol after the name, and before the type.

In-Chapter Exercise

2.   Find an example of a template unit file on your Raspberry Pi OS.

2.4 Targets

Targets, or target units, are the same as all other systemd unit types. They collect units together using dependencies (for changes in state such as booting or shutdown), and create standard, or user-defined names, for synchronization of dependencies between units.

As an example of their use, the processes that start up the system and shut it down are used by systemd with the sequential (not hard-wired) use of target units.

2.4.1 Basic Target Concepts

systemd can boot, do system service management, and perform other functions for the Raspberry Pi OS by using standard and named target units. For example, the target graphical.target provides a multiuser system with

TABLE 2.2

systemd Important Targets

default.target	The target that is booted by default. Not a real target, but a symbolic link to another target like graphical.target.
emergency.target	Starts an emergency shell on the console. Only used at the boot prompt as systemd.unit=emergency.target.
graphical.target	The default target in a desktop system GUI installation. Starts a system with network, multiuser support, and a display manager.
halt.target	Shuts down the system.
multi-user.target	Starts a multiuser system with network.
reboot.target	Reboots the system.
rescue.target	Starts a single-user system without network.

network connectivity *and* a graphical display manager. An interdependent set of units with unit dependencies can group controls related to system state, and provides a way of establishing custom system state controls.

Table 2.2 shows some critical systemd target units.

Following are listings and descriptions of some other special system target units. For a full list, refer to the man page on your system for systemd.special. Incidentally, these target states are the equivalents of "run levels" found in the older legacy Linux init system(s).

basic.target

A special target unit that does the basic boot-up operation. systemd automatically adds dependencies of the types Requires= and After= for this target unit. This starts all local mount points plus /var, /tmp and /var/tmp, swap devices, sockets, timers, path units, and other initialization processes necessary for necessary daemons.

ctrl-alt-del.target

This target starts whenever Control+Alt+Del is pressed on the console. It's aliased through a symbolic link to reboot.target.

default.target

The bootup default systemd unit. It's aliased through a symbolic link to multi-user.target or graphical.target.

emergency.target

The special target unit that starts an emergency shell on the main console. Similar to rescue.target, but which also starts the most basic services and mounts all file systems.

exit.target

The special service unit for shutting down the system, or the user service manager.

final.target

Target that is used during system shutdown and may be used to start late services after all normal services are already terminated and all mounts unmounted.

graphical.target

A special target unit for graphical login and operation, the default target on Raspberry Pi systems that use a GUI-based desktop.

Note
This target requires multi-user.target as a dependency.

halt.target

Target unit for shutting down and halting the system.

kexec.target

Target unit for shutting down and rebooting the system via kexec.

multi-user.target

Target unit for setting up a multi-user system with a text-only console interface.
    Primarily used in server machines. This target is a dependency required by graphical.target.

poweroff.target

Target unit for shutting down and powering off the system.

reboot.target

Target unit for shutting down and rebooting the system.

rescue.target

Target unit that starts the base system processes (including the system mount points.) and starts a rescue shell.

shutdown.target

Target unit that stops all services upon system shutdown.

slices.target

Target unit that establishes all slice units that become active after booting.

sockets.target

Target unit that configures all socket units that become active after booting.

sysinit.target

Target that starts the services needed for system initialization.

system-update.target

Target unit that manages off-line system updates.

timers.target

Target unit that manages all timers that become active after booting.

umount.target

Target unit that unmounts all mount points and automount points upon system shutdown.

2.4.2 A Target Example: Clock-Time-Based Running of a Script File

Question:　Why would you want to do this, as an ordinary user?

Answer:　Because at some particular time of the day, you want the system to automatically backup critical directories and files on designated media, via some automating shell script, like Bash, or perhaps a Python3 script file.

"Monotonic Scheduling" of events can be thought of as basing an event happening on the system in clock time. Clock time is designated in minutes, hours, days, weeks, etc. The following example creates a timer unit that relies on a specific target unit to execute a script file on a *daily* basis. The service which needs to be run daily can be designated as a dependency of this target.

The script file, which is named **your_script**, is made into a service, via the creation of a service unit file. **your_script** can have arguments when it is run, as shown below. Also, you must set the permissions on **your_script**, with **chmod 755**, so that it will execute properly when it is a service!

To get more information about how systemd specifies the time, see the man page for systemd.time.

1. Use the following command to create a directory that will hold the calendar-based timer unit:

```
$ sudo mkdir /etc/systemd/system/timer_daily.target.wants
```

2. The following timer unit file will need to be created, using the nano text editor, in the path specified below:

   $ **sudo nano /etc/systemd/system/timer_daily.timer**

   ```
   [Unit]
   Description=Daily Timer for Events

   [Timer]
   OnBootSec=5min
   OnUnitActiveSec=1d
   Unit=timer_daily.target

   [Install]
   WantedBy=basic.target
   ```

3. Create the target unit, with the nano text editor, in the specified directory:

   $ **sudo** nano /etc/systemd/system/timer_daily.target

   ```
   [Unit]
   Description=Daily Timer Target
   StopWhenUnneeded=yes
   ```

4. Now that we have a timer unit and timer target file created, adding events to this target involves placing an event into the /etc/systemd/system/timer_daily.target.wants folder.

   For any particular event to take place daily, create a service unit file for the particular event in the /etc/systemd/system/timer_daily.target.wants folder.

   For example, if you wish to run your_script.service daily (which for example, runs a Bash script named your_script), create the following file with the nano text editor:

   $ **sudo nano /etc/systemd/system/timer_daily.target.wants/your_\
   script.service**
   ```
   [Unit]
   Description=Whatever your script file does

   [Service]
   User=bob
   Type=Simple
   Nice=19
   IOSchedulingClass=2
   IOSchedulingPriority=7
   ExecStart=/home/bob/your_script -arg1 -arg2
   ```

   Use more ExecStart lines in the above file if you want to start more than one event daily.

5. Start and enable the daily timer:

    $ **sudo systemctl start timer_daily.timer**
    $ **sudo systemctl enable timer_daily.timer**

In-Chapter Exercise

3. Using the five previously mentioned steps, take a Bash script of your own, and have systemd execute it daily.

2.4.3 Unit Management with Additional Commands

So far, we have been working with services and displaying information about the unit and unit files that systemd is maintaining. However, we can find out more specific information about units using some additional commands. The following topics provide that specific information, by using the commands shown.

Displaying a Unit File
To display the unit file that systemd has loaded into its system, you can use the cat command. For example, to see the unit file for the sshd daemon, type the following:

```
$ sudo systemctl cat sshd
# /lib/systemd/system/ssh.service
[Unit]
Description=OpenBSD Secure Shell server
Documentation=man:sshd(8) man:sshd_config(5)
After=network.target auditd.service
ConditionPathExists=!/etc/ssh/sshd_not_to_be_run

[Service]
EnvironmentFile=-/etc/default/ssh
ExecStartPre=/usr/sbin/sshd -t
ExecStart=/usr/sbin/sshd -D $SSHD_OPTS
ExecReload=/usr/sbin/sshd -t
ExecReload=/bin/kill -HUP $MAINPID
KillMode=process
Restart=on-failure
RestartPreventExitStatus=255
Type=notify
RuntimeDirectory=sshd
RuntimeDirectoryMode=0755

[Install]
WantedBy=multi-user.target
Alias=sshd.service
$
```

The output is the unit file as available to the currently running systemd process. This can be critical if you have recently modified unit files or are overriding certain options in a unit file installed and built by the package management system.

Displaying Dependencies
To see a unit's dependency tree, you can use the list-dependencies command:

$ **sudo systemctl list-dependencies sshd.service**

This will display a hierarchy mapping the dependencies that must be dealt with in order to start the unit in question. Dependencies, in this context, include those units that are either required by or wanted by the units above it.

```
sshd.service
● ├─.mount
● ├─system.slice
● ├─sysinit.target
● │ ├─apparmor.service
● │ ├─dev-hugepages.mount
● │ ├─dev-mqueue.mount
● │ ├─fake-hwclock.service
● │ ├─keyboard-setup.service
● │ ├─kmod-static-nodes.service
● │ ├─plymouth-read-write.service
● │ ├─plymouth-start.service
● │ ├─proc-sys-fs-binfmt_misc.automount
● │ ├─sys-fs-fuse-connections.mount
● │ ├─sys-kernel-config.mount
● │ ├─sys-kernel-debug.mount
● │ ├─sys-kernel-tracing.mount
● │ ├─systemd-ask-password-console.path
● │ ├─systemd-binfmt.service
● │ ├─systemd-boot-system-token.service
● │ ├─systemd-hwdb-update.service
● │ ├─systemd-journal-flush.service
● │ ├─systemd-journald.service
● │ ├─systemd-machine-id-commit.service
● │ ├─systemd-modules-load.service
● │ ├─systemd-pstore.service
● │ ├─systemd-random-seed.service
● │ ├─systemd-sysctl.service
● │ ├─systemd-sysusers.service
● │ ├─systemd-timesyncd.service
● │ ├─systemd-tmpfiles-setup-dev.service
● │ ├─systemd-tmpfiles-setup.service
● │ ├─systemd-udev-trigger.service
● │ ├─systemd-udevd.service
● │ ├─systemd-update-utmp.service
● │ ├─cryptsetup.target
● │ └─local-fs.target
```

-     ├─.mount
-     ├─boot.mount
-     ├─systemd-fsck-root.service
-     └─systemd-remount-fs.service
-     └─swap.target

The recursive dependencies are only displayed for .target units, which indicate system states. To recursively list all dependencies, include the --all flag.

To show reverse dependencies (units that depend on the specified unit), you can add the – reverse flag to the command. Other flags that are useful are the - - before and - - after flags, which can be used to show units that depend on the specified unit starting before and after themselves, respectively.

Checking Unit Properties
To see the low-level properties of a unit, you can use the show command. This will display a list of properties that are set for the specified unit using a key=value format:

$ sudo systemctl show sshd.service
```
Type=notify
Restart=on-failure
NotifyAccess=main
RestartUSec=100ms
TimeoutStartUSec=1min 30s
TimeoutStopUSec=1min 30s
RuntimeMaxUSec=infinity
WatchdogUSec=0
WatchdogTimestamp=Mon 2016-08-08 15:51:56 PDT
WatchdogTimestampMonotonic=8131498
FailureAction=none
PermissionsStartOnly=no
RootDirectoryStartOnly=no
RemainAfterExit=no
GuessMainPID=yes
MainPID=914
```

Output truncated...

If you want to display a single property, you can use the -p flag with the property name. For example, to see the conflicts that the sshd.service unit has, you can type:

$ sudo systemctl show sshd.service -p Conflicts
```
Conflicts=shutdown.target
$
```

Masking and Unmasking Units
systemd has the ability to mark a unit as completely unstartable, automatically or manually, by linking it to /dev/null. This is called "masking" the unit, and is done with the mask command:

$ sudo systemctl mask nginx.service

This will prevent the nginx service from being started, automatically or manually, for as long as it is masked.

If you check the list-unit-files, you will see the service is now listed as masked:

$ sudo systemctl list-unit-files

If you attempt to start the service, you will see a message like this:

$ sudo systemctl start nginx.service
Failed to start nginx.service: Unit nginx.service is masked.
$

To unmask a unit, making it available for use again, simply use the unmask command:

$ sudo systemctl unmask nginx.service

This will return the unit to its previous state, allowing it to be started or enabled.

Editing Unit Files
While the specific format for all unit files is outside of the scope of this chapter, systemctl provides several built-in mechanisms for editing and modifying unit files if you need to change them. The edit command, by default, will open a unit file snippet for the unit in question:

$ sudo systemctl edit nginx.service

This will be a blank file that can be used to override or add directives to the unit definition. A directory will be created within the /etc/systemd/system directory, which contains the name of the unit with .d appended. For instance, for the nginx.service, a directory called nginx.service.d will be created.

Within this directory, a snippet will be created called override.conf. When the unit is loaded, systemd will, in memory, merge the override snippet with the full unit file. The snippet's directives will take precedence over those found in the original unit file.

If you wish to edit the full unit file instead of creating a snippet, you can pass the --full flag:

$ sudo systemctl edit --full nginx.service

This will load the current unit file into the default editor, where it can be modified. On our Raspberry Pi system, the default editor was nano. When you save and exit the editor, the saved file will be written to /etc/systemd/system, which will take precedence over the system's unit definition, found in /lib/systemd/system.

To remove any changes you made, either delete the unit's .d configuration directory or the modified service file from /etc/systemd/system. For example, to remove a snippet, we could type:

$ **sudo rm -r /etc/systemd/system/nginx.service.d**

To remove a full modified unit file, we would type:

$ **sudo rm /etc/systemd/system/nginx.service**

After deleting the file or directory, you should reload the systemd process so that it no longer tries to reference these files and reverts back to using the system copies. The following command does this:

$ **sudo systemctl daemon-reload**

In-Chapter Exercise

4. To get practice with the service management commands presented in the above section, execute them on your system, using the nginx service rather than sshd.

2.5 Practicing on Target Units

Systemd "target" states are instanced by target unit text files. Target units filenames end with the .target file extension, and are used to basically collect and create other systemd units through dependencies.

The graphical.target unit, which is used to instantiate or create a GUI session as a Raspberry Pi desktop system, starts many other system services on our Raspberry Pi system. It also starts the multi-user.target unit, because that target is a dependency of graphical.target. The multi-user.target unit starts many other critical system services, such as NetworkManager (NetworkManager.service,) or D-Bus (dbus.service), and is, or becomes, a milestone target unit.

2.5.1 Viewing the Default Target

To find out which target unit is the final target which determines the operating state of the system, you can use the following command:

$ **sudo systemctl get-default**
graphical.target
$

This executes the symbolic link located at /etc/systemd/system/default. target, and displays the result.

Note

The default target unit can be different from the current target that defines the current state of the system!

2.5.2 Viewing All Targets

To list all currently loaded target units, use the following:

$ **sudo systemctl list-units --type target**

For each target unit, this command displays its full name (UNIT) followed by a note on whether the unit has been loaded (LOAD), its high-level (ACTIVE) and low-level (SUB) unit activation state, and a short description (DESCRIPTION).

By default, the systemctl list-units command displays only active units. If you want to list all loaded units regardless of their state, run this command with the --all or -a command line option:

$ **sudo systemctl list-units --type target --all**

When we executed this command on our Raspberry Pi Os system, we got the following output:

$ **systemctl list-units --type target --all**

UNIT	LOAD	ACTIVE	SUB	DESCRIPTION
basic.target	loaded	active	active	Basic System
cryptsetup.target	loaded	active	active	Encrypted Volumes
emergency.target	loaded	inactive	dead	Emergency Mode
getty.target	loaded	active	active	Login Prompts
graphical.target	loaded	active	active	Graphical Interface
local-fs-pre.target	loaded	active	active	Local File Systems (Pre)
local-fs.target	loaded	active	active	Local File Systems
multi-user.target	loaded	active	active	Multi-User System
network-online.target	loaded	active	active	Network is Online
network-pre.target	loaded	active	active	Network (Pre)
network.target	loaded	active	active	Network
nfs-client.target	loaded	active	active	NFS client services
nss-user-lookup.target	loaded	active	active	User and Group Name Lookups
paths.target	loaded	active	active	Paths
remote-fs-pre.target	loaded	active	active	Remote File Systems (Pre)
remote-fs.target	loaded	active	active	Remote File Systems
rescue.target	loaded	inactive	dead	Rescue Mode
rpcbind.target	loaded	inactive	dead	RPC Port Mapper
shutdown.target	loaded	inactive	dead	Shutdown
slices.target	loaded	active	active	Slices
sockets.target	loaded	active	active	Sockets
swap.target	loaded	active	active	Swap

sysinit.target	loaded	active	active System Initialization
• syslog.target	not-found		inactive dead syslog.target
time-sync.target	loaded	active	active System Time Synchronized
timers.target	loaded	active	active Timers
umount.target	loaded	inactive	dead Unmount All Filesystems
zfs.target	loaded	active	active ZFS startup target

LOAD   = Reflects whether the unit definition was properly loaded.
ACTIVE = The high-level unit activation state, i.e. generalization of SUB.
SUB   = The low-level unit activation state, values depend on unit type.

28 loaded units listed.
To show all installed unit files use 'systemctl list-unit-files'.
$

2.5.2.1 Viewing the Currently Loaded Targets

To list all currently loaded target units, use the following command:

$ sudo systemctl list-units --type target

The following command illustrates the systemd logging facility (which has effectively replaced older, more traditional logging mechanisms) known as *journald*. The command that displays various aspects of systemd-style logging is the **journalctl** command. We describe journalctl in detail in Section 2.6.2. To use journalctl, along with the **grep** command, to list the current target, type the following:

$ sudo journalctl | grep Reached | tail -3
Apr 24 10:14:20 raspberrypi systemd[1]: Reached target Graphical Interface.
Apr 27 06:14:07 raspberrypi systemd[765]: Reached target Printer.
Apr 27 06:14:07 raspberrypi systemd[1]: Reached target Printer.
$

The output of the above command shows the current target unit and the two previous to it.

2.5.3 Changing the Current Target by Isolating Targets

It is possible to start all of the units associated with a target at once, and stop all units that are not part of the dependency tree for that target. This is similar to changing the runlevel in older, legacy init systems.

For instance, if you are operating in a GUI environment, with graphical. target currently defining the system state, you can shut down the graphical system, and put the system into a multi-user, Character User Interface (CUI) state by what is termed "isolating" the multi-user.target. This is achieved with the **isolate** command. Since graphical.target (lower down on the dependency tree) depends on multi-user.target, all of the graphical units below multi-user.target will be terminated.

But you need to look very carefully at the dependencies of the target you are isolating before doing this, to make sure that you are not stopping vital system services, that would make the system unuseable. To do this, use the following command:

$ **sudo systemctl list-dependencies multi-user.target**

To switch over to a different target unit in the current session, type the following command:

$ **sudo systemctl isolate name.target**

Replace **name** with the name of the target unit you want to use (for example, multi-user). This command starts the target unit named multi-user.target, and all dependent units, and immediately terminates all other units. To turn off the graphical user interface and change to the multi-user.target unit in the current session, type the following command:

$ **sudo systemctl isolate multi-user.target**

Note and Caveat
Note: When you execute this command, make sure that you don't have running programs, such as an opened document in LibreOffice! Switching target states will terminate those running programs ungracefully, and, in the case of LibreOffice, will require you to recover those documents.
Caveat: After executing the above command on our Raspberry Pi system, at the time of the writing of this book, it was necessary to change the virtual terminal to another virtual terminal (tty1 through 7 were the possibilities), such as tty1 by holding down the following keystroke sequence at one time

<Ctrl>+<Alt>+F1

where **F1** represents the function key F1 on your keyboard.
You are then logged into the system now running in the multi-user.target state, in a text-only, Character User Interface (CUI). This caveat was necessary because the active graphical display manager (lightdm), and the normal virtual terminal for display of X Window System programs on our desktop, did not hook up tty7 (the default screen display in a graphical.target state) to the display screen! So we simply switched our virtual display to tty2 with the keystroke sequence above to facilitate the target isolation.
After we tried the next command:

$ **sudo systemctl isolate graphical.target**

on our system, the display switched to graphical.target automatically after a few seconds.

So, to switch back to a graphical.target state, type the following command:

$ **sudo systemctl isolate graphical.target**

Question: If you hold down **<Ctrl>+<Alt>+F2** while the graphical.target is active (i.e., you have a desktop environment on-screen) and switch to a virtual terminal (tty 2), have you switched to the multi-user.target as well? And what command or commands would show you the savings in system resources by shifting to a multi-user.target state versus being in the graphical. target state?

Answer: No, the way to conserve system resources is to use **sudo systemctl isolate multi-user.target**. Just switching to another tty, and even logging in there, doesn't effect the target state the system is in, or the number of resources used by services in that target state. And of the commands like **ps -aux | less**, **htop, top**, our favorite is the **pstree** command. It shows the significant differences in running processes for the multi-user.target and graphical. target states. Of course, Webmin also achieves that.

2.5.3.1 Changing the Default Target

To have the system use a different default target unit when it starts up, type the following command:

$ **sudo systemctl set-default name.target**

Substitute **name** with the name of the target unit you want to be the new default (such as multi-user). This replaces the /etc/systemd/system/ default.target file with a symbolic link to /usr/lib/systemd/system/name. target, where **name** is the name of the target unit you want to have be the new default.

To configure the system to use the multi-user.target unit by default, type the following command:

$ **sudo systemctl set-default multi-user.target**

After a restart of the system, you will exclusively be able to login via a text-only, CUI. To permanently change back to a graphical.target state at restart, type the following command:

$ **sudo systemctl set-default graphical.target**

2.5.4 Changing to Rescue Mode

An ordinary, unprivileged user of a Raspberry Pi system would not have recourse to use the commands found in this section, and the following section. Most of the time, the system is operating normally, and also starts up normally.

Rescue mode allows a valuable, single-user environment to be in place to repair the system, when it is unable to complete the regular Boot and Startup processes. In rescue mode, the system attempts to mount all local file systems and start some important system services, but it does *not* activate any network interfaces, or allow multiple users to be logged into the system at the same time.

To change the current target and enter rescue mode in the current session, type the following command:

$ sudo systemctl rescue
Welcome to rescue mode! After logging in, type
journalctl -xb to view system logs,
systemctl reboot to reboot,
systemctl default or the key combination <Ctrl>+D to boot into default mode:
Give root password for maintenance (or press <Ctrl>+D to continue):

This command is similar to **systemctl isolate rescue.target**, but it also sends a warning message to all users that are currently logged into the system. To prevent systemd from sending this message, type this command with the --no-wall command option:

$ sudo systemctl --no-wall rescue

2.5.5 Changing to Emergency Mode

Emergency mode is exactly the state it sounds like – the most minimal environment possible that allows for the repair of the system. Even, believe it or not, in instances when the system is unable to enter rescue mode itself! In emergency mode, the system mounts the root file system in read-only mode and does not attempt to mount any other local file systems. Like rescue mode, it does not activate network interfaces and only starts a few essential services.

To change the away from the current target, and enter emergency mode, type the following command:

$ sudo systemctl emergency
Welcome to emergency mode!
After logging in, type journalctl -xb to view system logs,
systemctl reboot to reboot,
systemctl default or <Ctrl>+D to boot into default mode.
Give root password for maintenance (or press Control-D to continue):

This command is similar to **systemctl isolate emergency.target**, but it can also send an informative message to all users that are currently logged into the system. To prevent systemd from sending this message, run this command with the --no-wall command line option:

$ **sudo systemctl --no-wall emergency**

The above two sections, which allow you to change the system state to rescue or emergency modes, are most likely to be used when the system is not working correctly, or when there is a performance-oriented problem. But then what does an ordinary user do when a normal boot into either multi-user. target or graphical.target cannot be done at all, for whatever reason? There are several options, which we do not cover here in detail, to interrupt the boot process, or boot into previous kernel versions. A listing of these situations is as follows:

a. Power or hardware-related issues.

b. Entering GRUB2 recovery mode.

c. Booting into previous "boot environments."

d. If using the Zettabyte File System(ZFS) on zpools, using ZFS Recovery Mode.

2.5.6 Practice in Working with Targets

Following is a short command line practice session that allows you to work with the **systemctl** command, and the important options shown in the preceding sections, to effect systemd target states.

1. Check the default systemd.target:

    $ **sudo systemctl get-default**
    graphical.target
    $

2. List the target units, and determine the current systemd target with the Linux multiple command joining **who -r** with options, and **grep**:

    $ sudo systemctl list-units --type=target |grep active |egrep "graphical|multi|re\
       scue|emergency"
    graphical.target loaded active active Graphical Interface
    multi-user.target loaded active active Multi-User System

The following command checks the target state we are currently in:

$ **sudo who -r**
   run-level 5 2017-08-10 13:50
$

Note
The legacy run-level 5 designation corresponds to the graphical.target state.

3. Now we can change the systemd target to multi-user.target, use the multiple command **systemctl list-units**, conjoining **grep** and **egrep** to check units availability and status, and finally, the who -r command to find the run level:

$ **sudo systemctl set-default multi-user.target**

Removed symlink /etc/systemd/system/default.target.
Created symlink from /etc/systemd/system/default.target to /lib/systemd/system/multi-user.target.

```
$ sudo systemctl list-units --type=target | grep active | egrep "graphical|multi\
|rescue|emergency"
graphical.target loaded active active Graphical Interface
multi-user.target   loaded active Multi-User System
$ sudo who -r
   run-level 5  2022-11-15 06:37
$
```

Dependencies between targets imply one systemd target can be part of another systemd target. Both graphical. target includes multi-user.target, and multi-user.target depend on various other targets. Now check the systemd target dependencies using the following **systemctl list-dependencies** command, which checks the dependencies for systemd multi-user.target:

```
$ sudo systemctl list-dependencies multi-user.target |grep target
multi-user.target
●  ├─basic.target
●  │ ├─paths.target
●  │ ├─slices.target
●  │ ├─sockets.target
●  │ ├─sysinit.target
●  │ │ ├─cryptsetup.target
●  │ │ ├─local-fs.target
●  │ │ └─swap.target
●  │ └─timers.target
●  ├─getty.target
●  ├─nfs-client.target
●  │ └─remote-fs-pre.target
●  ├─remote-fs.target
●  │ └─nfs-client.target
●  │   └─remote-fs-pre.target
●  └─zfs.target
●  ├─zfs-import.target
●  └─zfs-volumes.target
$
```

To list the available systemd targets on the system, use the following command:

$ sudo systemctl list-units --type=target

UNIT	LOAD	ACTIVE	SUB	DESCRIPTION
basic.target	loaded	active	active	Basic System
cryptsetup.target	loaded	active	active	Local Encrypted Volumes
getty.target	loaded	active	active	Login Prompts
graphical.target	loaded	active	active	Graphical Interface
local-fs-pre.target	loaded	active	active	Local File Systems (Pre)
local-fs.target	loaded	active	active	Local File Systems
multi-user.target	loaded	active	active	Multi-User System
network-online.target	loaded	active	active	Network is Online
network.target	loaded	active	active	Network
nfs-client.target	loaded	active	active	NFS client services
paths.target	loaded	active	active	Paths
remote-fs-pre.target	loaded	active	active	Remote File Systems (Pre)
remote-fs.target	loaded	active	active	Remote File Systems
slices.target	loaded	active	active	Slices
sockets.target	loaded	active	active	Sockets
swap.target	loaded	active	active	Swap
sysinit.target	loaded	active	active	System Initialization
time-set.target	loaded	active	active	System Time Set
time-sync.target	loaded	active	active	System Time Synchronized
timers.target	loaded	active	active	Timers
zfs-import.target	loaded	active	active	ZFS pool import target
zfs-volumes.target	loaded	active	active	ZFS volumes are ready
zfs.target	loaded	active	active	ZFS startup target

LOAD = Reflects whether the unit definition was properly loaded.
ACTIVE = The high-level unit activation state, i.e. generalization of SUB.
SUB = The low-level unit activation state, values depend on unit type.
23 loaded units listed. Pass --all to see loaded but inactive units, too.
To show all installed unit files use 'systemctl list-unit-files'.

4. Reboot the system using the **systemctl reboot** command. Since we set the default systemd target to multi-user.target, the system will restart into that target state.

   $ sudo systemctl reboot
   Output truncated...

5. Once the system has restarted, check the systemd target units and the currently active target state.

**$ sudo systemctl list-units --type=target |grep active |egrep "graphical|multi|r\
escue|emergency"**

basic.target	loaded active active	Basic System
cryptsetup.target	loaded active active	Encrypted Volumes
getty.target	loaded active active	Login Prompts
local-fs-pre.target	loaded active active	Local File Systems (Pre)
local-fs.target	loaded active active	Local File Systems

mail-transport-agent.target	loaded active active Mail Transport Agent
multi-user.target	loaded active active Multi-User System
network-online.target	loaded active active Network is Online
network-pre.target	loaded active active Network (Pre)
network.target	loaded active active Network
paths.target	loaded active active Paths
remote-fs-pre.target	loaded active active Remote File Systems (Pre)
remote-fs.target	loaded active active Remote File Systems
slices.target	loaded active active Slices
sockets.target	loaded active active Sockets
swap.target	loaded active active Swap
sysinit.target	loaded active active System Initialization
time-sync.target	loaded active active System Time Synchronized
timers.target	loaded active active Timers
zfs.target	loaded active active ZFS startup target

20 loaded units listed. Pass --all to see loaded but inactive units, too.

$ **sudo who -r**
    run-level 3 2022-11-15 07:37

Since we are now in the multi-user.target state, multi-user.target is shown bolded in the above output. Also, the **sudo who -r** command shows us we are in runlevel 3, the legacy equivalent of the multi-user.target state.

2.5.7 Other systemctl Options that Work with Target Units

Targets, as defined and illustrated above, are unit files that describe the system state, or points of synchronization. Like other units, they can be identified by the file extension .target.

Targets are used to coordinate and group units together.

This brings the system to some desired states, which then allows use of case-dictated functionality. For example, the Raspberry Pi OS on hardware that is configured as a server, with a text-only CUI, does not have the performance overhead, which is essentially a wasted resource, of a graphical display manager, or desktop environment.

Targets are used as a coordination point, that makes desired functionality available, allowing the system administrator to designate the "milestone" state (which might consist of many inter-dependent targets,) rather than designating individual units to start to produce that state.

Target unit files specify, in their content configuration, that they are WantedBy=, or RequiredBy= some individual unit file, thus establishing dependency relationships. Units that must be made available can specify this condition using the Wants=, Requires=, and After= designations to indicate that particular dependency relationship.

2.5.8 Using Target Shortcuts

There are target units available for critical events, such as powering off the system, or rebooting. The **systemctl** command has options that give you faster and better methods to allow execution of those critical events.

To halt the system, you can use the halt command:

$ sudo systemctl halt

To initiate a full shutdown, you can use the poweroff command:

$ sudo systemctl poweroff

A restart can be started with the reboot command:

$ sudo systemctl reboot

The above three commands notify logged-in users that the critical event is about to occur (that is very important in a multi-user system, where many users might be in the middle of critical operations!,) something is running, or isolating a particular target will *not* do.

Note
Ordinary Linux system commands will tie together the necessary operations to accomplish the above state changes on the system, so that they will work properly with systemd-controlled state changes.

For example, an ordinary Linux command that will do this, to reboot the system, is simply:

$ sudo reboot

In-Chapter Exercise

5. You want to ssh into a newly-installed Raspberry Pi system from another machine on your LAN or intranet. When you attempt that, you get some obscure error message that denies you access via ssh to the new machine. Out of the multitude of debugging scenarios you could go through to find out why you are getting the error, you could use one single systemd command while sitting at the new machine to find out whether the sshd daemon is running, or even installed. Then proceed to solve your problem quickly and easily from there. What systemd command from the above sections gives that expedient procedure?

2.6 Other Important systemd Commands

As can be seen above, the **systemctl** command affects Units and Targets. But systemd has other important commands that provide control of many system functions. The following sections detail the use of some of these other important systemd commands.

2.6.1 Cgroups

Control groups (cgroups), included as part of systemd in the Linux kernel, allow you to create prioritized, and structured groups of processes running on your system. They are invoked by the systemd **systemctl** command. Considering the various ways of using cgroups, the most important one is to monitor and control Raspberry Pi OS resources. Cgroup monitoring, assessment, and control is used via systemd unit files. It can be transient or persistent.

The **systemd-run** command is used to create and start a transient unit as its own cgroup self-contained module, and then run a Linux command in that unit.

To create persistent cgroups, it is necessary to build service unit files for them in the /etc/systemd/system directory. That directory is the standard location for user-installed and user-defined services in systemd.

The objective of this section is to provide a pictorial description of the cgroup "tree," give some basic definitions, further describe the structure of cgroup unit types, and illustrate their standard arrangement. We also define Linux "namespaces," point you to a system programming example of namespace creation, and provide sources of further documentation for you to explore.

2.6.1.1 Default Cgroup Hierarchies for System Resource Control

To start, we show an instructive diagram, one which you can obtain on your own Raspberry Pi system with the **systemd-cgls** command. Following are the truncated results of that command on our Raspberry Pi system:

```
$ systemd-cgls
Control group /:
Control group /:
-.slice
  ├─user.slice
  │ └─user-1000.slice
  │   ├─user@1000.service
  │   │ ├─app.slice
  │   │ │ ├─gvfs-goa-volume-monitor.service
  │   │ │ │ └─1046 /usr/libexec/gvfs-goa-volume-monitor
  │   │ │ └─pulseaudio.service
```

```
          │ │ │ │  └─781 /usr/bin/pulseaudio --daemonize=no --log-target=journal
          │ │ │ └─gvfs-daemon.service
          │ │ │   ├─ 879 /usr/libexec/gvfsd
          │ │ │   ├─ 885 /usr/libexec/gvfsd-fuse /run/user/1000/gvfs -f
          │ │ │   ├─1066 /usr/libexec/gvfsd-trash --spawner :1.8 /org/gtk/gvfs/exec_spaw/0
          │ │ │   ├─63616 /usr/libexec/gvfsd-network --spawner :1.8 /org/gtk/gvfs/exec_spaw/2
          │ │ │   └─63630 /usr/libexec/gvfsd-dnssd --spawner :1.8 /org/gtk/gvfs/exec_spaw/4
...
└─init.scope
          │ │      ├─765 /lib/systemd/systemd --user
          │ │      └─766 (sd-pam)
          │ ├─session-3.scope
          │ ├─1219 /bin/login -f
          │ └─1492 -bash
          └─session-1.scope
          │   └─ 760 lightdm --session-child 14 17
...
├─systemd-timesyncd.service
│ └─446 /lib/systemd/systemd-timesyncd
├─avahi-daemon.service
│ ├─481 avahi-daemon: running [raspberrypi.local]
│ └─485 avahi-daemon: chroot helper
├─systemd-logind.service
└─518 /lib/systemd/systemd-logind
```

In-Chapter Exercises

6. Compare the output of the above **systemd-cgls** command with the **pstree** command output. How are they similar in both structure and content? How are they different? Execute the **pstree** command and the systemd-cgls command on your Raspberry Pi system, and compare the output you get to the output we show, in terms of fine-grained similarities and differences. What options of the **pstree** command can give displays of PID's, similar to the output of the **systemd-cgls** command?

****For Experts****

7. Are PID and cgroup number the same for all processes and threads? Write a system program that creates multiple persistent threads with the fork() system call, and then examine the cgroup numbers assigned to those threads.

Next, we give you some basic definitions that more fully describe the objects found in the **systemd-cgls** command's output graphics.

Slice – A group of units that organizes them in some way.

Service – A process, or a group of processes, which is started using a service unit configuration file.

For example, systemd-logins.service is a service.

Scope – Processes that are started and stopped by transient processes that use the *fork() system call*, and are registered by systemd at runtime. All user sessions are a good example of this.

In the command output text above, init.scope, and session-c1.scope are examples.

Slices, services, and scopes, are most importantly created by the system administrator, or by system programs. By default, systemd, and the operating system, start up mandatory and essential services automatically at system startup, dictated by the final target state that the system will run in.

Three slices are created by default:

- -.slice — the root slice;
- system.slice — the default path location for all system services;
- user.slice — the default path location for all user sessions;

In-Chapter Exercise

****For Experts****

8.   Are the threads you created for In-Chapter Exercise 7. slices, services, or scope units? Why?

To summarize, looking at the output of the **systemd-cgls** commands above, the root of the cgroup tree is the root slice, -.slice. The first major branch, aside from the system.slice, is the user.slice, with a number of scopes under that for user sessions. Proceeding down the tree, there are a number of other slices grouped under the major "branch" known as the system.slice, for example, avahi-daemon.service, cron.service, cups.service, ssh.service, etc. That is a capsule overview of the tree.

It is useful to list loaded slice unit types, by using the following command:

```
$ systemctl list-units --type=slice
```

UNIT	LOAD	ACTIVE	SUB	DESCRIPTION
-.slice	loaded	active	active	Root Slice
system-configure\x2dprinter.slice	loaded	active	active	system-configure\x2dprinter.slice
system-bthelper.slice	loaded	active	active	system-bthelper.slice
system-getty.slice	loaded	active	active	system-getty.slice
system-modprobe.slice	loaded	active	active	system-modprobe.slice
system-systemd\x2dfsck.slice	loaded	active	active	system-systemd\x2dfsck. slice
system.slice	loaded	active	active	System Slice
user-1000.slice	loaded	active	active	User Slice of UID 1000
user.slice	loaded	active	active	User and Session Slice

LOAD   = Reflects whether the unit definition was properly loaded.
ACTIVE = The high-level unit activation state, i.e. generalization of SUB.
SUB   = The low-level unit activation state, values depend on unit type.
9 loaded units listed. Pass --all to see loaded but inactive units, too.
To show all installed unit files use 'systemctl list-unit-files'.
$

2.6.1.2 *Additional Cgroup Reference Resources*

To find more information about resource control under systemd, the unit hierarchy, as well as the kernel resource controllers, refer to the materials listed below:

Cgroup-Related systemd Documentation
The following man pages give you more information on systemd cgroups:

systemd.resource-control – describes the configuration options for resource control
     shared by system units.
systemd.unit – describes common options of all unit configuration files.
systemd.slice – provides general information about .slice units.
systemd.scope – provides general information about .scope units.
systemd.service – provides general information about .service units.

Additionally, you can install the kernel documentation on cgroups, by using the following command on your Raspberry Pi OS system:

```
$ sudo  apt install linux-doc
Reading package lists... Done
Building dependency tree... Done
Reading state information... Done
The following packages were automatically installed and are no longer required:
    geoclue-2.0 ipcalc kaccounts-providers kactivities-bin kactivitymanagerd
    kdeconnect kded5 keditbookmarks kinit kio kpackagelauncherqml kpackagetool5
Output truncated...
Use 'sudo apt autoremove' to remove them.
The following additional packages will be installed:
    linux-doc-5.10
The following NEW packages will be installed:
    linux-doc linux-doc-5.10.179-1
0 upgraded, 2 newly installed, 0 to remove and 0 not upgraded.
Need to get 30.3 MB of archives.
After this operation, 167 MB of additional disk space will be used.
Do you want to continue? [Y/n] Y
Output truncated...
$
```

Once the documentation for the kernel has been downloaded, you can access and view the cgroups-specific content by viewing the **cgroups** man page on your system.

2.6.1.3 Linux Namespaces

There is a kernel-level construct in Raspberry Pi OS Linux, appropriately called "namespaces", which segregates and isolates the cgroup processes seen above in Section 2.6.1, and their system resources, in a separate and protected environment. This allows them to operate in their own process environments on the system. A very close analogy of namespaces, which you might be familiar with, is the concept of a variable's "scope" in a high level computer programming language, such as C or Python.

Namespaces use the *clone* system call to accomplish this process isolation. The biggest and most important use of namespaces is in the system-level creation, and maintenance, of Linux containers, such as LXD/LXC. For complete reference information on namespaces, consult the man pages on your Raspberry Pi system for *namespaces(7)*, and *user_namespaces(7)* – particularly the EXAMPLE on the user_namespaces man page, which gives an excellent and instructive C language system programming implementation of the clone system call used to create a child process that executes a shell command in a new namespace.

2.6.2 Journal Logging

System logging using log files is extremely useful for system administration. The logs record activity and events on a Raspberry Pi Linux system. Journal logging with systemd is very similar to the traditional methods available for logging. They are created so that the system administrator can carefully, systematically, and periodically audit the general operation of the system, especially with regard to performance enhancements that have been made and to maintain system security.

2.6.2.1 systemd Journal Log Messages

The systemd journal is created and managed by a special daemon, named journald, which channels all of the messages produced by the facilities and programs such as the kernel, initrd, systemd services, etc. into a database record structure. The systemd journal is a single, centralized management program for collecting together logs, regardless of where the log messages themselves are generated.

A critical, as well as controversial aspect of systemd journal logging, is that the log files are stored as binary data, and can be searched by processes deploying a specialized database traversal program. *They are not plain text files*. Previous legacy system logs were text files that could be viewed easily as such, or even edited in a text editor such as nano, Vi, or emacs.

Storing the log information in a binary format mandates that the log information be displayed in useful output formats specific to proprietary database management technologies. Simply stated, using that proprietary technology is a major drawback. But logs can be displayed using the **journalctl** command that we show in the next section.

2.6.2.2 *Using the* journalctl *Command to Query the Journal*

The **journalctl** command is a convenient way of querying entries in the journal database. Following is a synopsis of the command, extracted from the journalctl manpage

journalctl · Query the systemd journal

Syntax:
    journalctl [options...] [matches...]

Purpose:
journalctl may be used to query the contents of the systemd journal as written by systemd-journald.service.
If called without options or arguments, it will show the full contents of the journal, starting with the oldest entry collected.
All users are granted access to their private per-user journals. However, by default, only root users who are members of a few special groups are granted access to the system journal and the journals of other users.

    Commonly Used Features:

-a, --all	Show all fields in full, even if they include unprintable characters or are very long.
-f, --follow	Show only the most recent journal entries, and continuously print new entries as they are appended to the journal.
-r, --reverse	Reverse output so that the newest entries are displayed first.
-u, --unit=UNIT|PATTERN	Show messages for the specified systemd unit UNIT (such as a service unit), or for any of the units matched by PATTERN.
-S, --since=, -U, --until=	Start showing entries on or newer than the specified date, or on or older than the specified date, respectively. Date specifications should be of the format "2012-10-30 18:17:16".

To get more information about the use of the **journalctl** command, particularly about the structure that the command uses to query the journal, examine the **man journalctl** command contents as necessary on your system.

2.6.2.3 *Journal Logging Basics and Applied to the Webserver2 Program*

In this section, we show how to use the **journalctl** command and its options and arguments to do some basic systemd-style journal query operations. We then apply a set of those commands and options to a program named "webserver2". That program generates systemd-style journal log output.

Our use of the **journalctl** command applied to that program's journal output is relevant in this section, so as to better and more practically illustrate the use of **journalctl** options and arguments to a real application.

2.6.2.3.1 Basic Log Viewing

To see the logs that the journald daemon has collected, use the **journalctl** command.

When used without any options or arguments, every journal entry that is in the system will be displayed. The oldest entries will be first in the listing:

```
$ journalctl
-- Journal begins at Mon 2022-04-04 07:52:30 PDT, ends at Thu 2022-11-17 05:17:01
   PST. --
Apr 04 07:52:30 raspberrypi kernel: Booting Linux on physical CPU 0x0000000000
   [0x410fd083]
Apr 04 07:52:30 raspberrypi kernel: Linux version 5.15.32-v8+ (dom@buildbot)
   (aarch64-linux>
Apr 04 07:52:30 raspberrypi kernel: random: fast init done
Apr 04 07:52:30 raspberrypi kernel: Machine model: Raspberry Pi 400 Rev 1.0
Output truncated...
```

But what if you want to see the journal with the newest entry first? Use the **–r** (reverse) option on the basic **journalctl** command.

```
$ journalctl -r
-- Journal begins at Mon 2022-04-04 07:52:30 PDT, ends at Thu 2022-11-17 05:17:01
   PST. --
Nov 17 05:17:01 raspberrypi CRON[36470]: pam_unix(cron:session): session closed
   for user root
Nov 17 05:17:01 raspberrypi CRON[36471]: (root) CMD (  cd / && run-parts --report /
   etc/cron>
Nov 17 05:17:01 raspberrypi CRON[36470]: pam_unix(cron:session): session opened
   for user >
Nov 17 05:04:28 raspberrypi systemd-logind[519]: Removed session 83.
Nov 17 05:04:28 raspberrypi systemd-logind[519]: Session 83 logged out. Waiting for
   processes to exit.
Nov 17 05:04:28 raspberrypi systemd[1]: session-83.scope: Succeeded.
Nov 17 05:04:28 raspberrypi sshd[36257]: pam_unix(sshd:session): session closed
   for user bob
Output truncated...
```

In-Chapter Exercise

9. From the output of the above two commands executed on your Raspberry Pi system, what can you tell about the most recent current boot time, and the current time?

2.6.2.3.2 Journal Query Structures

The main purpose of collecting the log information together from many sources, thus centralizing them in one place, such as in the journal, is to be able to quickly and easily look at and take action based on the entries in the log that are important to you for some reason. That could be true of an ordinary desktop user, or a server system administrator.

Because of this, the most important use features of the **journalctl** command's options, and arguments, are its methods of ordering, and making inquiries into the journal, or separating out more useful, understandable, and compact information from it. Following are some of the ways these searches through the log can be done.

For example, the journal has many "field headings" that can be used for inquiry. Each of these fields acts as an index, or key, to specific kinds or sets of entries in the journal. Some of those fields are passed to it from the process being logged, and some are applied by the daemon journald, with data it gathers from the system at the time the log is from.

A leading underscore indicates that a field is of the latter type. The journal automatically records and indexes logging for that type of query. You can get more information about all of the available journal fields by typing:

$ **man systemd-.journal-fields**

2.6.2.3.3 Querying by Time

You can also see parts of the log in a "from-to" display. You would most likely want to do this when the system has been operating for a long time without a reboot. You can do an inquiry by using the **--since** and **--until** options, which limit the entries displayed to those after, or before some specified given times.

The time parameters are in a variety of formats. For absolute time values, you should use the following format:

YYYY-MM-DD HH:MM:SS

For example, we can see all of the entries since 2022-04-04 07:52:30 PDT using this command:

$ **journalctl --since "2022-04-04 07:52:30 PDT"**

If parts of the above time specification argument are left off, standard defaults are used instead. For example, if the date is omitted, the current date will be used. If the time component is missing, "00:00:00" (midnight) will be used. The seconds field can be left off to default to "00":

$ **journalctl --since "2022-04-04 " --until "2022-04-04 08:30 PDT"**

The journal also accepts some relative values, and English-language shortcuts. For example, you can use the words "yesterday," "today," "tomorrow," or "now." You do relative times by placing these symbols before arguments: "-" or "+" to a numbered value or using words like "ago."

To get the data from yesterday, use this command:

$ journalctl --since yesterday

If you used another system monitoring tool, and it gave information about a service interruption starting at 11:00 PM and continuing until an hour ago, you could type:

$ journalctl --since 11:00 --until "1 hour ago"

2.6.2.3.4 *Querying by Unit*

The most useful, and practical way of querying, is by designating the service unit's name you are interested in. You use the **-u** option to query by unit.

For example, to see all of the logs from the webserver2 unit on your system, use the following command:

$ journalctl -u webserver2.service

You can perform compound queries by adding arguments to the above unit query by unit name. To query by time and name, to check on how the status of the service you are interested in, use the following command:

$ journalctl -u webserver2.service --since today

Compound querying is useful when you want to compare log entries from related units running on the system. For example, if you want to compare log entries from your webserver2 service to the status of another unit, you can view the entries from both in chronological order by using the following compound query statement:

**$ journalctl -u webserver2.service -u systemd-logind.service --since \
  yesterday**

This allows you to study the interactions between different programs and debug targets and the interaction of dependencies, instead of just individual, isolated units.

2.6.2.3.5 *Querying by Process, User, or Group ID*

Several services may fork many child processes to accomplish their purposes. If you know the exact PID of a process you are interested in, you can perform a journalctl query by PID. To do this, execute the query by specifying the

_PID field. For example, if the PID we're interested in is 1, use the following command:

$ journalctl _PID=1

You can also show all of the entries logged from a specific user, or group. This is done with the _UID or _GID filters. For example, if webserver2 is being run by the user bob, you can find the user ID with the following command:

$ id -u bob
1000
$

Then, you can use the ID that was returned to structure a query command based on the results, as follows:

$ journalctl _UID=1000 --since today

The **-F** option of the **journalctl** command is used to show all of the available values for a given journal field. To see which group IDs the systemd journal has entries for, use the following command:

$ journalctl -F _GID
0
1000
7
123
65534
109
116
110
113
$

The above output shows all of the values that the journal has stored for the group ID field. This can help you construct your queries with the Group ID field.

2.6.2.3.6 Querying by Component Path

You can apply a filter to the query by providing a pathname. If the path-name leads to an executable image, journalctl will display all of the entries that are related to that particular executable image. For example, to find log entries that involve the webserver2 executable program, use the following command:

$ journalctl /home/bob/webserver2

where the path to the executable image is /home/bob, and the name of the executable program is webserver2.

Usually, if a unit file is available for the executable, this method is more understandable and gives useful information to someone trying to achieve system administration tasks, such as security intrusions (entries from associated child processes, etc.). However, this does not always yield useful information.

2.6.2.3.7 Querying by Priority

One query filter that system administrators are very interested in is message priority. While it is useful to log information at a very verbose level, when actually trying to read and interpret the observed and available information, listing low-priority logs can be obscure and useless.

You can use journalctl to display only messages of a specified priority or above by using the **-p** option. This allows you to filter out lower-priority messages. For instance, to show only entries logged at the error level or above, you can type:

```
$ journalctl --b -p err
-- Journal begins at Mon 2022-04-04 07:52:30 PDT, ends at Thu 2022-11-17 08:17:02 \
   PST. --
Nov 15 06:37:22 raspberrypi systemd-modules-load[145]: Failed to find module 'lp'
Nov 15 06:37:22 raspberrypi blkmapd[165]: open pipe file /run/rpc_pipefs/nfs/ \
   blocklayout faile>
Nov 15 06:37:22 raspberrypi systemd-modules-load[145]: Failed to find module \
   'ppdev'
Nov 15 06:37:22 raspberrypi systemd-modules-load[145]: Failed to find module \
   'parport_pc'
Output truncated ...
```

This will display all messages marked as error, critical, alert, or emergency. The journal implements the legacy UNIX/Linux syslog message levels. You can use either the priority name, or its corresponding numeric value. In order of highest to lowest priority, these are shown in Table 2.3.

The above numbers or names can be used interchangeably with the **-p** option. Selecting a priority will display messages marked at the specified level and those above it.

In-Chapter Exercise

10. What does the --b directive in the previous command do, as far as a compound query?

2.6.2.4 Query Output Display

The above queries showed particular kinds of log entry outputs. There are other ways we can add options and addendums to the queries. The journalctl output is more condensed and legible, thus a more readable display. Organized in a more understandable way if you want to cull certain information from it.

TABLE 2.3

systemd Error Priorities

Priority	Name	Description and Possible Action(s) To Be Taken
0	emerg	Emergency- A "panic" condition - notify system administration.
1	alert	Alert- Notify system administrator who can fix the problem. Example: loss of backup ISP connection.
2	crit	Critical- Failure in a primary system. Fix crit problems before alert problems. Example: loss of disk subsystem.
3	err	Error- Non-urgent failures, should be sent to developers or development admins.
4	warning	Warning- Not an error, but shows that an error will occur if action is not taken, e.g. file system nearly full.
5	notice	Notice- Unusual events, but not error conditions. No immediate action required.
6	info	Information- Normal operating messages - No action required.
7	debug	Debug- Info useful for developers for debugging the app, not useful during operations.

Note

In certain output displays below, exiting, or stopping, the display of journal entries can be done by typing **q** on the command line.

To display a certain number of log entries, you can use the **-n** option. By default, it will display the most recent 10 entries:

$ journalctl -n

You can also specify the number of entries you'd like to see, with a number after the **-n**:

$ journalctl -n 15

2.6.2.4.1 Displaying Log Entries in Real Time

To show the content of the journal in real time, and see the logs as they are being written, use the **-f** option

$ journalctl -f

Adjusting how journalctl displays log data shrinking or expanding can be achieved by using the following option. By default, journalctl will show the entire entry in the pager, left-to-right, allowing the entries to trail off to the right of the screen. This rightward-extensive display data can be seen by pressing the right arrow key. If you'd rather have the output truncated, inserting an ellipsis where information has been removed, you can use the **--no-full** option:

$ journalctl - -no-full

-- Journal begins at Mon 2022-04-04 07:52:30 PDT, ends at Thu 2022-11-17 08:17:02 PST. --

Apr 04 07:52:30 raspberrypi kernel: Booting Linux on physical CPU 0x0000000000 [0x410fd083]

Apr 04 07:52:30 raspberrypi kernel: Linux version 5.15.32-v8+ (dom@buildbot) (aarch64-lin...T>

Apr 04 07:52:30 raspberrypi kernel: random: fast init done

Apr 04 07:52:30 raspberrypi kernel: Machine model: Raspberry Pi 400 Rev 1.0

Apr 04 07:52:30 raspberrypi kernel: efi: UEFI not found.

Apr 04 07:52:30 raspberrypi kernel: Reserved memory: created CMA memory pool at 0x0000000...20 MiB

Apr 04 07:52:30 raspberrypi kernel: OF: reserved mem: initialized node linux,cma, compati...a-pool

Apr 04 07:52:30 raspberrypi kernel: Zone ranges:

Apr 04 07:52:30 raspberrypi kernel: DMA [mem 0x0000000000000000-0x000000003fffffff]

Apr 04 07:52:30 raspberrypi kernel: DMA32 [mem 0x0000000040000000-0x00000000fbffffff]

Output truncated ...

You can also specify to journalctl to display all of its information, no matter whether it includes unprintable characters. We can do this with the **-a** option:

$ journalctl -a

By default, journalctl displays the output of a query in a "paged" manner, one screenful at a time. To be able to process the data with text manipulation tools, such as a text editor, or LibreOffice Writer for example, you can output to standard output, redirecting it into a post-processing program, or to a disk file. You can do this with the --no-pager option. In the following example, we redirect the pager output to a file named "page1":

$ journalctl --no-pager > page1

2.6.2.4.2 *Query Output Formats*

If you are post-processing journal log entries with some particular program, as mentioned above, you will have an easier time parsing the data into that program if it is in a more amenable format. The journal can be displayed its output in a variety of formats. You can do this using the **-o**, option with a format specifier.

For example, you can output the journal entries in JSON format with the following command:

$ journalctl -b -u webserver2 -o json

TABLE 2.4

journalctl Output Formats

cat	Displays only the message field itself.
export	A binary format suitable for transferring or backing up.
json	Standard JSON with one entry per line.
json-pretty	JSON formatted for better human-readability
json-sse	JSON formatted output wrapped to make add server-sent event compatible
short	The default syslog style output
short-iso	The default format augmented to show ISO 8601 wallclock timestamps.
short-monotonic	The default format with monotonic timestamps.
short-precise	The default format with microsecond precision
verbose	Shows every journal field available for the entry, including those usually hidden internally.

This is useful for parsing with certain utility programs. You could use the json-pretty format to get a better handle on the data structure before passing it off to the JSON consumer:

$ **journalctl -b -u webserver2 -o json-pretty**

Table 2.4 shows the formats that might be used for such a display.

These options allow you to display the journal entries in whatever format best suits how you want to do the post-processing treatment of the content of the journal.

2.6.2.5 Journal Maintenance

It may become necessary to not only look through older boot environments, and correlate the logs found in them with the most current boot logs, but to delete older, obsolete log entries. Log and journal maintenance is an important aspect of system administration.

Note

At the time this book was written, "vacuuming", or cleaning out journal log files, only works on archived files and corrupted files, and does not work on active log files!

You can find out the amount of space that the active and archived journals are currently occupying on disk by using the --disk-usage option of the **journalctl** command:

$ **journalctl --disk-usage**

Archived and active journals take up 48.0M in the file system.

The active journal logs cannot be pruned.

When this facility becomes available for active journal logs, there are basically two different ways you will be able to do that.

1. If you use the --vacuum-size option, you can shrink your journal by indicating a size. This will remove only old archived entries that are corrupted or empty, until the total journal space taken up on disk is at the requested size:

$ sudo journalctl --vacuum-size=1M
sudo journalctl --vacuum-size=1M
Deleted archived journal /var/log/journal/42ef46612dc64ec2bf13b9704a661ec8/
   user-1000@0005fa1821e06e36-c096421281b7ec8d.journal~ (8.0M).
Deleted archived journal /var/log/journal/42ef46612dc64ec2bf13b9704a661ec8/ sys
   tem@0005fa1821194676-6ee6ae817589e0dc.journal~ (16.0M).
Vacuuming done, freed 24.0M of archived journals from /var/log/journal/42ef46612d
   c64ec2bf13b9704a661ec8.
Vacuuming done, freed 0B of archived journals from /run/log/journal.
Vacuuming done, freed 0B of archived journals from /var/log/journal.
$

2. Another way that you can prune the archived journal log is by specifying a cutoff time with the **--vacuum-time** option. Any entries beyond that time are deleted. This allows you to keep the entries that have been created after a specific time.

For instance, to keep entries from the last year, you can type:

$ sudo journalctl --vacuum-time=1years

Limiting Journal Expansion
You can limit how much persistent storage on disk the journal can take up. This can be done by editing the /etc/systemd/journald.conf file. The following items in that file can be used to limit the journal growth:

SystemMaxUse=: The maximum disk space that can be used by the journal in persistent storage.
SystemKeepFree=: The amount of space that the journal should leave free when adding journal entries to persistent storage.
SystemMaxFileSize=: How large individual journal files can grow to in persistent storage before being rotated.
RuntimeMaxUse=: The maximum disk space that can be used in volatile storage (within the /run file system).
RuntimeKeepFree=: The amount of space to be set aside for other uses when writing data to volatile storage (within the /run file system).
RuntimeMaxFileSize=: The amount of space that an individual journal file can take up in volatile storage (within the /run file system) before being rotated.

2.6.2.6 Boot Process Querying

Using the journal, you can examine logs of the present boot record and its progress, and past boot records. This is useful from a system administration perspective, when something goes wrong with the boot process, or when software or hardware on the system fails to start or operate properly after the system boots and is in the steady state condition.

2.6.2.6.1 Querying Past Boots

To display the information from the current boot, there are times when past boot sequence records would be helpful to examine and compare to the current one. The journal can save information from many previous boots, and the **journalctl** command can be made to display that information in an effective and concise comparative way. Note that in order for you to retain journal information from past boots, you must complete the procedures shown in this section first.

To enable persistent boot information, you can do the following:

1. Create the directory to store the journal with the following command:

   $ **sudo mkdir -p /var/log/journal**

2. Edit the journal configuration file with the editor of your choice:

   $ **sudo nano /etc/systemd/journald.conf**
   Under the [journal] section, uncomment (remove the # sign) the Storage=
     option, and set it to "persistent" to enable persistent logging:
   /etc/systemd/journald.conf
   . . .
   [Journal]
   Storage=persistent

When retaining previous boots via persistence is enabled on your system, the journalctl command provides some options for working with boots as a unit. To see the boots that journald knows about, use the --list-boots option with journalctl:

$ **journalctl --list-boots**
0 d536f728b3da464cbf4e740e95adffda Mon 2023-04-24 10:13:44 PDT—Sun
  2023-04-30 12:30:15 PDT
$

The above command will display a line for each boot, as shown in Table 2.5.

To display more verbose information from these boots, you can use information from either the first or second column. To see the journal from the previous boot, use the -1 relative pointer with the -b flag:

$ **journalctl -b 0**

TABLE 2.5

systemctl Boot Information

0	The first column is the offset for the boot from 0, the current boot environment.
0 d536f728b3da464cbf4e740e95adffda	An absolute reference, the boot ID is in the second column.
Mon 2023-04-24 10:13:44 PDT—Sun 2023-04-30 12:30:15 PDT	The time that the boot session spans, with two time specifications (from-to).

You can also use the boot ID to call back the same data from boot 0:

$ journalctl -b d536f728b3da464cbf4e740e95adffda

2.6.2.6.2 The Current Boot

To display journal logs from the current boot, use the following command:

$ journalctl -b

This will show you all of the journal entries that have been collected since the most recent reboot, particularly if you have done the procedures in the previous section and then rebooted a number of times. You can then monitor information about your current environment.

2.6.2.6.3 Displaying Kernel Messages

Kernel messages related to booting, those usually found in dmesg output, can be retrieved from the journal as well. To display only these messages, we can add the -k or --dmesg flags to the **journalctl** command:

$ journalctl -k

By default, this will display the kernel messages from the current boot. You can specify an alternative boot environment using the normal boot selection specifications above, being sure that a persistent boot environment was enabled. For instance, to get the messages from five boots ago (if they exist in the journal!,) you could type:

$ journalctl -k -b -5

In-Chapter Exercises

11. A new app you have installed refuses to run on your Raspberry Pi system. Out of the multitude of debugging scenarios you could go through to find out why that app is misbehaving, you could use a single systemd command to check the most recent record of system activity, and then solve the problem with the app quickly and easily from there.

Which specific command in the previous sections most compactly provides you with the procedure to expedite your viewing of recent system activity?

12. To get practice with the **journalctl** commands from the previous section, query the boot record from three previous system boots (if there are that many!) from the current boot environment.

2.6.3 systemd Timers

systemd takes on many of the functions and facilities that legacy Cron did, via support for clock-time-based, and calendar-time-based events.

From a system administrator's perspective, systemd can do Cron-like scheduling of system events. We give examples below of clock-time-based running of a single script, and calendar-based scheduling of events.

In order to get a complete description of how systemd deals with time-based specifications and operations, see the man page for systemd.time.

2.6.3.1 An Example of Clock-Time-Based Running of a Script

If you have a script /usr/local/bin/myscript that you want to run every hour, do the following steps:

1. Create a service unit file, named myscript.service, with your favorite text editor. Save it in /etc/systemd/system/, with the following content:

```
[Unit]
Description=Whatever MyScript Does

[Service]
Type=simple
ExecStart=/home/bob/myscript
```

Note that it is important to set the Type variable to be "simple," not "oneshot." If you specify "oneshot", the script will be run the first time, and then systemd will not run it again, and will turn off the timer.

2. Create the following timer unit file, in the same directory as the service unit file above.

```
[Unit]
Description=Runs myscript every hour

[Timer]
# Time to wait after booting before we run first time
OnBootSec=10min
# Time between running each consecutive time
OnUnitActiveSec=1h
Unit=myscript.service

[Install]
WantedBy=multi-user.target
```

3. To start and enable the service:

    $ **sudo systemctl start myscript.timer**

    and to enable it for every subsequent boot:

    $ **sudo systemctl enable myscript.timer**

In-Chapter Exercises

13. ```
    #!/bin/bash
    # My first script converted into a service
    echo "Hello World!"
    ```

If the above script file in your home directory on your Raspberry Pi system (which you have named myscript) is made into a service with the three steps shown above, how can you get the message "Hello World!" to display every 10 minutes on the stdout of a terminal?

14. (a) What command do you use to stop the service? (b) What command do you use to ensure the service does not run on every subsequent boot?

2.6.3.2 Example of Calendar-Based Running of the above Script File

If you want to start the service shown in Section 2.6.3.1 according to a calendar event, and not a clock-based interval specification, create a new timer unit, and link the service unit file from that example to that new timer unit.

1. Create the timer unit with your favorite text editor (or nano if you,) using the following command:

    $ **sudo nano /etc/systemd/system/cal.timer**

    Then put this text into that file

    ```
    [Unit]
    Description=Calendar-based timer

    [Timer]
    OnCalendar=Mon-Fri *-*-* 00:00:00
    Unit=myscript.service

    [Install]
    WantedBy=basic.target
    ```

The service file and the timer unit file are put in the /etc/systemd/system/ folder.

2. To start the calendar timer

    $ **sudo systemctl start cal.timer**
    ```

and to enable it for every subsequent boot:

$ **sudo systemctl enable cal.timer**

In-Chapter Exercise

15. What does the time stamp Mon-Fri *-*-* 00:00:00 in the above example specify for the running of the script file?

2.7 A Python3-Based Webserver as a "New-Style Daemon"

For our purposes here in these sections of the chapter, a "new-style" daemon, program, app, or method is one that is systemd-controlled. This example deploys a special Python3 module that easily creates a webserver daemon, and puts this module under the control of systemd as a new-style daemon. You don't absolutely need to have any Python knowledge, just to follow along with the steps shown below:

1. Place a valid index.html file in your home directory. Our home directory in the steps below is /home/bob. Additionally, our very simple index.html file is this

```
<!DOCTYPE HTML PUBLIC "-//W3C//DTD HTML 4.0 Transitional//EN">
<html>
<head>
        <meta http-equiv="content-type" content="text/html; charset=utf-8"/>
        <title></title>
        <meta name="generator" content="LibreOffice 4.3.5.2.0 (FreeBSD)"/>
        <meta name="created" content="2015-04-25T18:47:03.316903354"/>
        <meta name="changed" content="2015-04-25T18:48:11.213818830"/>
<link href="/home/bob/favicon.ico" rel="icon" type="image/x-icon" />
</head>
<body lang="en-US" dir="ltr" style="background: transparent">
<p>Under Construction</p>
</body>
</html>
```

2. Create a service unit file for the webserver in /etc/systemd/system, named simp.service, with the following content. We used the command **sudo nano simp.service** to achieve this:

```
[Service]
ExecStart=/usr/bin/python3 -m http.server -d /home/bob 8000
```

3. To start the service, use the following command:

   $ **sudo systemctl start simp.service**

4. To view the status of the service, type the following:

   $ **systemctl status simp.service**

   • simp.service
     Loaded: loaded (/etc/systemd/system/simp.service; static)
     Active: active (running) since Tue 2022-11-22 08:48:25 PST; 16s ago
    Main PID: 141711 (python3)
     Tasks: 1 (limit: 4164)
        CPU: 191ms
     CGroup: /system.slice/simp.service
             └─141711 python3 -m http.server -d /home/bob 8000

   Nov 22 08:48:25 raspberrypi systemd[1]: Started simp.service.
   $

5. To view the web page this service provides, in a web browser on your local machine, type-in the URL 127.0.0.1:8000

The index.html file is now displayed in your browser.

6. To stop the service, type the following command:

   $ **sudo systemctl stop simp.service**

In-Chapter Exercise

16. (a). Modify the service file for simp.service, so that the Python3 built-in webserver is exposed on port 8001. Also, modify the contents of the index.html file code so that it is customized to your liking. Add things like more text, images, links to other pages, etc. Name the service simp2, and complete the 6 steps shown above to make it into a systemd-controlled service. Then run the services simp and simp2 simultaneously, and with your favorite Web browser, browse to ports 8000 and 8001. What do you see there?
   (b). How can you expose the ports 8000 and 8001 to the Internet safely, so that from a remote site, you can see the webpages you've created for this Exercise?

The above examples illustrated how simple Bourne shell script files, and a Python built-in, can be made into daemon services under the control and monitoring of systemd. The first and second examples illustrated how to make a shell script a daemon by adding a service unit file for it in /etc/ systemd/system. The third example illustrated how to make a simple Python built-in, that runs a Python-based webserver application, into a systemd service.

2.7.1 systemd Methods of Changing the Activation Behavior of a New-Style Daemon

There are several other "new-style" techniques and methods that can be applied instead of, or to replace an old-style daemon (a traditional UNIX or Linux daemon,) to update it to be systemd-compliant and more effectively, and efficiently controlled by systemd.

These include the following general ways of achieving that:

Boot-Based Activation
"Old-style" daemons are started when the system boots, and/or by individual script files on a per-service basis, using UNIX BSD or SysV initialization. This is the traditional method of service activation, used before systemd's installation in the kernel. systemd uses a modernized version of activation, both when the system boots, and at runtime, using minimal service description files we have described in the sections above.

Socket-Based Activation
The chief advantage of socket-based activation of daemons is, most importantly, the simplification of configuration and the program development process. In socket-based activation, the creation and binding of listening sockets happens in systemd. Using initialization and service unit files for daemon configuration, systemd installs the sockets, and then assigns them to the systemd-started process when some triggering event occurs.

Bus-Based Activation
When the D-Bus InterProcess Communication (IPC) system is used, new-style daemons deploy bus activation so that they are automatically activated when a client application accesses their IPC interfaces, or channels.

Device-Based Activation
New-style daemons that manage a particular type or class of hardware, like disk volumes or ZFS datasets, are activated only when the hardware of the respective kind is plugged in, or otherwise becomes available.

Path-Based Activation
systemd provides a way to bind service activation to file system changes. This is implemented using path-based activation configured in path unit files, as illustrated and described in the man page for systemd.path.

Timer-Based Activation

New-style daemons can implement clean-up jobs that are intended to be executed in regular intervals. In systemd, this is implemented via timer unit files as shown in examples above, as described in the man page for systemd.timer.

It is possible, and preferable, for services to be activated by more than one of the above methods.

Examples of this are Wi-Fi, Bluetooth, and CUPS printer services, which can be made active when their respective devices are plugged in, or when activity is first seen on a particular port.

We provide a simple example of socket-based activation in Section 2.7.1.1.

2.7.1.1 A Simple Sockets-Based Activation Example

Note

Part of the efficiency and speed advantage systemd gives the Raspberry Pi OS is the ability to delay the start of services and daemons until they are actually needed, instead of running all of them when the system boots and enters the steady operating state.

Sockets-based activation for a daemon, such as a web server, means that when a request is made on a specified port that the web server is hooked to, the web server then starts as a daemon. It then services all requests made on that port.

In this example, we use the special **systemd-activate** command, which is usually used to test sockets-based activation, to achieve our objectives. **systemd-activate** "listens" on a port.

Following are steps you can easily take to make a web server application start when a HTTP request is made on a particular port of your choosing. You can change the port numbers shown in the example steps below to any ephemeral ports you want.

1. *****Optional***** Place a valid index.html file in your home directory on your Raspberry Pi OS system, if you haven't already done so for the example above in Section 2.7. Our home directory in the steps below is /home/bob. Additionally, our very simple index.html file is this:

```
<!DOCTYPE HTML PUBLIC "-//W3C//DTD HTML 4.0 Transitional//EN">
<html>
<head>
        <meta http-equiv="content-type" content="text/html; charset=utf-8"/>
        <title></title>
        <meta name="generator" content="LibreOffice 4.3.5.2.0 (FreeBSD)"/>
        <meta name="created" content="2015-04-25T18:47:03.316903354"/>
        <meta name="changed" content="2015-04-25T18:48:11.213818830"/>
        <link href="/home/bob/favicon.ico" rel="icon" type="image/x-icon" />
</head>
<body lang="en-US" dir="ltr" style="background: transparent">
<p>Under Construction</p>
</body>
</html>
```

2. Type the following command (where instead of the path /home/bob, you substitute the path to the directory where you placed the index. html file:

```
$ systemd-socket-activate -l 2000 -a python3 -m http.server -d \
  /home/bob 8096
Listening on [::]:2000 as 3.
```

This command awaits a request on port 2000, and then when one comes in (from a web browser, for example), it executes the command shown after the -a option to activate the Python3 http.server webserver built-in application. So basically you are using the **systemd-socket-activate** command to activate port 2000, and then coupling Python3 to this activation to run the http.server built-in application on port 8096.

3. To test this activation, with your favorite web browser, set the URL to

    http://your_ip_address:2000.

Our local network web address was 192.168.1.2.

Note You will get an error in the browser, or the browser will spin for a while. No worries!
In the terminal window you typed the command into, this will be displayed

```
Listening on [::]:2000 as 3.
Communication attempt on fd 3.
Connection from 192.168.1.2:38070 to [::ffff:192.168.1.2]:2000
Spawned python3 (python3 -m http.server -d /home/bob 8096) as PID 129730.
Execing python3 (python3 -m http.server -d /home/bob 8096)
Serving HTTP on 0.0.0.0 port 8096 (http://0.0.0.0:8096/) ...
```

You just "primed" the systemd-socket-activate program, and it has spawned the Python3 http.server application! You can check this by using the **ps -aux** command in another terminal window at this point.

4. Set your browser's URL to http://your_ip_address:8096, and press Enter. You have accessed the Python3 http.server on port 8096. To check this, use the **ps -aux** command again. It should now show two processes running: the systemd-socket-activate process, and the Python3 http.server process, which was socket-activated. Plus, perhaps a couple of Web browser processes as well.

5. Something similar to this will now show in the terminal window from Step 2:

```
192.168.1.2 - - [30/Apr/2023 15:39:13] "GET / HTTP/1.1" 200 -
192.168.1.2 - - [30/Apr/2023 15:39:13] code 404, message File not found
192.168.1.2 - - [30/Apr/2023 15:39:13] "GET /favicon.ico HTTP/1.1" 404 -
```

Whatever is in the directory you set in Step 1. above will be displayed. If the directory contains files, it will show you a listing of the files in the directory. And if there is a valid HTTP-formatted index.html file in that directory, as optionally shown in Step, your web browser will show its valid HTML contents in the browser window.

6. To terminate the Python3 built-in http.server, hold down **<Ctrl> + C** on the keyboard in the terminal window you typed the command from Step 2. You'll get a Keyboard interrupt received, exiting message.

One of the obvious drawbacks of this example is that the Python3 built-in http.server web server does not stop running after requests have stopped coming into it on port 8096. It's not *socket-deactivated*. Building a timeout into this simple example would be an interesting exercise, so that the web server is not always running. And, as you can see, the Simple Sockets-Based Activation Example is not a rigorous and thorough explication of socket-based activation, but it gives you the idea behind it using a single, and very simple, systemd command.

In-Chapter Exercises

17. How would you terminate the simple sockets-based activation example you created above from the command line?
18. Use the **ncat** command (from the nmap tools) to achieve the same results as the systemd-socket-activate program example above, except instead of a Python3 webserver program, launch a bash shell.

(Hint: On a server, use **ncat** to both listen on a port, and then start the bash shell when a request comes in on that port, and on a client connect to the server on that port)

2.8 Chapter Summary

In this chapter, we provided a complete overview of the superkernel known as systemd, which essentially controls everything on the Raspberry Pi OS system, including the Linux kernel itself. We covered the following basic systemd, and other Linux commands- id -u, journalctl, ncat, nmap, systemctl, systemd-activate, systemd-cgls, **systemd** socket activate, who -r

Questions, Problems, and Projects

Chapter 0

1. Create a directory called Raspberry in your home directory. What command line did you use to do this?

2. Give a command line for displaying the files **lab1, lab2, lab3,** and **lab4.** Can you give two more command lines that do the same thing? What is the command line for displaying the files **lab1.c, lab2.c, lab3.c,** and **lab4.c**? (Hint: use shell metacharacters.)

3. Give a command line for printing all the files in your home directory that start with the string memo and end with **.ps** on a printer called **upmpr.** What command line did you use to do this?

4. Give the command line for nicknaming the command **who -H** as **W.** Give both Bash and C shell versions. Where would you put it if you want it to execute every time you start a new shell?

5. Type the command **man ls > ~/Raspberry/ls.man** on your system. This command will put the man page for the **ls** command in the **ls. man** file in your Raspberry directory (the one you created in Problem 1). Give the command for printing two copies of this file on a printer in your lab. What command line would you use to achieve this printing?

6. What is the **mesg** value set to for your environment? If it is on, how would you turn it off for your current session? How would you set it off for every login?

7. What does the command **lpr -Pqpr [0-9]*.jpg** do? Explain your answer.

8. Use the **passwd** command to change your password. If you are on a network, be aware that you might have to use the **yppasswd** command to modify your network login password. Also, make sure you abide by the rules set up by your system administrator for coming up with good passwords!

9. Using the correct terminology (e.g., command, option, option argument, and command argument), identify the constituent parts of the following Raspberry Pi OS single commands.

   ls -la *.exe
   lpr -Pwpr file27
   chmod g+rwx *.*

10. View the man pages for each of the useful commands listed in Table 0.2. Which part of the man pages is most descriptive for you? Which of

the options shown on each of the man pages is the most useful for beginners? Explain.

11. How many users are logged on to your system at this time? What command did you use to discover this?

12. Determine the name of the operating system that your computer runs. What command did you use to discover this?

13. Give the command line for displaying manual pages for the socket, read, and connect system calls on your system.

Advanced Questions and Problems

14. Following is a typical /etc/profile configuration file, this particular one is from a default installation on our Raspberry Pi system:

```
# /etc/profile: system-wide .profile file for the Bourne shell (sh(1))
# and Bourne compatible shells (bash(1), ksh(1), ash(1), ...).

if [ "$(id -u)" -eq 0 ]; then
  PATH="/usr/local/sbin:/usr/local/bin:/usr/sbin:/usr/bin:/sbin:/bin"
else
  PATH="/usr/local/sbin:/usr/local/bin:/usr/sbin:/usr/bin:/sbin:/bin:/usr/\
    local/games:/usr/games"
fi
export PATH

if [ "${PS1-}" ]; then
  if [ "${BASH-}" ] && [ "$BASH" != "/bin/sh" ]; then
    # The file bash.bashrc already sets the default PS1.
    # PS1='\h:\w\$ '
    if [ -f /etc/bash.bashrc ]; then
      . /etc/bash.bashrc
    fi
  else
    if [ "$(id -u)" -eq 0 ]; then
      PS1='# '
    else
      PS1='$ '
    fi
  fi
fi

if [ -d /etc/profile.d ]; then
  for i in /etc/profile.d/*.sh; do
    if [ -r $i ]; then
      . $i
    fi
  done
  unset i
fi
```

Write an explanatory sentence in your own words describing exactly what you consider important lines in the file accomplish, including the comments (the lines that begin with the pound sign #). Examine this file on your Raspberry Pi system. How does it compare, line-for-line, with the one above? We assume here that, by default, Bash is both the interactive and login shell on your system.

15. What is the default umask setting in an ordinary, non-privileged account on your Raspberry Pi system, from both a login and non-login shell? Describe in your own words what the umask setting is, and how it is applied to newly-created directories and files. Is the umask set in /etc/profile on your Raspberry Pi system? If not, where can the umask be set most effectively on a persistent basis, for a particular single user, both in a login and non-login shell?

16. Assume that all users, when they log into your Raspberry Pi system, have Bash as their default shell. What file sets the shell prompt for them on your Raspberry Pi system? Is it the file illustrated in Problem 14? Describe the lines in the file that actually specify the shell prompt, and give a short description of the components of those lines. Experiment to find out which file accomplishes the actual shell prompt setting for ordinary users (for both interactive or login shells), and write an explicit description of what you have discovered.

Additionally, set the shell prompt for yourself in the current interactive shell, so that it contains the following:

A display of just the date/time.

A display of the date and time, hostname and current directory.

A display where the entire prompt is in red text, along with hostname and current directory.

Then make those changes persistent for yourself in both login and interactive shells. Finally, undo the persistent changes.

As a follow-up, design your own shell prompt so that it contains the information you want in a useful display given your use case(s), and make that designed prompt persistent for yourself on your Raspberry Pi system.

17. Give a sequential list of the exact commands you would use to make the TC shell the default login shell for your user account on your Raspberry Pi system. Is the TC shell installed by default on your Raspberry Pi system? If not, how would you install it on a Debian-family or CentOS system? Give the exact commands for installation of not only the TC shell, but any of the other 4 major Raspberry Pi OS shells available.

18. Execute all of the compound command Examples provided at the web link explainshell.com, and then use the output shown to explain all

of them in your own words. Try executing the Examples with meaningful arguments on your Raspberry Pi system, if possible.

Project 1

After completing Problems 14 through 16, gather your findings together in a summary report that details the default settings (within the scope of the files you have examined and in the context of those problems) of the Bash environment on your Raspberry Pi system. For example, which actual file takes precedence by default, and what components of the Bash environment are set in that file? What are the critical default settings in the Bash environment, and what actual files on your Raspberry Pi system affect them?

Chapter 1

1. ***Note*** At the time of the writing of this book, the Raspberry Pi foundation supported a "Lite" release of the Raspberry Pi OS, which can be the basis for a "server' install. It comes with a terminal console interface instead of a desktop. On this platform, 99% of "server" apps run on it.

    Write a brief outline of how to install the "server", non-GUI-interface of the Raspberry Pi OS, on your computer hardware. Briefly detail exactly how the "Lite" installation procedure differed from a Desktop distribution installation. If you didn't do the installation, find out from the system manager how the installation was done, and why it was done in that way.

2. After doing Problem 1, do the following steps on the server edition in order to complete the requirements for this problem:

    a. If you have not already done so, download, install, and test the vsftpd service on your system, as shown in Example 1.2.

    b. Use the **adduser** command to create a new user account on your Linux system with the following configuration:

```
$ sudo adduser ftp2
Adding user `ftp2' ...
Adding new group `ftp2' (1004) ...
Adding new user `ftp2' (1003) with group `ftp2' ...
Creating home directory `/home/ftp2' ...
Copying files from `/etc/skel' ...
Enter new UNIX password: YYY
Retype new UNIX password: YYY
```

```
passwd: password updated successfully
Changing the user information for ftp2
Enter the new value, or press ENTER for the default
        Full Name []:
        Room Number []:
        Work Phone []:
        Home Phone []:
        Other []:
Is the information correct? [Y/n] Y
$
```

    c. Test your new user account locally on your LAN by using the command **ftp 0** with username **ftp2**. Test it from the Internet. Put files in the users account, and retrieve files from that account locally from another account and from the Internet.

3. After doing Problems 1 and 2 for a server edition install, and given the steps needed to accomplish user account management, make a table or chart of what users and groups need to be added to your system, and what their default account parameters and group memberships should be. What command can you use to identify all existing groups on the system? Use the batch mode account creation technique to implement the users and groups from the table or chart you created.

4. Do the same operations as in Examples 1.3 and 1.4, *except* use externally-mounted USB3 bus SATA SSDs, flash drives, or PCIe M.2 modules instead of the drive types specified in those Examples.

In the case of duplicating Example 1.3, you might be adding an externally-mounted USB3 bus SATA SSD. In the case of duplicating Example 1.4, you will be doing that on an externally mounted USB3 SATA SSD or PCIe M.2 module.

Following are some advisories about how to complete the duplicate of Example 1.3 successfully

Make sure you know the logical device name of your system disk, such as /dev/sda. Don't do this problems steps by mistake using that drive! If you do, you will render the system unbootable!

5. Execute Example 1.5 on available hardware. What would be the security and archival advantages of creating a mdadm RAID1, mirrored pair of SATA hard disks? To follow up on Example 1.5, repeat the Example using a selected higher order of RAID on the requisite number of readily available multiple disks in your array.

6. Add a shared network printer to your Linux system *without* a direct USB connection, and outline the steps necessary to get the printer to actually work, given your installation type.

7. Rewrite the following bash and Tcsh scripts in Python 3:

```
#!/bin/bash
if [ -d "/usr/bin" ] ; then
   echo "/usr/bin is a directory"
else
    echo "/usr/bin is not a directory"
fi
```

```
#!/bin/bash
echo "Enter input: \c"
read line
echo "You entered: $line"
echo "Enter another line: \c"
read word1 word2 word3
echo "The first word is: $word1:"
echo "The second word is: $word2:"
echo "The rest of the line is: $word3:"
exit 0
```

```
#!/bin/bash
echo "The command name is: $0."
echo "The number of command line arguments passed as parameters\
    is: $#."
echo "The value of the command line arguments are: $1 $2 $3 $4 $5\
    $6 $7 $8 $9."
echo "Another way to display values of all the arguments: $@."
echo "Yet another way is: $*."
exit 0
```

```
#!/bin/tcsh
if ( ( $#argv == 0 ) || ( $#argv > 1 ) ) then
   echo "Usage: $0 ordinary_file"
   exit 1
endif
if ( -f $1 ) then
   set filename = $argv[1]
   set fileinfo = `ls -il $filename`
   set inode = $fileinfo[1]
   set size = $fileinfo[6]
   echo "File Name:        $filename"
   echo "Inode Number:     $inode"
   echo "Size (bytes):     $size"
   exit 0
else
   echo "$0: argument must be an ordinary file"
   exit 1
endif
```

8. What is the meaning of the term archive?

9. What is the **tar** command used for? Give all its uses.

10. You want to create a tar archive of a project that contains several directories, sub-directories, and files, and save the archive on a USB flash drive mounted on your system so that you can distribute the archive to your friends. (a) What is the pathname to a USB flash drive mounted on your system? (b) How would you designate a USB flash drive as the destination for where the tar archive would be created, as an argument to the **tar** command? How would you encrypt the USB flash drive so that only people with the passphrase can see what is on it?

11. If you have not encrypted the USB flash drive, what are the access permissions for the files on the USB flash drive from Problem 10?

12. Give a command line for creating a tar archive of your current directory.

13. Give commands for compressing and keeping the archive from Problem 12 in the backups directory in your home directory.

14. Give commands for restoring the backup file in Problem 13 in the ~/ backups directory.

15. Give a command line for copying your home directory to a directory called home.back so that access privileges and file modification time are preserved.

16. Why is the **tar** command preferred over the **cp -r** command for creating backup copies of directory hierarchies?

17. Suppose that you download a file, RaspberryPiBook.tar.Z from an ftp site. Give the sequence of commands for restoring this archive and installing it in your ~/RaspberryPiBook directory.

18. Use the **tar** command to create a compressed archive of a directory of your choosing in a new directory you create named backups under your home directory. Name the compressed archive **something.tar.gz,** where something is the name of the directory you chose to backup. Show the command lines that you used to perform these tasks.

19. Use the **tar** command to restore the compressed tar archive ~/backups/ courses.tar.gz you produced in Problem 18 above, into a new directory named mirrors under your home directory. Show the command lines that you used to perform these tasks.

20. Use the Raspberry Pi OS Menu choice Accessories > SD Card Copier to clone your system microSD card onto another adequate-sized microSD card. Make sure the target microSD card has a large enough capacity to achieve the cloning! To test the clone, gracefully shut down your system, and remove the original system microSD card. Then replace it with the cloned target, and restart the system.

***Hint: In order for us to achieve this easily, we mounted an adequate size microSD card in a Vanja OTG/USB Multi-Function Card Reader/Writer, plugged that device into a USB port on our Pi 400, and used the SD Card Copier facility to do the cloning.

21. Mansoor is working with Bob on a project. He needs to be able to read, write, create, and delete files related to the project, which are located in the Project directory in Bob's home directory. Bob and Mansoor are ordinary users without administrative privileges. They wish to do this project without contacting the system administrator to request new groups, group membership changes, sudo changes, etc. When the project is over, Bob will remove the modified permissions on his home and the Project directory for user "mansoor" himself, instead of contacting the system administrator.

On your own Raspberry Pi system, in conjunction with another user, use ACLs to accomplish the following (substituting valid usernames on your system for Bob and Mansoor):

a. Create a project directory under Bob's home directory named "Project".

b. Set the ACL on Bob's home directory so Mansoor has read, write, and execute privileges on it.

c. Set the ACL on the Project directory so that Mansoor has rwxo privileges on it.

d. Have Bob create some files in the Project directory.

e. Have Mansoor make Bob's home directory the current directory.

f. Have Mansoor test whether or not he can-

   delete files in Bob's home directory,

   delete the Project directory from Bob's home directory,

   list, create new files, or remove the files that Bob put in the Project directory.

g. Have Bob revoke Mansoor's x privileges on Bob's home directory and the directory Project.

h. Have Mansoor test the revocation of modify privileges from step g.

i. Why can Mansoor still see the files in Bob's home directory, and the files in the **Project** directory, but not delete or modify any files in those directories after step g?

j. What command(s) would Bob have to execute to deny Mansoor access to his home directory?

Note
Show verification of ACL settings at as many steps as necessary to validate what you have done.

22. If you give a set of users permissions to a project directory using ACLs, how can you ensure that sub-directories that are created by the project manager beneath that project directory provide the same access privileges to those users?

23. Create a project directory on your system and create a git repository in it for any number of local users on your computer system. Then use ACLs to give access to the project directory to the users that are collaborating in the project. This should allow those users to push to and pull from the git repository. Have your allowed users test the repository. Also test the security of the repository, i.e., can non-allowed users access it?

24. After completion of Chapter 1, Section 1.15, Procedures I, II, and III, use the nfs4-acl-tools to accomplish the same things that are done in the example on a remote NFS UNIX file system, such as on a FreeBSD or Solaris 11.4 server mounted on your local Raspberry Pi OS system. In order to do this, you must first install the nfs4-acl-tools on your local system. Then install and use a UNIX-based NFS server on another machine on your network which has an NFSv4 file system, and on your local machine install an NFS client. Connect client to server, and mount the remote file system on your machine. Finally, use the nsf4-acl-tools to set and view ACL inheritance on the files on the remote machine, as is done in Procedures I, II, and III.

How do you know ahead of time that the remote NFS file system is capable of NFSv4-compliant ACLs? Then answer these questions:

a. Are there any system calls that directly affect ACLs, and what are their names and functions?

b. What are some examples of system calls that deal with the file access mode parameter?

25. Do all Use Cases from Chapter 1, Section 1.16.2 on your Raspberry Pi system, and note the results.

26. Use gufw to do all Use Cases in Chapter 1, Section 1.16.2 on your Raspberry Pi system, and remark on how much easier (or harder) it is to accomplish the same things you did in Problem 25 in gufw.

27. Do all the steps shown in Chapter 1, Section 1.16.5, Example 1.13 on your Raspberry Pi system, and interpret the log entries in the Journal as shown in that section. Use gufw to construct the rule shown in step 1:

sudo ufw deny in log-all from 192.168.0.8

Furthermore, try different forms of entry, such as vsftp and http on different standard and ephemeral ports, and note what is present in Journal log entry components for each.

28.

    a.   On our Raspberry Pi system, CUPS is active when no printer is plugged in or attached. That can be seen by using the command **systemctl status cups.service**. Examine the cups.service systemd service unit file in /lib/systemd/system, and write a short paragraph-long description, in your own words, for why CUPS is active when no powered-on printers are attached to the system. This question assumes that CUPS is installed on your system, according to the requirements shown in Section, and that it is enabled at system boot.

    b.   How would you make CUPS *unavailable*, or inactive when no printer is plugged-in or attached?

29. Execute all of the steps of Example 1.5 up to step 8, using two USB flash drives mounted on your computer. You can put more data into /mnt/raid1 for testing purposes.

Then, do the following parts of that Example:

    a.   Add a third USB flash drive equivalent in size to the originals into the RAID1 array md0. On our Raspberry Pi system, it was named /dev/sdd. Do steps 2 and 3 on the newly added flash drive.

    b.   Check the integrity of the data placed in /mnt/raid1.

    c.   Replace /dev/sdc with the new flash drive /dev/sdd, and wait for the array to be resynced. On our Raspberry Pi system, this took about 30 minutes.

    d.   Again, check the integrity of any data you may have placed in /mnt/raid1.

    e.   Execute step 12 to remove the RAID1 array, and zero out the flash drives so that they can be reused as FAT32 formatted drives.

Extras for Experts

30. Execute the following steps of the user and group creation method, in detail for your Raspberry Pi system, according to the following constraints:

    a.   Your systems capabilities to accommodate additional persistent media,

    b.   whether or not you want to use a traditional partitioning/file system creation/file system mounting –based approach,

    c.   your security model, in terms of how it isolates users and groups from one another,

d. your system performance model as it affects users and groups,

e. how many users and groups you plan to accommodate.

For example, you can add one or more additional hard drives to your system, limit the privileges you want ordinary users to have, allow them to run their own executable programs from their home directories, and have a small-scale set of user accounts and groups.

The user and group creation method is as follows:

Step 1. A second persistent medium, such as an internally-mounted SATA hard drive, an externally-mounted USB-bus device, or some other medium connected that uses some other bus architecture, must be added to your system. See the basic traditional approach of doing this in Section 1.5.3.

You can also create "home" directories on that drive as well, that will become the home directories for new users that you add to the system as needed.

Step 2. When you are using the **adduser** command to add individual new users, if you use the --home option, you can specify that the new user's home directory be the same directory you created in Step 1. To use a template for larger-scale account creation, you can use the **newuser** command. You can also customize the default "skeleton" file that is used by the **adduser** command, so that it uniformly provisions newly-created user accounts, groups, etc., so that all new accounts have their home directories on the new hard disk.

Step 3. If you manipulate the ownership permissions of the directories from steps 1 and 2, the new user will own and have access to the directories on the second hard disk. This is achieved by a privileged user via the **chmod** and **chown** commands. But you must also consider the impact of these permission changes on your system's security model.

By tailoring the home directory and file security so it is in conformance with your security model, via traditional file access permissions, or via Access Control Lists (ACL's) as shown in Section 1.15 above, you can ensure that users and groups are limited and structured to conform to both the security model, and any performance use case(s) designed by you.

31. Using the following system program, named killer.c, and the general procedure of Chapter 1, Example 1.17, give an unprivileged user the capability of terminating any process on your system with the killer.c executable-version system program.

```
/* killer.c: killer signal pid */

#include <sys/types.h>

int main(int argc, char *argv[])
{
      pid_t pid;
      int signal;

    if (argc != 3) {
      printf("Inappropriate number of command line arguments.\n");
      exit(0);
    }
    pid = atoi(argv[1]);
    signal = atoi(argv[2]);
      if (kill(pid, signal) == -1) {
          perror("Kill failed");
          exit(1);
      }
      exit(0);
}
```

Compile the above system program, and run it as follows:

```
$ gcc -w killer.c -o killer
$ sudo apt-get install csh
Output truncated...
$ csh

% ps
PID    TTY     TIME     CMD
15995 pts/3   00:00:00 bash
16693 pts/3   00:00:00 csh
16695 pts/3   00:00:00 ps
% ./killer 16693 2

% ps
PID    TTY     TIME     CMD
15995 pts/3   00:00:00 bash
16693 pts/3   00:00:00 csh
16702 pts/3   00:00:00 ps
% ./killer 16693 9
Killed

$ ps
PID    TTY     TIME     CMD
15995 pts/3   00:00:00 bash
16704 pts/3   00:00:00 ps
$
```

Note

Your process ID numbers in the above instructions will be different than what is shown here. Also, we assume that the gcc compiler is installed already on your Raspberry Pi system, which it is by default on our systems.

The **killer.c** program in the above session takes a PID and a signal number as command line arguments, and uses the kill() system call to send the specified signal to the process with the given PID. After compiling the program and saving the executable code in the file called killer, install the C shell, start a C shell process and use the **ps** command to see the PID of the new C shell process. We then use the killer program to send signal number 2 (SIGINT) to the new C shell process (PID 16693). The output of the **ps** command shows that, as expected, the C shell does not terminate. When we send signal number 9 (SIGKILL; sure kill) to the new C shell process, the shell terminates. The SIGHUP signal would also terminate the shell process.

Project 1

After completing the Requirements of Chapter 1, Example 1.9, automate the Python3 script file using a systemd timer so that it runs on a schedule that is useful to you.

Chapter 2

1. Answer the following as completely as you can:
   a. Is a systemd unit a target, or can it be a target? b. Is a systemd target a unit, or can it be a unit?
   This question is aimed at getting you to think about the conceptual organization of systemd, as shown in Figure 2.1, as well as the details of what units and targets are.

2. How can you easily verify that the milestone boot targets shown in Figure 2.2 are reached in the order local-fs-pre.target, sysinit.target, basic.target, multi-user.target, and graphical.target shown in that figure, when your system boots? The basic assumption here is that you are booting into a Raspberry Pi OS desktop environment, but you can also describe verification on the basis of using a CUI text-only set of systemd commands.

3. What systemctl command can be used to change your Raspberry Pi system from the final target state graphical.target to multi-user.target, and then change the final target state back to graphical.target. Test these operations on your system.

4. Take a Bash script file that is useful to you, and turn it into a systemd-controlled service that executes at an appropriately-timed interval. Place the script file in your home directory on the system, and set permissions on it properly. Start, stop, restart, and edit the operation of the service with the appropriate systemctl commands.

5. Compare the information and logs found in /var/log to the contents of the journal, excluding the directory /var/log/journal if that exists. Prepare a report of the significant similarities and differences that you notice, particularly with respect to searching, rotating, and retention of the logs.

6.

Part 1. Write a simple Bash script file that can repeatedly back up a single source directory under your home directory, to a target directory that is either on a USB-mounted thumb drive on the system, or to a remote computer on your LAN. Use the tar command and appropriate options, to compress the target archived directory, or use the scp or rsync commands to create an uncompressed backup on the target. Be sure to name the backup on the target with some meaningful label, to differentiate sequential backups that you make, and make sure you test this script file to see that it works correctly!

In order to help you complete this problem, and to refresh your memory about how to do copying operations with the **scp**, **ssh**, and **rsync** commands, we repeat some examples of those copying operations here.

Following is a condensed collection of examples that use scp, ssh/dd, and rsync to copy files and directories locally and remotely. It is understood in these examples that you have permission access to the local files and directories, and that you have permission access to the remote locations as well.

a. An example of using secure copy (scp) to copy all the files in the directory webserver2 to a remote directory of the same name.

$ scp webserver2/*.* bob@192.168.0.25:/home/bob/webserver2/

b. An example of extracting the remote file backup.tar file at /home/bob in 512 byte blocks and streaming it through dd to the current working directory on the system you typed this command.

**$ ssh bob@192.168.0.13:/home/bob "dd if=backup.tar ibs=512"\
    tar xvBf –**

c. An example of using rsync to copy an entire directory named syncdir in the current working directory locally to a mounted USB thumbdrive named USBint:

$ rsync -av syncdir /media/bob/USBint')

d. An example of using rsync to copy an entire directory named syncdir2 in the current working directory in push mode, remotely to an OS X machine:

$ rsync -av -e ssh syncdir2 bob@192.168.0.7:/Users/b/unix3e

e. An example of using **rsync** to copy a file named rsynctest from the current working directory to the local destination on a thumb drive named USBint is

$ rsync -av rsynctest /home/bob/USBint

Part 2. To make the above script file practical and useful for you, make it a systemd service that can be run on some regular basis (to be determined by you). So, for example, you could time the service to run daily at 9:00 PM. Make sure to enable this service so it is persistent across boots!

7. Examine the man page for the **systemctl** command on your system, and write a short report that describes its syntax, purpose, options and option arguments, and sub-commands that pertain to units and unit files.
8. It would be helpful if you could "rewind" the system into a previously saved boot environment. How would that be possible, using what you know of systemd and the Raspberry Pi OS? Sketch a way of doing that.
9. Write a brief description of why you would change the system state into the following targets:

   poweroff.target, rescue.target, multi-user.target, graphical.target, reboot.target, emergency.target.
10. Determine which systemd commands must be run as root, using the sudo command, and which do not require root privilege. Produce a table of those commands. Explain exactly what your strategy was in finding out the information that allowed you to answer this question.

Advanced Questions, Problems, and Projects

11. What is the snapshot feature of systemd, and how and why do you use it? What other Raspberry Pi OS facilities, programs, and systems have similar capabilities, and how does their implementations compare in detail to systemd snapshots?
12. In terms of starting up your system, what does systemd do when the target units in Figure 2.2 *cannot* be reached, for whatever reason? What strategies can be deployed, and what specific systemd tactics can be used, to start up the system when these targets cannot be reached? In other words, what path of execution can be followed, and why? Does the system immediately enter into rescue or emergency mode? What are systemd's error-handling capabilities, as far as system startup go? How did you find this out? And most importantly, how can you use your answers to these questions as a trouble-shooting guide on your Linux system, when the requisite target states cannot be reached?

Project 1

To practice with changing the system state to rescue and emergency modes, use the commands in Sections 2.5.4 and 2.5.6, to achieve what is shown there on your system. And when your system goes into those states, carefully explore and document the capabilities of rescue and emergency mode operations. For example, what file system commands and facilities do you have available to you in those modes? Can you mount external media while the system is in those modes, so that you can save and backup important user data files? It would be very useful to become familiar with these two system state targets (by experimenting with bringing your Linux system into these states!), so that if an emergency happens, you can recover from it.

Project 2

Take the following Python rolling-backup program script, and use the methods of this chapter to run it on your Linux system. As shown in those sections, implement the Python script as a clock-time-based or calendar-based systemd service. Modify the Python code so that the service runs at time intervals that are useful for you.

Also, make sure you change the source and target directories in the Python code so that they suit your specific needs, and work with the file system structure of your Linux system. For those familiar with Python programming, use any enhancements to it that you feel would make the script file more "Pythonic".

```
#!/usr/local/bin/python
import os
import shutil
target = "/home/bob/USBint/" #Target directory, or where you are \
  backing up to
i = 1
while i <= 5:
    temp_path = target + str(i) + "/"
    if not os.path.exists( temp_path ):
        try:
            os.makedirs( temp_path )
            print "Created  " + temp_path
        except:
            print " Could not create  " + temp_path
    i = i + 1
print "Deleting the oldest archive"
shutil.rmtree( target + "5" )
print "Recycle the backups"
os.rename( target + "4", target + "5" )
os.rename( target + "3", target + "4" )
os.rename( target + "2", target + "3" )
# Do the backups
os.system('cp -a ' + target + "1" + " " + target + "2")
os.system('rsync -av /home/bob/python/' + " " + target + "1") #Source \
  directory here
```

Project 3

Convert the Python script file shown in Project 2 to a Bash script file that does exactly the same thing. Then, as specified in Project 2, use systemd to enable the Bash script to run at a time interval that is useful for you. Also, change the source and target directories to suit your specific use case needs, and Raspberry Pi system configuration as well.

Project 4

According to the steps shown in Section 2.7.1.1 A Simple Sockets-Based Activation Example, create a simple webserver with the Python built in, on an LXC container, and expose it in a public IP address, using bridging, so that it can be viewed on the Internet.

Note
Be careful to set the parameters of your router firewall correctly, as well as the firewall of the LXC container, so that hackers can't penetrate both your network, the LXC container, and the Raspberry Pi OS system you're using as an Internet server.

Index

A

B

C

Printed in the United States
by Baker & Taylor Publisher Services